All Teams Are Not Created Equal

This book is dedicated to
Earl, Mary, and Mae Ketchum

All Teams Are Not Created Equal

HOW EMPLOYEE EMPOWERMENT REALLY WORKS

Lyman D. Ketchum
Eric Trist

 SAGE PUBLICATIONS
International Educational and Professional Publisher
Newbury Park London New Delhi

For information address:

SAGE Publications, Inc.
2455 Teller Road
Newbury Park, California 91320

SAGE Publications Ltd.
6 Bonhill Street
London EC2A 4PU
United Kingdom

SAGE Publications India Pvt. Ltd.
M-32 Market
Greater Kailash I
New Delhi 110 048 India

Printed in the United States of America

Library of Congress Cataloging-in-Publication Data

Ketchum, Lyman D.
    All teams are not created equal : how employee empowerment really works / Lyman D. Ketchum, Eric Trist.
        p.   cm.
    Includes bibliographical references (p.   ) and
index.
    ISBN 0–8039–4652–X (cloth)
    1. Organizational effectiveness. 2. Industrial organization.
3. Work groups. 4. Job enrichment. 5. Quality of work life.
I. Trist, E. L. II. Title.
HD58.9.K45 1992
658.4—dc20   91–45355

92 93 94 95 10 9 8 7 6 5 4 3 2 1

Sage Production Editor: Astrid Virding

Contents

Part II Center-Out: A New Change Model

Part III New Plant Start-Ups

Part VI Conclusion

PART I

Inertia in Crisis

ONE

Understanding the Problem

In recent decades, businesses and other institutions in the industrialized world have experienced an increasing number of problems relating to the performance of their organizations. Productivity falls far short of what it could be, the safety of their workers and of the public at large is compromised, and the quality of their products and services cannot be relied upon as it once could.

These problems may be considered as first-level, or first-order, problems. The forces generating them are powerful, deeply rooted, complex, and long in development.

The immediate source, however, of these first-level problems is people; the behavior of the people who make up the organizations—those who do the work and those who manage them. How they behave can be called a second level or order of problems. Any first-line supervisor can come up with a ready list of these: absenteeism, lack of commitment, lack of initiative, failure to concentrate on the job, use of drugs and alcohol. More senior managers easily list the shortcomings of those serving in a managerial capacity even though the organization performance implications are less visible.

The first- and second-order problems are not new. One major corporation reported that in the period between 1961 and 1969 absenteeism rose 56%, turnover 76%, grievances 38%, and disciplinary layoffs 46%. Productivity gain declined, and at one point absolute productivity decreased.

By the late 1970s it was apparent that something was wrong and that it was not limited to workers and supervisors in manufacturing plants but extended to people in all organizations.

Nor was the problem limited to young people. Conventional wisdom of the early 1970s had it that important and unprecedented societal changes in the sixties—principally in values, expectations, affluence, and increased education—had brought about behavior changes in young workers, and the 1972 strike at the General Motors plant at Lordstown, OH, became the symbol of the clash between technology and the rising expectations of the younger generation. But Irving Bluestone, then vice president of the United Auto Workers, noted that while Lordstown was "a young people's plant," a strike was also in progress at Norwood, one of General Motors's oldest plants. "There is a large, large number proportionately of the older folk," he said, "who are saying exactly the same thing [as the younger workers]."

Despite these early warnings, problems of organizational performance have continued and proliferated. For example, in 1987 IBM estimated that it would take $2.66 billion of additional revenue to generate the same amount of profit that could be realized if each employee were responsible for saving $1,000 a year by removing product defects. Yet managers in general either seemed to ignore the signs that something was wrong or reacted in ways that have proved ineffective.

Few people would disagree that the second-order problems of employee behavior are the cause of the first-order performance failings. There is no doubt about the bad behavior. But the differences of opinion on why it is there and what to do about it span a wide spectrum.

For some the solution is coercion. Laggards must be made to see the error of their ways. They must be coerced into satisfactory attendance and task performance. They must stop using drugs and alcohol. The Office of Technology Assessment estimates that more than 10 million workers in 1988 were subject to concealed telephone and computer observation and that "the number of surveillance systems sold to businesses rose nearly threefold to 70,000 from 1985 to 1988" (Lopez, 1990).[1] In the meantime, efforts to automate the production process must be redoubled so that production can be made goof proof and fail safe. Peopleless factories are the goal; machines don't take coffee breaks and overstay them.

A large percentage of U.S. managers operate in the belief that behavior in the workplace is primarily a function of character traits. Hire right and you won't have trouble. If the wrong kind pass the hiring screen, coerce them into "right" behavior. If that fails, fire. Those holding this view put great store on the five Ps—piecework, pay-for-performance, penalties (such as loss of pay), productivity bonuses, and profit sharing. Inevitably, they place heavy dependence on rules. "In difficult times you need to find people who have the right work ethics," says Mr. Ed Vick, president and chief executive of Levine, Huntley, Vick & Beaver. "People who don't show that ethic—you've got to get rid of them. There's no place to hide in an environment like this" (Stern, 1991).[2] The same article, headlined "As the Going Gets Tougher, More Bosses Are Getting Tough with Their Workers," affirmed that getting tough might be a trend, citing Westcon, Inc.; IBM; Sears, Roebuck & Company; and KPMG Peat Marwick.

Corporate restructurers tend to take a narrow economic view. Thin out the management ranks; thin out all ranks; cut 15% across the board. This remedy is a current favorite in the buy-out scheme. Control is put into new investor hands, and in the belief that there is fat everywhere the new bosses direct operating management to reduce the staff by some magic number.

Further along the spectrum is a smaller number of concerned managers seeking solutions in a variety of less severe approaches. Remedies in many forms have emerged and are touted in acronyms and alphabet programs; one brochure for a productivity conference advertised VAM™, TEI™, and T.E.A.M.S. Advocates of employee ownership see a direct relationship between financial stake in the company and everyday behavior. Communication programs abound: "Let 'em know the trouble we're in and they'll behave differently." The U.S. Department of Labor and many others promote labor-management cooperation, but this step is generally taken only in desperation, when the enterprise has its back to the wall. During the early 1980s, "quality circles"—volunteer worker discussion groups with limited scope of responsibility and authority—were the rage. They worked in Japan, and for a time airline flights to Japan were filled with U.S. managers seeking answers there.

A cover story in *Business Week* (Byrne & Jackson, 1986) titled "Business Fads: What's In—and Out; Executives Latch on to Any Management Idea That Looks Like a Quick Fix," spoke to the propensity of companies to use otherwise good ideas "as gimmicks to evade the basic challenges they face." All too often these remedies ask people to change in some way. Referring to programs designed to help employees handle stress, the National Institute for Occupational Safety and Health made note of the ineffectiveness of these programs when no efforts are made to reduce "organizational" sources of stress, and that doing so was "blaming the victims" (1987). A recent study by the University of Wisconsin Industrial Engineering Department and Communications Workers of America indicates that electronic monitoring of employee performance was related to increased levels of tension, anxiety, depression, anger, and fatigue (Smith, Sainfort, Rogers, & LeGrande, 1990).

A THIRD-LEVEL DIAGNOSIS: THERE IS SOMETHING WRONG WITH THE ORGANIZATION OF WORK

At the far end of the spectrum is a still smaller minority of managers who are taking a different direction. They acknowledge that yes, there are serious performance problems, which are the result of an equally serious problem of behavior on the part of the people in the organization. But they are looking beyond this second-order problem. Their approach is based on the belief that uncommitted behavior is not necessarily natural. When people are chronically absent, unalert, and uninformed, look for a deeper problem. Their hypothesis is that in industrialized societies this third-order problem lies in a mismatch between the characteristics of people and the organizational characteristics of workplaces. While individual character traits are not to be ignored, there is a strong relationship between behavior on the job and the way work is organized. We create the workplace, and the workplace creates us.

According to this small group of managers, the third-order diagnosis of a mismatch between people and the organization of work represents pragmatism of the highest kind. For them, it is not practical just to complain about people's loss of the work ethic and ignore the reasons why people are uncommitted. They look for ways in which the *work experience,* rather than the people, can be changed to produce a better match.

GOOD WORK AND BAD WORK

What, then, are these characteristics of the work organizations that determine whether or not a worker is committed? There is remarkable agreement among groups from different levels, different technologies, and different companies throughout the United States. Nor do the similarities end at our shorelines. What applies here applies throughout the industrialized world and, where bureaucracies exist, in developing countries. A clear picture of what constitutes good and bad work experience can be put together by asking a group of people to respond to the following four questions:

What was it like working on the best job you ever had?
What was it like working on the worst job you ever had?
What was it like working for the best boss you ever had?
What was it like working for the worst boss you ever had?

Their responses bring into sharp focus what constitutes good work and bad work experience. For example, the following comments were made by a group of working officers of a local union:

Best job: "Not an assembly-line type thing." "Good working conditions and pay." "Had good knowledge of job through extensive training and freedom to make decisions." "Had responsibility." "There wasn't close supervision." "It was not confining in proximity to other workers." "I had proper equipment."

Worst job: "The weather (outside job) was hot or cold, often wet." "I was on call 24 hours a day." "There was constant pressure to meet deadlines." "It was manual labor to the exclusion of using what we had learned in high school; it was mindless." "There was no room for advancement." "Poor ventilation." "Poor supervision." "Safety conditions poor-to-nonexistent."

Best boss: "Interested in the company (quality, production, status in community, general well-being)." "Gave me freedom to perform my job (gave help when I asked)." "Didn't always hunt for someone to blame, backed his people." "Treated workers as humans, not machines. Took into account workers' outside lives as he dealt with us." "Open to suggestions and cared about what I thought." "Fair and straightforward." "Understood the problems and tried to do something about them up to the limits of his power and authority." "He was given considerable decision-making latitude by his boss." "I could depend on him not to change his position in the third step of our grievance process." "He expected me to do my job without my being watched closely." "He maintained a reasonable balance between his job and the rest of his life." "His word was good." "He knew my performance and my potential capability."

Worst boss: "He was always looking over my shoulder. He gave me no leeway, wanted to be both foreman and operator."

"He used child psychology, behaved like a parent saying, 'I know what is best for you.' " "He didn't communicate well. It was hard to understand what he was trying to convey." "He didn't care what the real problem was. He didn't grasp what I was telling him was going wrong." "He covered his backside." "He preferred sending the problem down the line to solving it in his unit." "He reacted poorly under pressure, began fault-finding instead of logical problem-solving."

When people are asked, as a follow-up to the above questions, "How productive were you in these situations?" and "What proportion of your relevant talents were utilized?" they invariably report that in the worst-boss and worst-job situations they were less productive by far and that they were vastly underutilized.

The problem of unsatisfactory work experience is by no means limited to hourly paid people. A group of middle managers in another plant had these responses:

Best job: "Control and responsibility for performing the job." "Freedom of movement." "Had resources necessary to complete the job." "Challenge in the job big enough to cause a certain amount of doubt." "Was able to see things being accomplished." "Accountability—took credit." "Was able to work with people."

Best boss: "Permitted subordinate to make own decisions." "Knew his area of responsibility and made decisions on his own within that area." "You knew where you stood with him." "He was close enough to guide and direct when necessary through informal communication." "Could be trusted and he in turn trusted subordinates." "Kept subordinates well informed." "Followed chains of command." "Gave recognition when deserved."

The worst-job and worst-boss questions brought out mirror-images of these responses.

From responses like these, it is possible to identify certain basic needs that people at all levels of an organization require from their work:

> To join with others in a common task;
> To have some latitude to make decisions;
> To receive recognition for one's contributions;
> To learn and go on learning;
> To make reasonable use of one's intellect;
> To receive information about how one is doing and what is going on in and beyond one's immediate area; and
> To feel that one's contributions fit into a logical whole.

From their classical studies in the sixties and early seventies, Emery (1964, 1976) and Trist (1978) compiled a list of psychological requirements that must be met if commitment to work is to develop. These intrinsic factors include:

> The need for the job to be reasonably demanding in terms other than sheer endurance and to provide a minimum of variety (not necessarily novelty, which is too much for some people though the spice of life for others). This is to recognize enfranchisement in problem solving as a human right.

> The need to be able to learn on the job on a continuing basis. Again, this is a question of neither too much nor too little, but of matching solutions to personal requirements. This is to recognize personal growth as a human right.

> The need for some area of decision making that the individual can call his own. This recognizes the opportunity to use one's own judgment as a human right.

> The need for some degree of social support and recognition in the workplace, from both fellow workers and bosses. This recognizes "group belongingness" as a human right.

Table 1.1 Properties of Jobs

Conditions of Employment	The Job Itself
Socio-economic factors (extrinsic)	Psycho-social factors (intrinsic)
Fair and adequate pay	Variety and challenge
Job security	Continuous learning
Benefits	Discretion, autonomy
Safety	Recognition and support
Health	Meaningful social contribution
Due process	Desirable future

The need to be able to relate what one does and what one produces to one's social life. That is, to have a meaningful occupational identity that gives a man or woman dignity. This recognizes the opportunity to contribute to society as a human right.

The need to feel that the job leads to some sort of desirable future (not necessarily promotion). It may involve training or redeployment—a career at shop floor level leading to the development of greater skill. It includes being able to participate in choosing that future. This recognizes hope as a human right.

In addition to these intrinsic motivations, both Emery (1964, 1976) and Trist (1978) recognized the importance of continuing the consideration of the extrinsic factors. Trist identified these as fair and adequate pay, job security, benefits, safety, health, and due process (see Table 1.1).

These psychological needs and associated human rights provide a high quality of work experience. This is often referred to as *quality of work life* (QWL). It is not confined to any one level of employment. Managers also need a high QWL. It must be recognized, however, that it is not always possible to meet these needs to the same extent in all work settings; nor, indeed, do all kinds of people need them to the same degree—individual differences are considerable. Furthermore, these needs cannot always be judged from conscious expression such as that given in responses to attitude surveys about job satisfaction. Where there is no expectation that any of the jobs open will offer much chance of learning, a person will soon learn to "forget" such a requirement. It is difficult to accept as real something one has not yet experienced. Nevertheless, a high QWL may still be built in terms of these factors—so long as the factors on the extrinsic list are also satisfied. Together they constitute the necessary and sufficient conditions for a good work experience at the job or task level.

The failure to meet workers' intrinsic needs can be seen in a set of responses to interview questions posed to a group of workers at a 40-year-old unionized plant (A. Ketchum, 1971).

On variety:

"They take away variety by saying, 'All you need to know is if this goes or doesn't go.' " "We are treated like a machine. If we knew where the products are going, each person might have more job pride." "We are confined to a table 56 x 62, go around and around like a dog chasing his tail. It's rather boring, in other words."

On stress:

"Stress comes from not knowing when you can feel satisfied with the number of cycles you ran in a shift."

On problem-solving:

"That's for the foreman and the maintenance department."

On information received:

"The foreman keeps information to himself, and he's not available." "We never have any cost information, only guesses." "What little we get is because someone slips and says something they shouldn't." "I've been working here 20 years and don't know what unit costs are." "They keep us ignorant on purpose." "If I had more information, it would let me know something about my job security."

On quality:

"We don't get any information, and what little we get is from Quality Control." "The attitude is, if we can pull the wool over QC's eyes, let's do it." "When you buy a product on the market these days, you get bad quality. I can see where [a large consumer merchandising company] is having its problems based on what I see here at the plant."

On opportunities to learn:

"What I have learned I have learned on my own. I don't think they want us to know how it operates entirely." "When I first came to work here, I tried to get the foreman to take us to the chemical area. Finally one night we got the safety person to take us down there." "I joined a tour of family members one time so I would know more than my 12-year-old son who was on the tour."

On decision making and influencing policies:

"Nothing that I'd say would make any difference anyway." "Supervisors don't listen, and engineers don't ask." "As far as work rules, safety rules, and procedures are concerned, someone else decides." "Anything unusual and we have to call the foreman. It seems useless to do this with a lot of things. They should ask us what we think. Now they just jam it down our throats, so naturally we jam it back down theirs." "They make the rules, we bend them."

The impact of the quality of the work experience goes beyond the workplace. The interviewer questioning the workers quoted above strove to find out how their work lives were related to their lives away from work. In their responses to the statement "I talk about my work with my family," shame, an exceedingly strong emotion, was clearly evident. Those who talked with their family made the point that they did not talk about the work itself but only about things like benefits. They didn't feel their families would be interested in their repetitive jobs and they seemed embarrassed by the actual work they did. A similar probe was made regarding how they talked about work with friends. Many said they never brought it up. If asked, they simply gave the name of the company and the product.

THE CONSEQUENCES OF "BAD" WORK EXPERIENCE

What happens when people's needs are not met in their work experience? In initial indoctrination activities for a new unit of an established plant, a group of new hires from a variety of industries were asked that question. Their responses—immediate, personal, and freely offered—included expressions such as "felt placid and robot-like" . . . "felt useless" . . . "bored" . . . "resentful" . . . "used all my energies on outside activities" . . . "stopped trying" . . . "daydreaming" . . . "got stubborn" . . . "hated to come to work" . . . "worked unsafely" . . . "made up rumors." With these responses, can it be doubted that absenteeism should have been high, commitment low, and workers ill-informed and only marginally alert?

This case has a happy ending. These people, for whom the lack of need satisfaction was a common condition, went on to take their places in a redesigned workplace, one in which they were treated as resources, in which they got information, made decisions, went on learning and developing their capabilities. Their work experience was radically changed, so their behavior at work changed. They became committed. Gone was the anger, the boredom, the apathy, and the other negatives they had expressed about their previous work experience. They became highly productive. Thus, commitment is a bargain. *Commitment to work is still central to*

people's lives, but the commitment is conditional on the work experience.
As essential as money is, money alone is not enough.

COMMITMENT TODAY

Commitment, always important, became even more critical with the rise of continuous processing, which changed what is required of the worker. As work became more interdependent, worker decisions became more important. Today, production processes move more rapidly, and things happen so fast that there is no time to get the supervisor to correct a problem. Pressure in vessels is higher, and more hazardous materials are involved. Separate units are more closely integrated, so that a delay in one unit has consequences in many others.

Workers today must therefore have greater knowledge and information if the production process is to function without interruption. Failure to anticipate has costs and risks of unacceptable dimensions. Only the committed anticipate. Similarly, incorrect interventions in the process can yield similar outcomes. Supervision cannot remedy such problems.

Another problem in advanced technology: Work—however interesting—that puts too few demands on the worker. Especially problematic are long periods of time when there is little to do. Vigilance and idleness do not coexist.

A LOOK AHEAD

At this point in the early 1990s, the third-order problem of a mismatch between the characteristics of people and the characteristics of conventionally organized work that yields "bad" work experience remains real and evident. "Bad" work experience leads to the second-order problem, the failure of people to do what needs to be done. The second-order problem has in turn led to the first order of problems, increasing operating difficulties in business enterprises, including difficulties in the areas of safety, reliability, and productivity. We have a basis for distinguishing between "bad" work and "good" work. The chapters that follow describe how "good" work is designed and how the change from "bad" to "good" is implemented in both new and existing workplaces. Special emphasis is given to the past, present and future role of senior managers in the remaking of whole organizations.

NOTES

1. Reprinted by permission of *The Wall Street Journal,* © 1990 Dow Jones & Company, Inc. All rights reserved worldwide.
2. Reprinted by permission of *The Wall Street Journal,* © 1991 Dow Jones & Company, Inc. All rights reserved worldwide.

T W O

Designing "Good" Work: The Beginnings

By the early 1970s, proponents of what we have called the third-order diagnosis of problems of organizational performance, the mismatch between people and work, were putting their ideas into practice. New plants based on innovative principles of work design began to appear, led by Procter & Gamble's Lima, OH, plant in 1970 and General Foods's Gaines pet food plant in Topeka in early 1971. Over the next five years came Alcoa's magnesium ingot plant in Addy, WA, General Motors's Delco Remy Division battery plant in Fitzgerald, GA, and GM's Packard Electric Division wire harness plant in Brookhaven, MS, Butler Manufacturing's plant in Storey City, IA, and Cummins Engines's plant in Jamestown, NY.

DESIGNING INNOVATIVE PLANTS

These new plants were conceived not by dreamers or theoreticians but by practical people, mostly plant managers or executives to whom the plant managers reported. They were attempting to solve problems that had proved intractable to other approaches.

Dissatisfied with what they had experienced (or, as some described it, endured), they had seen that the old ways weren't working and a remedy would require a drastically new approach.

The basis for this new approach can be seen in the charge given by the first author to the design team for the Gaines pet food plant. First, planning was to be based on the philosophical belief that employees will best respond (be productive) when they have a high feeling of self-worth and of identification with the success of the organization. For these feelings to exist, employees must be treated not just as one element to be dealt with independently of other elements, but as part of a system. System analysis must encompass plant design, philosophy of management, organization, and staffing. The planners were admonished to erase all the givens and begin anew to devise a management system applicable in today's and tomorrow's environments. They were to have a sound reason for every design point and were to do nothing simply because it had always been done that way.

The plants that emerged from this new approach were different from traditional organizations in many ways. They were designed to achieve high levels of intrinsic motivation on the part of workers and to rely much less on the coercive motivation so widely practiced in factory systems. A major departure was in the area of specialization. Past management practice had narrowed the scope of jobs by exporting tasks from so-called production workers to specialists; maintenance of equipment, training of new workers, scheduling, and other functions were outside the purview of the production workers (see Figure 2.1). Although these aspects of the production process affected the quality of both the work life on the shop floor and the products themselves, the workers had no control over them.

In the new plants, this process was reversed. Many—and sometimes all—tasks traditionally handled by other departments were assigned to the production unit (see Figure 2.2). It was not an application of the favorite shibboleth of senior managers, "push the decisions to the lowest possible level"; rather, the principle was to

Figure 2.1

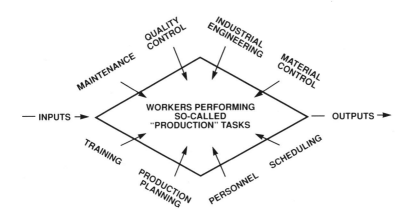

Figure 2.2

enable good decisions to be made at the point of action. Workers in these plants were required and permitted to make a wide range of important decisions—a large step in the direction of creating "good" work.

It was necessary to modify the methods of determining payment. Workers were paid on the basis of what they knew and could contribute, rather than what job they happened to be working on. This change made possible the development of multiskilled and self-deployable people so that a reservoir of needed skills was always present.

What managers in the new plants did was different from what they had been accustomed to doing in the old kind of organization. The management structure was flatter. And the purpose of management, as one design team expressed it, was "to enable people to do work," not to coerce. Rules were scarce. One plant manager said, "We will operate on only two rules: the golden rule and the rule of common sense."

The hiring process was specially designed to give applicants an opportunity to experience and understand what the designers were trying to create. Sometimes autonomy in the lower levels was sought even in the design process; one design team deliberately left issues open temporarily so that as hiring was done the new workers could participate in as many aspects of the design as possible.

This innovative designing resulted in work experience far different from what workers had been accustomed to. At a typical new plant, workers were organized into teams of 8 to 20 members. Although there was a team leader, a management person responsible for one or more teams, each team member had a sense of responsibility for the team's output. Members learned more than one of the skills associated with the team's production. As they added to their skills and knowledge of the process, their pay was increased. Variances from specifications were detected and corrective steps taken within the unit. The group was kept informed of what was occurring both within the process and in the larger environment of the plant. Personnel problems were dealt with within the group and were frequently resolved without recourse to higher authority.

Training of new team members was also done by the group, as was routine maintenance of equipment. Scheduling, materials coordination, and shift assignments were similarly handled by the group. Team meetings were held regularly in which members reviewed the performance of the team.

The successful plants were accomplishments of considerable magnitude and a tribute to the managers who created them. These managers had to learn a whole new way to manage. They often lacked the sponsorship and protection of senior management. That not all these projects succeeded was largely for this reason.

Conventional wisdom had it that "anyone could do it in a new plant" but that bringing about change in an existing plant was far harder. That view was not borne out in the experience of the select few who had the opportunity for comparison. One manager successful in existing-plant change and convinced that it would be easier in a new plant was to reverse his former opinion when he was assigned to create a new plant on a new site.

HOW THE NEW PLANTS DID

It is all well and good for workers to be content on the job, but what the managers of these plants had been seeking in their redesign of the workplace was a solution to the performance problems that had been plaguing them. Were they successful in increasing productivity, reliability, and safety on the part of their employees?

In fact, the bottom-line performance results of these new plants were phenomenal, so good that to many they were beyond belief. The Gaines pet food plant had the greatest year-to-year productivity increase of all GF plants, maintaining this record for years until the division was sold. As more and more such innovative plants were established, their amazing potential was confirmed. According to a *Business Week* report (Hoerr, Pollock, & Whiteside, 1986), Procter & Gamble's 18 "teamwork sites" are 30% to 40% more productive than their traditional counterparts and significantly more able to adapt quickly to the changing needs of the business. Companies have found that they require 25% to 30% fewer employees (both workers and managers) than in traditional organizations. Product quality is reliably better, and plant facilities are better utilized. Absenteeism is lower.

The new plants have proved better in other important ways. One company experiencing product sabotage in the retail distribution channel found it imperative to make packaging changes quickly. When it went to its two plants, one traditional and one innovative and both nonunion, they found the people in the innovative site much more responsive. Another company found its market share eroding when a competitor introduced an improved product made with new technology. By using plant employees as project engineers and expediters, the company scrapped the old technology and installed the new—its largest single capital investment ever—in record time, and the lost market share was regained.

A reporter from a large city newspaper, obviously accustomed to underdeveloped workers in the old kind of organization, visited the Gaines pet food plant in its early days. He came away with the opinion that some extraordinary people had been found and hired. In fact, this was not so. The workers had the same levels of education and experience as their counterparts in other plants, and nothing in their backgrounds or interviews suggested personal characteristics that would set them apart. What was different was the way their work was organized, which enabled them to develop to their fullest potentials and motivated them to commit their best efforts to the organization.

SOME PARADOXICAL COMPLICATIONS

Despite the proven success of the new, different-but-better manufacturing plants, there was no unseemly rush to emulate them. Instead, they and the people who produced them encountered considerable antipathy and even hostility. Misunderstandings about what had been created were frequent. There were pressures to conform. CEO blessings backfired. In short, the management world did not beat a path to the doors of those who had produced a better mousetrap.

People in the innovative units frequently experienced ill treatment at the hands of others in their own organizations. It came from managers at all levels, supervisors, workers, and union officials. In some cases these others seemed to see the innovative units as "rate busters."

In one instance the hourly paid plant safety coordinator from an innovative plant with top safety performance attended a corporation-wide meeting of managers charged with safety in their respective plants. In addition to making contributions of significance to the subject at hand (safety), he answered many questions about things back home. The interest level was high. Later, while being escorted on a tour of the host plant by one of the participants, the guide, remembering the discussions of back home conditions and events, confronted him with, "Tom, why are you lying?"

The production manager of another innovative plant found himself out of a job when his boss in the home office was replaced by a peer plant manager from a traditionally managed unit. In Norway, one highly successful innovator was derisively and condescendingly referred to by the corporate vice president of personnel as "the professor."

During a meeting of an organization of fellow innovators, one plant manager was heard to say, "This is the first time I have been able to talk about what I'm trying to do without seeing the other person's eyes glaze over."

"You, too!" exclaimed the other managers present.

The lack of understanding of what they were doing plagued those who had established or were trying to establish innovative workplaces. One manager, explaining the plans for such a unit to his newly appointed boss, was told, "All you are talking about is the Hawthorne Plan." His reply—"If you will explain to me what you think the Hawthorne Plan is, I will explain the differences"—

was repaid in retributions many times over. One division operations vice president persisted in his erroneous belief that workers
in a new innovative plant in this corporation enjoyed a guaranteed
annual wage and angrily declared, "I'll not have that in any of my
plants!" Another group, discussing a successful innovation that
had attracted considerable media attention, asked, "What do you
do once the network TV cameras have been withdrawn?" suggest-
ing that once the publicity died away the plant would become just
an ordinary one.

Among professionals in the field of management, the negative
reactions ranged from misunderstanding to downright rancor.
Managers who created the new sites were charged with being im-
moral for "running away" from the old plants to start new plants
in corn fields instead of changing the old plants. The term *greenfield
site* was coined to describe the flight, and it quickly became an ep-
ithet for the successful new sites. Further, it was charged that the
Gaines Topeka plant had hired "managers in workers' clothing"—
a neat trick, easier said than done, thought those at Gaines who
had hired all but one of the workers at the starting wage. People
with a stake in incentive pay schemes were particularly eager to
downgrade the importance of the design of work. The myth that
the Gaines Topeka plant had failed was propagated and is kept
alive even today.

There were well-intentioned misunderstandings as well. A division human resource manager exasperated the managers of the innovative site in his corporation by encouraging the managers of
other plants to visit the innovative one and carry back some feature
of it to implement in their own plants. He failed to recognize that
the innovative site was a systemic whole, made up of harmonious
parts that could not successfully be segmented and grafted onto a
very different whole. A cosmetic feature such as eliminating reserved parking places was easy to copy but insignificant in effecting
change. Other segmented thinking was evidenced by an organization development executive who had gained administrative control over a resource group originally put in place to help create new

site innovations and redesign old sites. This manager relegated the group to a stall in a compartmented "stable" that included foreman-training and team-building services. Work redesign, thought to affect only the hourly paid people, was described as "something for the unwashed."

Imitation encouraged by CEO pronouncement often created difficulties. The innovative plant manager would begin to receive calls and requests for visits from other plant managers, and not all the calls were complimentary.

A particularly ironic problem was created when division and corporate executives wanted the "different" organization to conform even when it was better because it was different. One innovative plant manager was beset by a quality assurance (QA) director who wanted a QA manager on the site and a division controller who wanted someone in the plant who was a controller and nothing else. The plant manager saw the systemic nature of his innovations, and, with little experience to guide him, he regarded almost any change as potentially knocking out a fundamental pin and causing the rest of the system to erode if not collapse. He therefore did battle on all fronts, and as a result the executives wanting to make the system conform in some "small" way labeled him unreasonable and intractable, at a considerable cost to his career.

There were other ways in which being different had its penalties. Once the Gaines plant in Topeka was on stream, outstripping other units in productivity and control of quality, the team leaders there, counterparts to first-line supervisors in the existing plants, became unpromotable. Corporate policy held that an individual could advance only so many job "points" at a time. But the Topeka organization was not a many-layered bureaucracy. For a team leader, the next step in the Topeka hierarchy was production manager, a jump in job points exceeding that allowed by corporate policy. Promotion in the Topeka system was therefore foreclosed. One would have to be promoted to a higher-level job in another plant. But here another corporate policy intervened: interplant transfers and promotions were restricted to people in jobs carrying more points than did the team leader job. Therefore, promotion to another plant was foreclosed. This is a superb example of the misfit of an innovative organization in a traditional bureaucratic organization.

COMPLICATIONS
IN REDESIGNING EXISTING UNITS

The same problems of antipathy, misunderstanding, and bureaucratic misfit were experienced by innovative managers and union officials attempting to redesign work in established plants. It wasn't that innovation couldn't be started; it couldn't be sustained, although some lasted three or four years. All too often the story had a great beginning, a vulnerable middle, and an ignominious end. The reasons for the failure to sustain were many and varied. There were no models of organization redesign in the United States; the successes were in new plants, beginning in the 1970s. Often, unanticipated external factors caused the fadeout. In no case, however, was the cause of the failure the workers themselves or the supervisors.

A typical episode of success leading to fadeout occurred at one of General Foods's largest plants, the Maxwell House division's plant in Hoboken, four years after the start-up of the Gaines plant in Topeka. It began as a joint labor-management endeavor. After considerable effort, work in one building on the site was redesigned. Six weeks after work had begun in the new way, all previous quality and production achievements had been substantially exceeded. Participants declared it a resounding success. As luck would have it, the redesigned unit produced an energy-intensive product, and when oil prices skyrocketed in the mid-seventies, the unit was shut down. The workers were dispersed throughout the plant on the basis of seniority. Local management, inexplicably prodded by division management, then switched from a joint labor-management quality-of-work-life thrust to an emphasis on creative problem-solving for everyone. Shortly thereafter, no vestige of this successful pioneering innovation remained.

In other organizations, innovation faded when key sponsors left the company. An innovative work redesign project in Harman Industries, headed up by Sydney Harman with the cooperation of Irving Bluestone of the UAW, could not survive the departure of Harman to become the Undersecretary of Commerce. In the H. J. Heinz Company, around 1976, a promising innovation came to a halt with the unrelated resignations of several key executives who had sponsored the effort.

A LITTLE BACKGROUND

The unexpected complications were not, as it turned out, an oddity—some events peculiar to specific times, places, and people. Nor were the managers in the early 1970s initiating projects to create innovative new sites and change existing sites the only ones disturbed about the first-order problems of organization performance. Many wrote of human needs in the workplace, but the solutions proposed were limited to change in managerial behavior.

Others were looking beyond the behavior of workers and managers and were examining work itself. As early as 1950, the second author with colleagues from the Tavistock Institute initiated studies in the mining industry in Great Britain that revealed that the reasons for worker dissatisfaction lay less in the pay pacts than in the form of organization under which the miners worked, which was one man, one task. In mines where there were multiskilled groups that together carried out all the tasks for the work cycle, interchanging roles and shifts, the level of productivity rose, volunteer absenteeism became a decimal point, accidents were halved, and turnover vanished.

Thus was revealed the power of the working group as a basic unit. Very dramatic was the increase in morale; people wanted to go to work. The older men came back to work on the face. The miners were excited, they collaborated with each other and with management. Less supervision was necessary and one level was eliminated altogether.

THE SOCIO-TECHNICAL SYSTEMS APPROACH

From these studies, Trist and Emery developed the theory of socio-technical systems. In this view, the organization is seen as made up of two different, independent but linked systems: the technical system, which includes the equipment and processes and follows the rules of physics, chemistry, and engineering, and the social system, which follows the rules of psychology, sociology, and politics.

The claims of these two systems are often in conflict. What is best for the technical system may not be best for the social system, and vice versa. The traditional workplace follows the technological imperative; people are expected to adapt to the technology whatever this may be and however it may have been designed. The result is what we have termed the mismatch between the characteristics of work and the characteristics of people.

The socio-technical systems approach recognizes that commitment to work is conditional on the work experience. In place of the assumption that people must always adapt to the technology, it assumes that there are different ways of using technology and that the technical system can be adapted to fit people. Those who design work from a socio-technical systems approach therefore search simultaneously in the two systems, the technical and the social, for the best match of solutions, a process called *joint optimization*, which we will examine more closely in Chapter 6.

A key feature of the socio-technical systems approach is *discovery*. Workers discover that work need not be demeaning, can be exciting. Supervisors discover that people can and will behave cooperatively. Managers and senior executives similarly make discoveries about the behavior of people and the functioning of organizations, discoveries that go against their long held assumptions. This element of discovery seems to be essential; no amount of instruction can effectively take its place. Yet making discoveries requires that a structure be in place within which to make them, a catch-22 that has been a formidable barrier to the dissemination of the socio-technical systems approach in new and existing work-places.

For a considerable period of time, inordinate considering their appropriateness, the socio-technical theories and their applications were little known in U.S. management circles. In the early 1970s this began to change.

THE NEWS SPREADS

In March 1971, a conference on "New Directions in the World of Work" (Price, 1972), sponsored by the W. E. Upjohn Institute for Employment Research, demonstrated that a small core of people were thinking about the problem of organizational performance in terms of the way work is designed. The 42 participants came from management, unions, federal government agencies, universities, business magazines, and the Ford Foundation. The stated purposes of the conference were:

To get as clear and comprehensive a view as possible of current problems in the world of work that have come to the attention of all
   the groups represented by the participants;

To consider how such problems affect all participants as individuals
   and as organizational representatives;

To study and evaluate a variety of new approaches that are being tried
   by industry, unions, government, and others to deal with work-
   centered problems; and

To identify and recommend how these approaches or others might be
   improved or more widely used—and by whom.

The Upjohn Institute conference was a revealing experience to many of those attending. The academics and others were astonished to learn what had been accomplished in such projects as Robert Ford's work in job enrichment at AT&T and the innovative Gaines pet food plant in Topeka, both of which were given detailed presentations. The practitioners were astonished to learn that such a field as socio-technical systems existed and that Davis and Trist had been teaching it at UCLA since 1967.

Nevertheless, the conference heralded deep-seated resistance to the idea that performance problems in organizations could be remedied by redesigning work. Consensus was not reached on any of the conference purposes. According to the conference report (Price, 1972), "There seemed to be two main reasons for this. The first was that the kinds of work problems emerging today seem to challenge fundamental management and union practices, as well as government policies—policies that were developed in an earlier era to meet a different set of conditions than now obtain." Secondly, "problems in work life look very different when seen from the perspective of each of the various interests represented at the conference table."

As a result of this and other conferences, the media gave extensive coverage to work redesign efforts. Articles in *Fortune* (Gooding, 1970), *Atlantic* ("Work in America," 1971), *Newsweek* ("Blue Collar Blues," 1971) and *U.S. News and World Report* ("Latest Moves," 1972), and books by Judson Gooding (1972) and Harold Shepard and Neil Herrick (1972) were followed in 1973 by a spate of articles in *The New York Times*, the *National Observer, Newsweek, Reader's Digest,* and the *Atlantic,* and a segment of NBC's "First Tuesday."

The federal government, too, was showing an interest. In his Labor Day address in 1971, President Nixon said,

> In our quest for a better environment, we must always remember that the most important part of the quality of life is the quality of work, and the new need for job satisfaction is the key to the quality of work. . . . We must make sure that technology does not dehumanize work but makes it more creative and rewarding for people who will operate the plants of the future. (Nixon, 1971)

Elliot Richardson, Secretary of Health, Education, and Welfare, created a special task force that produced a pathmaking book, *Work in America* (U.S. Department of Health, Education, and Welfare, 1973). In 1972, a subcommittee of the Senate Committee on Labor and Public Welfare (1972) held hearings on worker alienation, and shortly thereafter Neil Q. Herrick, of the Department of Labor, began a series of conferences to introduce the ideas to union leaders, senior managers, and officials of various government agencies.

With congressional backing, the National Commission on Productivity and the Quality of Working Life was formed to demonstrate to Congress and the nation at large that there was something wrong with the organization of work and that something could be done about it. The commission held a series of conferences in 1972 and 1973. The third conference was addressed by presidential aspirants Edward Kennedy and Charles Percy. Noting that the quality of work was an idea whose time had come, Senator Percy blamed rising job dissatisfaction on an entrenched, authoritarian industrial system in which managerial and labor institutions have too often become blind to the broader needs of our society. Percy sensed an imminent breakthrough in changing the ideas about work.

A key event in 1972 was the first International Conference on the Quality of Working Life. The conference produced two volumes of papers (Davis & Cherns, 1975) and proved an important force in the expansion of the field. Davis formed a Center for Quality of Working Life and began teaching two-week courses in sociotechnical systems for managers and union officials at UCLA. Regrettably, the term *quality of working life* and its abbreviation *QWL* came to receive a bad name because of a number of ideas that were promoted under its banner, especially the notion that workers could earn free time by producing their quota in less than the allotted time. QWL is nonetheless a useful term and will be used in this book in a holistic sense to mean the design of work to match people's intrinsic motivations to work, as well as extrinsic needs.

Still another source of dissemination of the innovative ideas was the innovative plants themselves, which became magnets for those wanting more information. Between March 1971 and August 1975, no fewer than 123 visits were made to the Gaines pet food plant in Topeka, mostly by small groups of educators, journalists, television crews, consultants, corporate executives, union officers and members, hospital executives, representatives of social agencies, engineers, students, and doctoral candidates. They came not only from the United States but from Sweden, Japan, the United Kingdom, Israel, Canada, West Germany, Belgium, France, and South Africa. The same thing happened at two Volvo plants in Scandinavia in which working teams of 15 to 20 members replaced assembly lines. Visits there soon became the vogue among U.S. managers.

THE RESPONSE OF CORPORATE MANAGEMENT TO THE EARLY INNOVATIONS

Given the surge of achievement and its attendant publicity and national support, one would have expected corporate managers to embrace innovations that so impressively improved the bottom line. Instead, these intelligent, sincere, dedicated, bottom-line-oriented-managers ignored, rejected, or even vigorously opposed them. In the vast majority of U.S. corporations there were no such innovations. In the few where innovations did occur, they were made on the periphery of the corporation, far from the center of power, primarily in manufacturing plants. Senior people were generally confronted with a fait accompli; in some cases the innovation was deliberately concealed from those in the executive suite.

By 1975 a pattern had emerged. Once the innovations on the periphery appeared, senior managers reacted in three ways.

(1) They permitted or caused the innovation on the periphery to fade out, leaving things pretty much as they were before.
(2) They permitted or caused the innovation on the periphery to be encapsulated, with little support for attempts to diffuse the ideas elsewhere in the company.
(3) They attempted to sustain the innovation and replicate it in other units on the periphery of the organization.

This third way was rare. An example of a management that responded in the third way is Procter and Gamble. P & G's innovative plant in Lima, OH, was the outcome of a three-week training program in socio-technical theory and applications jointly sponsored by P & G and Aluminum Company of Canada. Directing the program were Eric Trist and Louis Davis. Among the participants were Alcan vice president James Cameron and staff specialist Charles Krone from P & G headquarters. After the Lima plant success, P & G went on to build many more new socio-technically designed and managed plants. They now call this approach to management "advanced manufacturing systems."

The second response to the emergence of a successful manufacturing innovation was evident at General Foods, which became the prime and well-publicized example of encapsulation, contained innovation, and high opportunity costs. But by no means is GF the only place where such a phenomenon occurred.

The fade-out response had many variations. In one case, during a period of 10 years from the late 1960s to the late 1970s, about 70 QWL projects were tried out in a diversified manufacturing concern. All of these projects, some of which were conspicuously successful over periods up to four years and that had been initiated in their own area by line managers, had faded out except one in a new plant. An exhaustive study was made by the second author of this whole course of happenings and reviewed with four functional vice presidents and a number of senior staff specialists. Few of those present had been aware of the extent of the innovations and the positive results obtained. At the end of the discussion, nevertheless, it was apparent that no one favored taking the risk of trying to get support for QWL at the corporate level. Their systems of management practice had stood the test of time, they said, and in labor relations both sides knew where they stood. Some strong voices advocated letting other companies do the pioneer work. "We will hang back in the pack watching what they do and will learn from it. Then, if and when the time is ripe for us, we will mobilize the very considerable internal and external resources we can command and move forward quickly on a wide front."

UNIONS AND THE EARLY INNOVATIONS

The earliest innovative work sites in the United States began without unions. Plant managers at these sites doubted that what they wanted to do could be done with a union. And well-designed and well-managed sites have been highly resistant to union organizing attempts.

In many ways organized labor's early reception of the notion that something should be done about how work is organized paralleled that of management. Like managers, union leaders are individuals, with their own personal values, goals, and unique sets of life experiences that shape the way they perceive the world. And like managers, some make things happen, some watch what happens, and some wonder what happened. The typical union leader's work experience was in traditional workplaces; many of them had made their work life worthwhile through doing union activity, militant and otherwise. None had encountered and experienced work designed along the new principles.

A small minority, including Irving Bluestone of the UAW, Leon Schacter of the Amalgamated Food and Allied Workers Union, AFL-CIO, and Peter Diciccio of the IUEW, saw the need and the benefits of involvement as well as the risk of not being involved. Others were less knowledgeable and strongly resisted the ideas. While Bluestone was publicly active in advancing the concept of QWL, some of his colleagues were saying, "An assembly line is an assembly line. What we must do is get the worker more time off and money enough to enjoy the leisure time."

Some labor leaders opposed quality of working life programs on the grounds that if workers wanted them, they would ask for them. They had not. Therefore, the reasoning went, there is no demand for redesigned work. The vast majority of union members, like their leaders, had no discovery opportunities and would not know what to ask for or how to ask for it when they had not experienced it.

Union officials resented the framing of the problem by academics and managers. That most of the solutions proposed were coming from the management side implied to them that anti-union attitudes lay behind the job improvement initiatives. One conference report noted:

> The anxiety here reveals that union representatives are clearly suspicious of an analysis that challenges the fundamental precepts of the trade union. When you suggest that the basic problem has to do with the nature of the job and the way the plant is structured, rather than wages, fringes, and other things basic to the bargaining process, then union representatives understandably get nervous.

Work redesign called for some cooperation between labor and management. But union officials by their power of negotiation had to win good things for workers. Getting good things through collaboration was being asea in uncharted waters.

FROM 1975 ONWARD

Interest and awareness grew tremendously in the next 10 years. Whereas about 200 people, mostly academics, had attended the 1972 International Conference on the Quality of Working Life held at Harriman, NY, there were some 2,000 in attendance at the 1981 conference "QWL and the Eighties" in Toronto. Most of these were managers and union officials, often attending as teams. Many case studies of successful change efforts in unionized plants were presented.

General Motors and the UAW persisted with their redesign efforts in established plants. Proctor & Gamble maintained the innovations in their new plants and redesigned their old. Rohm and Haas, Tennessee, and the Aluminum Brick and Glass Workers showed the way in the Knoxville plant and became a magnet for those interested in redesigning established unionized plants.

Even today in the 1990s it must be noted that most of those in the management and union worlds in the United States have still not beaten a path to the doors of those who brought about successful changes in the workplace. Managers with plants in the early stages of redesign continue to ask:

- How do you gain initial understanding and support from division and corporate management?
- How do you maintain understanding and support of division and corporate management?
- How do you prove to upper levels that it is right?
- What do you do when corporate and division policies are contrary to local values and practices?
- What is the best approach to making the benefits of participative management known among hostile managers outside the innovative unit?

Similarly, a recent survey of a small group of executives who have plant managers of innovative plants reporting to them found them asking:

- How can I move the concepts into the corporate office and get some understanding there?
- How do I work on corporate task forces to study and "convert" the corporation?
- How do I get other managers interested when even a successful model within the corporation doesn't move them?
- How do you measure the improved performance and link it to the innovation?

These executives summarized their concerns in a single question: "How do we change the corporate structure/culture to reduce conflict with our innovative units and at the same time improve the operation of the corporate groups?"

From the time of the first successful QWL innovations to the present, there has been little or no change at the centers of organizations. When intensive change has been contemplated, preparation in the executive offices has been misguided, inadequate, or nonexistent. When change has faded out or become encapsulated, senior managers have failed to recognize and understand what was happening. Intensive change on the periphery has occurred in spite of the center, not because of it. Thus the change model practiced has been a *periphery-in* model, rather than a *center-out* model. And with such a change model, the change process has been slow and ineffective.

The opportunity costs of this slow and ineffective change process have been inestimable. These innovations at the periphery, while increasing in number, have not improved in quality. Stagnation develops. Senior management, content with the superior bottom-line results achieved in the innovations, permits them to exist without attainment of their full potential. Sometimes second-, third-, and fourth-generation site managers, content and unwilling to take risks, contribute to the problem. As a result, the state of the art has not advanced.

The behavior of intelligent and dedicated managers in resisting change that will improve their bottom line has not been in the best interest either of stockholders or of the larger society. Why, then, have so few been willing to embrace the idea that the answer to performance problems lies in redesigning work to meet the needs of people? And why are some companies in which some people are toiling to do just that so slow to accomplish it? The stakes are too great to leave these questions unexplained. Chapter 3 will take up the first question, and the chapters in Part II will answer the second and discuss a way of dealing with the problem.

THREE

Organizational Paradigm and Paradigm Shift: A Whole New Way of Thinking

The answer to a perplexing question in one field is often to be found in another seemingly unrelated field. Thus we turn to the history of the advancement of science for insights that help explain inertia in crisis.

According to Thomas Kuhn (1962), progress in science has not been a steady accretion of knowledge but has occurred in jumps, when phenomena have been observed that could not be explained by the existing body of ideas. For example, astronomers in Ptolemy's day held to a theory about the heavens based on the belief in the Earth as the center of the universe. The sun, moon, planets, and stars all revolved about the Earth. In time, with the development of improved instruments, astronomers began to observe planetary movements that could not be explained by this system of thought. A radically different set of theories had to be conceived to explain these new observations.

Kuhn used the word *paradigm* to represent *universally recognized scientific achievements that for a time provide model ideas, measurements, and solutions (theories) to a community of practitioners.* When new information is developed that is irreconcilable with such a set of accepted ideas, the change in scientific knowledge is not only major but discontinuous. The community of practitioners—be they scientists in a particular field such as astronomy or professionals in the field of management—must do more than learn new facts; they must unlearn much of what they had previously known. The entire body of theory must change. Kuhn called this a *paradigm shift.*

Unavoidably, a paradigm shift brings conflict. For a time the two incompatible paradigms compete for followers. Despite all the evidence of the truth of the new paradigm, many if not most in the community of practitioners will cling fiercely to the old.

ORGANIZATIONAL PARADIGMS

The concepts of *paradigm* and *paradigm shift* are central to understanding the failure of the "better mousetrap" theory—why managers, even those most oriented to the bottom line, reject the evidence of the benefits of the redesign of work and attack its successful practitioners.

An organization is an embodiment of shared ideas held in the heads and hearts of its members. It has values and beliefs, often referred to as its philosophy. It has axioms that are regarded as self-evident truths. It has theories and models that serve as conceptual maps. This commonly held body of ideas, values, axioms and theories constitute what we may call the organizational paradigm. It is used by the organization's members to explain to themselves and to others how the organization functions. It is the base from which organization leaders set organizational goals. It comes into play whenever members of the organization—separately or in groups—ponder, decide, or justify their actions. The organizational paradigm forms the base for policy formulation. It drives the organization's structure and processes and therefore the behavior of its members.

Table 3.1 Two Organizational Paradigms

Old	*New*
The technological imperative	Joint optimization of the technical and social systems
People as an extension of the machine	People as complementary to the machine
People as expendable spare parts	People as a resource to be developed
Maximum task breakdown, simple narrow skills	Optimum task grouping, multiple broad skills
External controls (supervisors, specialist staffs, procedures)	Internal controls (self-regulating subsystems)
Tall organization chart, autocratic style	Flat organization chart, participative style
Competition, gamesmanship	Collaboration, collegiality
Organization's purposes only	Members' and society's purposes also
Alienation	Commitment
Low risk-taking	Innovation

Since the beginning of the factory system in the United States, our enterprises have operated with a paradigm based on the values, beliefs, axioms, theories, and models that gave rise to scientific management. Today, however, an increasing number of practitioners are adopting a new, radically different paradigm. The innovations described in Chapter 2 flowed from values, theories, and models that are incompatible with the old. Advanced industrial societies are thus in the midst of an organizational paradigm shift. Table 3.1 contrasts the two paradigms. Noting the differences makes clear why the adoption of the new approach represents an organizational paradigm shift.

Our traditional organizations follow the technological imperative, which regards people as extensions of machines and therefore
as expendable spare parts. By contrast, the emergent paradigm is
founded on the principle of joint optimization, which regards people as complementary to the machine and values their unique capabilities for appreciative and evaluative judgment, a resource to
be developed for their own sake rather than to be degraded and
cast aside.

Traditional organizations are also characterized by maximum
work breakdown, which leads to circumscribed job descriptions
and single skills—the narrower the better. Workers in such roles
are often unable to manage the uncertainty, or variance, that char-
acterizes their immediate environment. They therefore require
strict external control. Layer upon layer of supervision comes into
existence supported by a wide variety of specialist staffs and formal procedures. A tall pyramidic organization results, which is auto-
cratically managed throughout, even if the paternalism is benign.
By contrast, the new paradigm is based on optimum task group-
ing, which encourages multiple broad skills. Workers in such a role
system (as opposed to a job system) become capable of a much
higher degree of internal control, having flexible group resources
to meet a greater degree of environmental variance. This leads to a
flat organization characterized by as much lateral as vertical communication. A participative management style emerges with the
various levels mutually articulated rather than arranged in a simple
hierarchy.

In the traditional organization each member has first of all to
compete with and defend himself or herself against everyone else,
whether as an individual or as a member of a functional group—
maintenance versus production, staff versus line. Rewards such as
promotion and privilege go to those who (in the metaphor introduced by Michael Maccoby, 1976) are "gamesmen"—those who
excel in playing the political game of the organization. Cooperation, though formally required wherever tasks are interdependent,

takes second place as a value. The new paradigm, by contrast, gives first place to coping with the manifold interdependencies that arise in complex organizations. It values collaboration between groups and collegiality within groups. It encourages the establishment of a negotiated order in which multiple and mutually agreed tradeoffs are continuously arrived at.

Traditional organizations serve only their own ends. They are, and indeed are supposed to be, selfish. The new paradigm imposes the additional task on them of aligning their own purposes with the purposes of the wider society and also with the purposes of their members. By so doing, organizations become both "environmentalized" and "humanized" (Ackoff, 1974)—and thus more truly purposeful—rather than remaining impersonal and mindless forces that increase environmental turbulence.

A change in all these regards from the old paradigm to the new brings into being conditions that allow commitment to grow and alienation to decrease. Equally important is the replacement of a climate of low risk-taking with one of innovation. This implies high trust and openness in relations. All these qualities are mandatory if we are to transform traditional technocratic bureaucracies into continuous adaptive learning systems.

PERSONAL PARADIGM CHANGE

This discussion of the substantial differences between the old paradigm and the new should begin to clarify why intelligent, dedicated managers, with few exceptions, have been unwilling to adopt widely publicized innovations that have demonstrated dramatic improvements in the bottom line. The newly designed innovative plants and the successful and permanent redesigns of established plants exemplify an organizational paradigm shift. The new paradigm on which they are based is incompatible with the old. Adopting the new has meant giving up the old. For most managers, such a change has been too great. They have been ready to initiate moderate organizational change, but not to create intensive change, which would require changes in their way of thinking, their roles, and their behavior. Most have clung to the old paradigm. To accept the new they must make a personal paradigm change, which means deep change in themselves.

Personal paradigm change usually takes place a little bit at a time. People change their way of thinking in small increments, largely from experiencing a new kind of work life.

To understand how difficult it is to adopt a new paradigm, we must consider the kind of learning that is needed for such a change. Learning in general may be categorized into two kinds, happy learning and unhappy learning. *Happy learning* is additive, an extension or a refinement of something one already knows. The knowledge gained is within one's existing personal paradigm. It may involve a modification of one's views, but not an extensive reorganization of one's values, beliefs, axioms, theories, and models. Acquiring a bit of useful information, recognizing why a machine has been malfunctioning and what to do about it, discovering a way of getting a point across to a group of trainees—all these are examples of happy learning. With happy learning, there is usually no reason for embarrassment or shame at not having had the knowledge previously. In short, happy learning makes one feel good.

Unhappy learning is very different. Unhappy learning does involve a reorganization of the values, beliefs, axioms, theories, and models that together make up one's personal paradigm, which has been built up slowly through one's life experiences. These form an essential part of one's identity. Formal training, conscious experimentation, not-so-conscious trial and error, induction, and deduction all play a part in the development of a personal paradigm.

Unhappy learning often involves unlearning—finding out that what one "knows for a fact" is not a fact at all. For example, a widely cherished axiom holds that most people don't want to or won't make decisions. This axiom derives from the common experience in the traditional work system, where, to be sure, there are many people who don't want to make decisions. But experience with re-designed workplaces has shown that these same people, when placed in new-paradigm organizations, do make decisions, important decisions. The willingness to make decisions turns out to be a product of the work experience. The axiom that people don't want to make decisions is revealed to be only a truth-in-context, the context of an organization driven by the old paradigm. Because most of us have experienced no other kind of work context, the belief has been reinforced.

Another form of unhappy learning associated with a paradigm shift involves finding out how much one doesn't know, discovering that there is a body of knowledge that one ought to know but doesn't. Learning of one's own ignorance can be frightening and/or depressing, especially when one first discovers that a paradigm change is in order. It can also be shaming. The plant manager, for example, who discovers that he or she knows less about a major development—such as socio-technical systems theory—than people at lower levels in the organization may suffer acute embarrassment. Embarrassment leads to shame, and shame can easily lead to anger and resentment.

One common reaction upon experiencing unhappy learning is to find someone to be angry with. The object of the anger may be a consultant, a peer, a boss, or a union official. It may be a team working in the new-paradigm mode. It may be "they" or the system. Sometimes it comes in resentment at words used to describe the new ideas; one corporate vice president took offense at the word "traditional" used to describe the old way of doing things and demanded, "Why don't you find another word, such as 'classic'?"

Because a personal paradigm change involves unhappy learning, for most people it is painful. It means giving up long-held assumptions and ways of thinking and doing, forsaking the haven of the familiar. One consciously and unconsciously stops doing certain things and begins instead to do other things. Giving up is usually accompanied by mourning, especially when that given up has

Table 3.2 Personal Paradigm Change

Give Up	New Reality
Feeling of having learned it all	Learning never stops
Reductionist thinking	Systems thinking
Dependence on procedures	Focus on results
False simplicity	Complexity
It is "they" who are to blame	Personal accountability
Virtue of being certain	Doubt
Belief in stability	Continuous change

been dearly held. One must also make a number of tradeoffs and accept new reality in return (see Table 3.2).

The Feeling of Having Learned It All. One trainer from an organization development department, after sitting through his first exposure to socio-technical theories and principles angrily exclaimed, "I just got these Maslow and Herzberg principles mastered and now you come along with this socio-technical stuff!" The realization can mean public humiliation; one highly respected professor of organizational behavior, taking issue with others at a conference, suddenly sensed a need to hedge and added, "Unless there is something going on which I don't know about."

Convenience of Reductionist Thinking. At issue is how we think— what we choose to see of the world and how we think the world works. Systems thinking is essential to understanding living things— organic wholes that function as they do because of the way the parts are arranged and interact with each other. Organizations exhibit properties of living systems, and therefore to manage them, change them, exist in them healthfully one must employ systems thinking. Our education has taught us an accounting, engineering, industrial management, and even a psychology geared to reductionist logic. In our "scientific" research, we isolate variables and try to determine what happens to "a" when we change "b." But in a living system or an organization, everything internal is connected to everything else and elements in the systems environment are making themselves felt. How "a" changes when you change "b" depends on what else is going on in and out of the system.

Dependence on Procedures as Measure of Effectiveness. Procedures are at the heart of a bureaucracy, where it is believed that if procedures are followed, results are sure to come. Rewards go to those who blindly follow procedures and remain safe as they do so. The new way recognizes the unenduring value of procedures in a rapidly changing environment and puts direct emphasis on results. "Why has it been done this way?" becomes the valued question. Demands on the individual rise commensurately. The implications of giving up dependence on procedures goes far beyond the boundaries of business organizations.

Simplicity. It is convenient to look for oversimplified answers to problems. The paradigm change means giving up the simple answers and accepting that answers may be more complicated and difficult to find. In a group of union stewards participating in a workshop exercise designed to make them aware of their assumptions and the consequences of these assumptions, one participant observed, "And all the time I thought the foreman was the problem."

It Is "They" Who Are to Blame. Difficulties in the workplace are no longer explained by reference to "those bad workers," "those bad union leaders," "those bad foremen," or "those bad managers." Such comfortable rationales are replaced by an acceptance of one's own responsibility along with that of others' for the nature of the workplace, of which the "bad" behavior is a function. Furthermore, one may also begin to apply the concept that "the product of work is people" to oneself and begin to wonder about one's own past life choices and personality development (Herbst, 1974).

Virtue of Being Certain. In the old way to be certain is to be virtuous. In the new way full accord is given to the notion that everything can't be known and new circumstances continuously arise. The possession of some doubt about the nature of things and the correct course to follow is not only natural but a virtue, a stimulus to greater effort to set forth the courses available from which to make a choice and to learn from having done so.

Belief in Stability. Unplanned, uncontrollable change is a feature of our society. Yet in all of us is a yearning for normalcy, a yearning for a return to stability. Not too many years ago the VP for finance of a Fortune 500 corporation, speaking of the volatility of the financial markets, concluded his address with,

> Our business and financial institutions have reacted admirably so far in an enormously difficult time. We have gained experience, seasoning, and toughness that should stand us in good stead, both while the current difficulties persist and after we move on—*as in time I am confident we will*—into a steadier, healthier, more rational environment.

The undeniable reality is that things have become even more unstable, more tumultuous and there are no signs of abatement. In a very real sense, it is these very conditions of environmental turbulence that have necessitated proposals for radical change in the organization at a time when there is in most every individual this yearning for a return to a stable state.

A LOOK AHEAD

Chapter 2 ended with the observation that the behavior of the vast majority of intelligent and dedicated U.S. managers in resisting something that would improve the performance of their organizations was paradoxical and not in the best interests of stockholders and the larger society. The question of why the better mousetrap theory failed was posed. In this chapter, the answer was shown to be rooted in the phenomenon of an organizational paradigm shift, in which two incompatible paradigms exist simultaneously, each competing for adherents. In a paradigm shift, *every* individual is confronted with the need to reexamine his or her ways of thinking. But self-confrontation is a painful process, one to be avoided if possible. It therefore seems that the strong and dynamic resistance to change shown by managers and others was an unavoidable phenomenon.

Currently, in spite of the increased visibility of the first-order problems and their consequences, too few interpret the landscape as requiring intensive change for the long-term solution. Professing to want team work without teams is little more than rhetoric. Professing empowerment without teams made by system change is not to know.

A second concern at this time is the slowness of those attempting to make system change. Until now the innovative projects have followed a *periphery-in* change model. That is, a single plant or unit at the periphery of an organization was designed or redesigned, independent of (and sometimes without the knowledge of) senior corporate officials at the center. At the time these early projects were initiated, there probably was no other way the changes could have been brought about. The periphery-in model, with its many disadvantages, has persisted as efforts to make intensive change have multiplied. With periphery-in, senior managers have left middle managers free to do nothing or to make changes not sufficiently deep or intensive. "Bad" work experience has persisted and years have been wasted. At best, the periphery-in model has yielded progress at far too slow a pace. At worst it has resulted in no change at all.

As a result the progress in bringing about change in the workplace has been slow, too slow in the light of the seriousness and urgency of the first-order problems of organizational performance. If one chooses to fix the beginning of the current organizational paradigm shift as the early 1950s, we have already traversed about 40 years. To be realistic, we must expect a good many years to elapse before the shift is complete.

A discouraging picture? Yes, given the way in which change has occurred thus far. If periphery-in continues to be the change model, far more than another 40 years will be required to complete the organizational paradigm shift.

A new model is required. If successful intensive change is to be made, and if its success is to be sustained, it must be made not just at the periphery but throughout the corporation. Senior management needs to be not only actively involved but at the very heart of the change. The change model needed is one that *begins* with senior management. This model is referred to as the *center-out* change model. A direct outgrowth of periphery-in experience, the new model can greatly speed up the rate of deep organization change. The balance of this book is devoted to a description of this new change model and its implementation and to consideration of the new model in its relationship to senior corporate management and the nonmanufacturing as well as the manufacturing sectors of the company. Chapters 7, 8, and 9 (Part III), and 10, 11, and 12 (Part IV), deal with plant-level applications of the model in new and existing plants respectively.

PART II

Center-Out: A New Change Model

FOUR

Senior Managers Appreciate

The center-out model can be used not only by companies in which there have been few or no intensive change initiatives but also by those companies that have been practicing periphery-in. A select few U.S. companies are now beginning a transition from periphery-in to center-out. Happily, several conditions currently prevail that contribute to the feasibility of both the redesign of work and the center-out change model.

Much knowledge has been gained through experience with periphery-in. The ranks of line and staff managers who have successfully innovated have swelled. Promotions have put some of them into positions of greater influence.

The increased use of statistics, of itself a good thing, has brought to many executive suites an altered attitude about learning something new. Now, everyone, including those in the executive suite, must learn new things and training is cascaded downward from the very top. Coupled with the changed attitude about learning is some movement toward a longer term perspective.

There is more change activity of all kinds. Besides indicating the level of concern, this can lead to more units making an odyssey similar to one described as, "We began with short interval scheduling, progressed to incentive pay, quality circles, just-in-time and then finally got to socio-technical systems." An example of a company-level odyssey is Corning. According to Corning's Senior Vice President and Corporate Director for Quality, a quality journey has three stages. The third, the World-Class Quality Stage, adds self-managed teamwork (Luther, 1991).

The labor movement has undergone significant change. Like the early innovating plant managers, the early union innovators such as Irving Bluestone and Leon Schacter were lonely, but today's union official who seeks new goals can find company within the labor movement. New breakthroughs have shown that work can be successfully redesigned in old, unionized plants. The U.S. Labor Department's Bureau of Labor-Management Relations and Cooperative Programs has been active in fostering change by sponsoring conferences, conducting and publicizing studies, and issuing reports on significant literature and events. Labor-management committees promoting cooperation at the area level have also come into being, on the pattern of an initiative by then Mayor Stanley Lundine of Jamestown, NY.

New resources are being developed by the educational system. The number of universities that teach socio-technical theory and methods, although not yet abundant, is increasing. Furthermore, the few who have been teaching these theories have been graduating PhDs for the past several years.

Public workshops now abound whereas at one time the two-week course on socio-technical systems at UCLA was about all that was to be had. For years the only networks that provided opportunity for executives engaged in change to link up with counterparts in other companies were sponsored and maintained by the first author. Networks recently have become commonplace.

The time is right for the center-out change model to emerge.

The "center" refers to the chief executive officer, the other corporate officers, and second echelon key executives reporting to them. Herein lies a problem in that this book is addressed to managers in companies ranging in size from large multinationals with many subsidiaries, to single division companies. Two matters have caused us to describe center-out as it applies to a medium sized single division company. The first relates to exposition. We endeavor to present a complex process in understandable terms, but if a very large company were chosen for the illustration the presentation would be unduly cumbersome because of the variety of organization types and structures existing in these very large companies. On the other hand, once one understands the principles of the center-out model described for a medium sized company, adaptation of the model to a particular large sized organization is easy.

The second reason for our choice of the medium sized company for exposition purposes arises in the urgency of getting on with the change process. There is a tradeoff between the ideal of beginning at the very center of an extremely large organization and the risks of taking such a very long time to remake it. An associated factor is the degree of decentralization common in very large organizations. There are many relatively autonomous centers and one can profitably apply the center-out change model to one or more relatively autonomous subsidiaries or business units.

Accordingly, the center-out model is depicted for a functionally organized, modest sized corporation with six manufacturing plants. Senior management includes a chairman of the board and chief executive officer, four outside directors, and vice presidents of marketing, finance, manufacturing, research and development, human resources, environmental affairs, and procurement. It is assumed here that initiatives toward intensive change are yet to be exerted.

In center-out, senior management is no longer passive but plays an active leadership role. The critical initial step of what we will call "getting it right at the center" is the development of an understanding of the fundamental reasons why intensive change is vital to the long-term success of the organization. From this understanding comes well-founded commitment and in this respect center-out differs dramatically from periphery-in in which senior management's commitment to intensive change—if it came at

Table 4.1 Appreciation: A Two-Step Process

- Seek facts. Facts are reality judgments.
- Uncover the significance of the facts. This involves value judgments.

Appreciation covers the enterprise itself and the environment, each in the past, present, and future.

---

all—came after lower- and middle-level managers had succeeded in creating good work that brought about improved bottom-line results. This initial step is a difficult, time-consuming process, yet without it any innovation is doomed to face the pitfalls of the periphery-in model.

THE APPRECIATION PROCESS

The essential process employed in the early steps of getting it right at the center is *appreciation* in the special meaning that Vickers (1965) gave this word. Appreciation in his sense must be distinguished from its senses of gratitude ("I appreciate your thoughtfulness") and growth in value ("Those stocks have appreciated considerably"). Vickers uses *appreciation* to mean a comprehensive process of gaining a deeper understanding of the world about us. It occurs in two steps. First, one seeks facts, which are judgments of reality. Second, one labors to uncover the significance of the facts, their relevance and importance for the organization. These are judgments of value (see Table 4.1).

Appreciation covers both the enterprise itself and the environment, and it deals with the past, the present, and the future. In the center-out model, appreciative activity explores where the organization has come from, is now in relation to today's environment, what the environment is likely to be 5 to 15 years (or even further) down the road, and what the organization will have to be like to survive in that future.

Appreciation is by no means easy for a group of senior executives to accomplish. The chief executive officer assembles the participants, but their presence together is no guarantee that work will be done. Because each executive has experienced ineffective groups unable to make decisions, perform analyses, or do effective work, all are likely to harbor a derisive attitude about collective capability. Instead of collaborating, they will display the competitive behavior that got them where they are. They will be oriented to the short term when a long-term perspective is called for. Part of the problem lies in the career system. Bower (1970) has noted that managers are rewarded for performance that is almost always defined in terms of short-run economic or technical results. In one group of functional vice presidents of a large U.S. corporation, who were meeting to consider how the organization might be made more adaptive to the future, one ventured the opinion that he saw no reason to spend time on the future: "Let's focus on profit." And in this roomful of intelligent managers, the attitude toward the short run was so prevalent that no one chose to challenge him. No more time was spent on the future that day.

Appreciation demands long spans of uninterrupted time. The deliberations are complex. Conflicts of values, personalities, and opinions will surface and have to be worked through. The best results are obtained by going off-site for three or four days and conducting proceedings informally in open dialogue. By going into retreat the participants can experience a process.

The key players at the center, also engaged in the day-to-day pursuits of running the business, will resist taking the time for appreciation. As someone has said, "Managers are so busy doing the urgent that they have no time for the important." Time and place aside, operational matters will tend to take precedence. What is operational is familiar territory and "safe." Difficult issues can be avoided with an operational agenda. But the entire group must be involved. Rules must be established that nothing is "right" or "wrong," but that judgments will come later. Everyone can look at things privately and collectively. In doing so as a group they come to a much more common understanding. A shared appreciation is far better than having secret beliefs unknown to each other.

Facilitation by professionals in this field is useful. Not to be overlooked is the nature of appreciation as a process. You don't appreciate off the top of your head or with your eyes lifted to heaven. First ideas are by no means the final ideas. Ideas at any point in time are not final but the best that can be done with the knowledge and information currently available.

Senior executives, acutely aware of the fragile and temporary nature of their positions, will correctly sense significant personal risks in the appreciation process. There are career risks, especially for older executives, who may be hanging on until retirement or for a special retirement package. There are risks to self-esteem. Unlearning is painful for almost anyone but especially so for these high-ranking executives, whose status adds to the stress. There is stress in contemplating changes in direction, emphasis, organizational structure, department mission, and priorities. And there is stress as potential obsolescence of one's knowledge, skills, and contacts becomes apparent and as one recognizes the possibility of losing power and influence.

Appreciation demands a broad view, yet the usual compartmented organization rewards managers for a parochial view. Each executive has a constituency with expectations for individual rewards and resources, and the executive's power with that constituency depends on success in obtaining those rewards and resources (Zaleznik, 1970).

The deliberations will be affected by the reception given to bad news, for much in appreciation is bad news. When the messenger bearing bad news is beheaded, candor and intensive searching cannot be expected to develop in the appreciating team. In one company, key members of the personnel department persuaded a senior executive to permit a survey of attitudes and perceptions of the top four or five levels of management. When he reviewed the results, his response was, "You have brought me my head on a platter." Within two years, only one of the group who did the survey remained with the corporation. The message to bad-news-bearers was clear.

Other barriers to appreciation will arise. Too often the unquantifiable is ignored and the quantifiable is given more importance than it should have. An inordinate reliance on certainty may have to be overcome. Many organizations seem to operate on the unwarranted assumption that once everything is known and planned for, then fully effective control, applied by management, will lead to the right outcome (Driggers, 1967).

Appreciation makes great demands on those at the center of power who are entrusted with stewardship. It is much easier not to change, to deal with presumed certainty rather than with the reality of uncertainty, to assume one can control the future instead of accepting the need to adapt to things beyond one's control. The effect of appreciation on the key managers is uneven and often gradual. The organizational logic of paradigm shift is not easily forthcoming the first time through. Commitment to intensive change may be quite tentative at the beginning, but it will build during the appreciation process.

MOTIVATIONS TO APPRECIATE: CONDITIONS AND INSIGHTS

It is appropriate to wonder why anyone would decide to undertake the difficult and time-consuming process of appreciation. Certain conditions and insights may provide the motivation.

Getting it right at the center may begin when senior management recognizes the necessity of taking a truly long-term perspective. There are many pressures on senior management to take a short-term view and the idea of a three-year plan being strategic is prevalent. Blaming Wall Street for this state of affairs is commonplace.

Crisis—having their backs against the wall—can be a prime force leading senior managements to ask the questions of appreciation

Table 4.2 Conditions and Insights That Can Lead to Appreciation

- Recognizing the necessity of taking a truly long-term perspective
- Having their backs against the wall
- Realizing that they have lost business opportunities due to preoccupation with internal problems
- Having been confronted with the business effectiveness of intensive innovation on the periphery

and go thereon to intensive innovation. Short of crisis is the condition beginning with being disturbed about what is happening within the corporation and in the wider environment, wondering where all this is likely to lead in the future. From abroad, mounting competition in price, quality, and variety may be spurring those at senior level to look for ways to improve performance.

For others it can be a realization that they have lost business opportunities because of being overly preoccupied with internal problems such as chronic labor disputes and stoppages, environmental pollution, and product recalls. Coincidentally they may have become disillusioned with the inadequacy of quick fixes that promised much but have delivered too little of permanence.

Occasionally the existence in the company of a plant in which work has been successfully redesigned will cause the CEO to consider going beyond mere replication of that success throughout the corporation's manufacturing plants. Surely, the CEO reasons, if we can gain in all areas of the company the commitment evident in the redesigned plant, the company will perform immensely better.

Appreciation is made up of several steps, but these may turn out not to be sequential. Inevitably topics will be taken up anew as both the scene and the executives' views change. Appreciation can begin with the present and continue with the future or can go back and forward between the two. It can begin with a wide scan of the broader environment or with the state of the organization itself. Most managers at the present time seem more comfortable with beginning with the present. In Australia, Merrelyn and Fred Emery

Table 4.3 Appreciating the Present

- What is it like up there? (Asked regarding the board of directors and the investment community)
- What is it like in this company, and how did it get this way? (This brings in the past)
- What is it like out there (in the environment) and how did it get that way?
- Is there a good "fit" between the enterprise and the environment or is there some mismatch? Could we be doing better than we are now doing?

(Emery & Emery, 1976) developed a form of appreciation that they called "the search conference." This is now becoming widely used in all industrial societies.

APPRECIATING THE PRESENT

In the more favored practice, appreciation begins with questions about the here-and-now (see Table 4.3).

What Is It Like Up There? This is an important political question. Few CEOs need to be reminded that the investment community must not be ignored, that there are limits to the power and latitude of corporate officers. Participation by outside directors is of great advantage here. Their presence will broaden the horizons of the appreciating group. Generally, directors are better able to surmise the reception awaiting the news that the company is embarking on a serious and long-term remaking of itself. Those in the investment community are more accustomed to old-paradigm thinking managements and their short-term outlook. Indeed, Wall Street deserves some of the blame for the short-term orientation but forward-looking managements should not use Wall Street as an excuse to do nothing. It will be difficult for many in the Wall Street community to appreciate the realities of a paradigm shift when it is their first exposure to the notion. They may not easily concede the time required to make deep change.

Regarding the paradigm shift, in the investment community some will soon realize that deep change is needed there, a realization that can trigger the wide range of emotions associated with confronting this reality.

What Is It Like in This Company, and How Did It Get This Way? You have to know where you are before you can figure out how to get where you're going. Also important is to know how the current state of affairs evolved. This historical perspective can help the group to identify the ideas that drive the organization's structure, processes, and behavior. Typically, senior management professes beliefs in the form of a philosophy statement or credo. What actually goes on in the organization, however, is generally in sharp contrast to this credo. Thus in addition to the *professed* organizational paradigm, there is an *operational* paradigm (Argyris & Schon, 1974). People throughout the organization feel the operational paradigm but are seldom able to articulate its presence. Proof that paradigms come in pairs—professed and operational—is found when consultants use the company credo or philosophy to gain support for change and get only snickers and turnoffs by managers at the plant level. Attitudes toward the professed organizational paradigm will range from blissful ignorance to Machiavellian cynicism.

The senior group at the center must study what actually goes on in the organization and from these data infer the values, beliefs, axioms, theories, and models that drive the organization. This search is unhappy learning of an intense kind. Some microsocial analysis—studying at the level of the individual why people do what they do—is unavoidable. Comparing the professed and operational paradigms is further painful learning. We will examine this process at length in subsequent chapters.

What Is It Like Out There, and How Did It Get That Way? The environment "out there" is broad-reaching, including not just the markets and competition and their implications for the enterprise but the physical, political, macroeconomic, legislative, and social aspects of the environment. As we saw earlier in the chapter, changing conditions are making intensive change in the workplace more feasible as well as more necessary. Trends can be distinguished from fads if one goes backward in time to identify already visible trends and make some judgments about the deeper causal factors and how they are connected.

Is There a Good "Fit" Between the Enterprise and the Environment, or Is There Some Mismatch? This is the "how are we doing?" aspect of the process. The group reviews how well the company is doing, how well it could be doing, and what needs to be done.

"How well is the company doing?" extends beyond the performance of manufacturing and encompasses selling, market research, purchasing, and finance. The appreciating group assesses the match with the environment in *all* relevant aspects.

A company must make what is wanted and sell it at a price the prospective user is willing to pay. This principle is followed well by most managers, and it is not the primary subject of this book.

Responsiveness to changing conditions is a cardinal need of a successful organization and must be included in the criteria of performance.

Regarding "Could we do better than we are now doing?" all too often managers and those who judge their performance only look to the past for a base against which to compare performance. One plant manager's perspective was jolted in a conversation with a Japanese counterpart. Over several years of diligent efforts his plant had shown considerable improvement in reducing the defect level, and he felt good about the accomplishments. When he compared his goal for the next few years with that of the Japanese organization, however, he found that his goal for defect-level reduction was far too complacent. A thorough technical analysis would have uncovered the sources of the defects and led him to thinking more in terms of what is possible. Asking what is really possible is likely to reveal unexpected opportunities.

Table 4.4 Appreciating the Future

- What do we *want* our company to be like?
- What is it going to be like out there in, say, 5, 10, 15 years or even longer?
- What *must* our company be like?

APPRECIATING THE FUTURE

Whatever the current state of the company, it cannot be evaluated except in relation to the future. All may be well but not so well as it might be, and not for so long as it may seem.

What Do We Want Our Company To Be Like? In appreciating the present it is inevitable that warts, besides the consequences of doing nothing, will come into view. These will relate to personal values, comfort, and effort. "Some things that go on are in significant conflict with my personal values. I would like it to be otherwise." "I don't like being required to . . . . ." "It takes far more effort to get things done than should be necessary." It is eminently right to search for ways to remove these warts but appreciation must *not* conclude with the question, "What do we want this company to be like in the future?" So doing ignores the matter of "fit" with the environment.

What Is It Going to Be Like Out There in, Say, 5, 10, 15 Years or Even Longer? Senior management must make some informed conjectures about how the environment will change. The long-term survival and well-being of the business will depend on these judgments, and even those playing catch-up are advised to carry out this step and repeat it regularly. Wishful thinking must not prevail. The managers may wish for some government regulation to decrease. They may hope that import restrictions will continue to protect their industry. They may wish for the return of a work ethic in which people will work hard no matter what the nature of the job, the boss, and the workplace. They may wish that labor unions will go away.

Already the key appreciating group has examined past trends in the environment, made some judgments about the deeper causal factors and how they are connected. Now they share their views on the trends they feel are likely to go on influencing the future during the next 10 to 15 years. They also identify new issues and trends that they feel are likely to emerge in this period. No one has a privileged insight into the future. Therefore, everyone's views carry equal weight. Scanning the wider environment in a futures' perspective is generalist work.

What Characteristics Must Our Company Have in Order to Thrive in This Conjectured Future Environment? The desired characteristics— the company with its warts removed—are examined against the backdrop of the anticipated environment. There must be a good match between these two if the company is to survive and prosper. Usually a compromise between what the management desires and the demands of the environment of the future is called for. A *goal state of affairs* begins to take shape.

Appreciation complements the usual and important business elements regarding market dominance, taking over other companies, introducing new products, and the like.

APPRECIATION OUTCOMES: KEY IDEAS

Appreciation is not complete without the formulation of some key ideas or postulates that will become the foundation for strategic decisions. Here are some that might well come out of the deliberative activity (see Table 4.5).

Unpredictability Is the Only Certainty of the Future. Senior management anticipates change, not changes. The best and most durable

Table 4.5 Key Ideas

- Unpredictability is the only certainty of the future
- Commitment is conditional on the work experience
- Achieving commitment means organization change in the magnitude of a paradigm shift
- An operational paradigm drives organizational structure, processes, and behavior
- The operational paradigm differs from a professed management philosophy
- Existing controls must be preserved until they are no longer necessary
- The eventual configuration of functional areas can be only partially known at this time
- The "experience gap" will constrain the pace of change
- Most of our people must undergo a significant personal paradigm change and this cannot be legislated
- Attitudes and relationships with unions must be reconsidered

---

organization is not one designed to function well in predicted conditions. Far better is one capable of rapid and effective response to whatever comes along. Such an organization requires committed people throughout, widespread multiple skill proficiency, and an absence of rigidity—the kind of organization that is driven by the new paradigm.

Commitment Is Conditional on the Work Experience. "Bad" quality work for people must be replaced by "good," and the knowledge required to do it must be readily available. The goal: "Everyone doing what needs to be done because they want to do it."

Achieving High Commitment Means Organization Change in the Magnitude of a Paradigm Shift. Modest change won't do. Canned programs off the shelf won't do. It will take intensive change and this is a long-term endeavor. Impatient though the senior executives may be, they must realize that large organizations are like supertankers: Once they are under way, it takes considerable time and distance to change their course. The rudder moves quickly and the bow will move, changing the heading of the ship, but for a time the vessel will continue sliding on its old course. Given the time it takes deliberately and intensively to alter the organization and the rapidity of the environmental change that necessitates organizational change, one must run fast just to stay even.

An Operational Paradigm Drives Organizational Structure, Processes, and Behavior. The appreciating group has searched out the operational paradigm of the organization. As they did so they probably discovered the value of having a cynic present. According to the *Devil's Dictionary* (Bierce, 1911), a cynic is "a blackguard whose faulty vision sees things as they are, not as they ought to be. Hence the custom among the Scythians of plucking out a cynic's eyes to improve his vision." Although the search will not be totally candid this first time through, the attempt is an important signal of new thinking that will have positive influence in the weeks and months to come when those outside the center of power are asked to engage in appreciation.

The Operational Paradigm Differs from a Professed Management Philosophy. This is more than a matter of profession of an ideal while living by other values. The paradigm has valuable theories and models that help make the ideals a reality. A philosophy will contain some statement to the effect that people are the company's most important asset. A paradigm will go further and consider, for example, the theory that a person needs to learn and go on learning and what happens when this need is not met. Thus the very senior group will be involved in some microsocial analysis, matters too important to be delegated to the human resource function.

Existing Controls Must Be Preserved Until They Are No Longer Necessary. A property inherent in all old-paradigm organizations is that controls at all levels are essential to its functioning. Dangerous and counterproductive norms are operative, and coercion must be preserved until it becomes unnecessary. In one meeting of a joint labor-management redesign task force, a technical process was being discussed. It became clear that a recommended procedure for relieving the pressure of a vessel was not being followed and that a hazardous condition was being created for all. After some beating about the bush, one worker blurted out, "Of course we don't, but you know we always try to get away with as much as possible here." Strong group norms such as this are major determinants of behavior and make a boss presence essential.

Controls must also stay in place in the management ranks. Rewards systems enticing managers to favor the short term at the expense of the longer and to take risks with quality, compliance, and environmental concerns are in place and are likely to stay in place for some time to come.

Thus, it becomes apparent that *center-out does not mean that intensive change in structure, processes, and behavior is made at once at the center and radiates outward like waves from a stone dropped into a pond.*

The Eventual Form of Functional Areas Can Be Only Partially Known at This Time. A key feature of scientific management has been the practice of exporting tasks from the province of workers and managers in the core production process within manufacturing to numerous compartments in the organization we refer to as *functional areas.* With the exporting came psychologically impoverishing work experiences, the resulting decline in commitment, and the need for more and more controls. A reimportation of tasks from the functional areas to those in the core process becomes the first order of business even though work for all people in the functional areas must someday be changed from "bad" to "good." This does not argue that people and their activities in one area of the company are more important than those in another. Nor is making product always the core process; although in this book we have chosen to describe companies in which making product is the core process.

Considerable uncertainty regarding what will become of jobs and people in the functional areas is unavoidable. There are no models to follow because whole or large parts of organizations based on the new paradigm do not yet exist. The center's acknowledgment and acceptance of this uncertainty and partial knowledge signals a significant change from the old of prescience and omnipotence in the executive suite to the principle that all of the answers are not known and that the organization members must search for the answers, that is, create the future. Truly, organization members become resources. This exemplifies a change that *does* emanate at the center and traverse outward toward the periphery.

The Experience Gap Will Constrain the Pace of Change. Imagine a riverboat pilot of the kind Samuel Clemens wrote about, who has plied a section of the river for many years and has learned every bend, every shoal, every current. Imagine that then a cataclysmic event has put the river in a new bed. Overnight much of the pilot's knowledge and experience have become useless.

It was put this way by a plant manager who created for a new employer a successful new state-of-the-art plant; "I worked 20 years for [a large, diversified manufacturing concern], took all their training courses, and then ran into this. I felt like my blinders were removed!" Because he did the up-front work on the new plant, this knowledgeable, experienced and successful practitioner in the old paradigm had little difficulty believing that the old way was deficient, the prospects of the new much better. Despite this, he was not equipped to manage in the new paradigm.

The circumstance this plant manager encountered as he passed the threshold separating the old paradigm from the new typifies the position of the vast majority of managers today. In his former employment he had made his way from a first-line supervisor up through line and staff positions to a key position in the plant. Along the way he was mentored by more experienced managers who also served as his role models. There was always someone around to watch over him and see to it that he did not make large mistakes. He was restrained if he began to stray. The experience in subordinate line and staff positions in the presence of mentors, monitors, and role models stood him in good stead in the day-to-day activities of his job. His judgment was formed and tempered by those experiences. Came a new position with opportunity to

Table 4.6 Managers and the New Paradigm

- Class Ones—embrace
- Class Twos—sanction
- Class Threes—tolerate
- Class Fours—ignore
- Class Fives—oppose
- Class Sixes—sabotage
---

create a new way plant. For him it was a relatively sudden paradigm shift. Despite his freshly developed proclivity for new-paradigm thinking, much of his valuable experience was rendered obsolete. In his new situation he could not harken back to personal experience as a team member, team manager, or middle manager in a state-of-the-art organization of "good" work and highly committed people. Nor was it possible for him to enter a state-of-the-art organization to acquire the missing experience.

Compounding the never-gained practice on the way up was the absence of much needed support in the higher levels of the new organization. There was no extensive new-paradigm organizational infrastructure—mentors, monitors, and role models—on which to rely. Gone, too, were the plant manager's organizational counterparts.

In the early phase of intensive change the experience gap is ubiquitous and no amount of senior management impatience will change its reality. Under the periphery-in model of change the handicaps of the experience gap resulted in limited success followed by fade-out or in outright failure. Center-out was fashioned to cope with the handicaps, not eliminate them. One makes haste slowly, prepares for accelerating the rate of redesign later.

Most of Our People Must Undergo a Significant Personal Paradigm Change, and This Cannot Be Legislated. This key idea deserves paramount attention. Experience with the periphery-in model has shown that managers fall into six classes with respect to the new paradigm (see Table 4.6).

In every successful innovation there has been at least one manager falling into the first class, those who embrace, advocate, and employ the new ideas.

The class twos are not so rare but there is considerable distance between them and class ones. Consenting, approving, endorsing, and sanctioning is far different from embracing and advocating. Retreat for class twos is always an option. They allow the onus of risk to be borne by someone else, usually an innovative plant manager.

Under class threes—the tolerators—the risk for the real innovators has been even greater. "It is okay to proceed," they say, "but don't let anything screw up." After the change is successfully carried off, they take credit by saying, "This innovation happened only because I let it happen." Another favorite saying: "The only reason this has been permitted is the better bottom line." The innovator is left to wonder what would happen should a glitch of any kind occur.

Class four managers ignore. Ignoring is not as benign as it may first appear. One tactic these managers use is to pretend there is nothing new or different about a different-but-better plant. When the new plant begins to outstrip other old-paradigm units, they make excuses for the old plants, thus demeaning the accomplishments of those in the innovative plant while condoning the failure of those in the old plants to change. One class four executive was seen to get very red in the neck every time comparative cost and quality data from old- and new-paradigm plants were reviewed.

Class five managers oppose. Some of them are bottom-line-macho managers who say the new paradigm is "not what made America (or 'this corporation') great," and "A red-blooded manager can be interested only in profits; any concern for the quality of work life of the organization members is a sign of weakness." It is perfectly natural for one unable or unwilling to try to make a paradigm change to use the new way as a license to fail. "It is not being done my way and your way won't work; if I do it your way and it doesn't work, it isn't my fault."

Class six managers sabotage. It is likely that they are ideologically rooted and not open to persuasion. Persistence is one notable characteristic. With the periphery-in model there are many of these, but they are beginning to become anachronisms.

In their appreciation efforts the senior managers may have encountered some from each class. Importantly, besides some personal paradigm change on the part of initiating managers, they will have gained valuable insights about the process. Because getting managers at all levels to buy-in to the new direction is central to the feasibility of intense change, the form of the field as regards these six classes needs to be appreciated and reappreciated in all change undertakings, and strategies amended accordingly.

Attitudes and Relationships with Unions Must Be Reconsidered. Generally in corporate America, attitudes toward trade unions range from sanguinity through stoicism to viewing organized labor as a cancerous tumor on the organization. Plant managers of nonunion plants in many companies are dead certain that their careers are seriously jeopardized if their plant becomes unionized.

Trade unions, a bulwark of a democracy, are searching for a recasting of role. The AFL-CIO now is officially for labor-management cooperation, for QWL and workplace democracy. Taking note of change, Secretary-Treasurer of the AFL-CIO Thomas Donahue (1989) says,

> We are as committed to dynamism as everyone else in society. And so we acknowledge that workers must change too and so must their union and we have been engaged in that process for a number of years. But management attitude must change as well. Neither workers nor their employees can build a secure future in splendid isolation from each other. . . . We can negotiate hard and represent well. We can cooperate on quality and productivity improvement simultaneously.

Work redesign can be done with unions and on more than one occasion during the redesign process the local union has become the major stimulus for continuing when management flagged.

When there is a union it is highly unlikely that redesign can be successful without their involvement.

The company without labor unions should ask what policies and actions are employed to keep the unions out and how these policies and actions affect the present, the choice of a goal paradigm, and the change process itself.

With the formulation of the key ideas that will guide the organization in a process of change and its ongoing functioning, the first step in the change process is complete. Insights about the process of personal paradigm change, its highs and lows and its unevenness, have been gained. Steps that immediately follow further manifest new values of the center-out change model.

New leadership is in evidence. Leadership of the old, setting the course and telling the organization to follow, one in which key words were *obey* and *comply*, is exchanged for a realization that all wisdom does not reside in the senior group; others are to be enrolled in the search process.

Appreciation is an art that begins with facts, and every person has a unique porthole of vision into the world inside the organization and beyond. Each person uses unique life experiences as a background against which to interpret the facts. Augmenting participation in the appreciation process affords a more complete and accurate picture of the present, making firmer the foundation from which to embark on the journey to the future. Similarly, expanded participation enhances conjecture about the future.

New leadership is deeply concerned about buy-in by people at all management levels. Many class ones are needed and few class fives and sixes can long be tolerated. Without widespread buy-in, the remaking of the organization is doomed for the present. Buy-in, a reflection of how one perceives the world, is in this sense purely voluntary. Finite limits of senior manager power of authority in matters of dictating how people shall think are quickly reached. People tend to support what they help to create and genuine participation in these basic matters is essential to success in developing support for the new direction.

Clearly, this is not participation for participation's sake. Asking other stakeholders to participate in this most important appreciation activity dispels the aura of one or a few "big brains" and installs in its stead the notion that people are valued resources. Setting a new tone of genuine participation is change that *will* radiate outward from the center toward the periphery.

The CEO, officers, and directors at the center are now well positioned to move on to the next step. Our next chapter is devoted to succeeding steps in the center-out change model.

FIVE

The Work of the Second Echelon

Accordingly, having completed the first pass at getting it right at the center, the CEO charters several groups to engage in supplemental appreciative activity. Each corporate officer (in our chosen example, vice presidents of marketing, finance, manufacturing, research and development, human resources, environmental affairs, and materials management) is directed separately to assemble key managers in his respective function to carry out the next step, appreciation validation and enhancement (see Figure 5.1).

The second echelon groups are asked to begin with the more senior group's tentative conclusions developed in the first pass at appreciation and the resolution to follow the center-out model of change. They are supplied with the key ideas, the paradigm believed to be operational in the company, and the goal paradigm, however sketchy and incomplete. They are to go beyond assimilating the ideas and the underlying beliefs, as they do so capitalizing on their unique perspectives gained from experience in their respective areas of the company. It is theirs to reason why (see Table 5.1). Considerable dialogue among the several second-echelon appreciating groups is called for.

The CEO must be adamant about the already reached conclusions while at the same time inviting challenges. Validation will

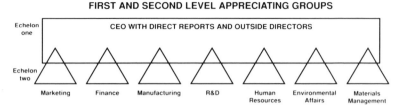

Figure 5.1 First- and Second-Level Appreciation Groups

Table 5.1 The Task for the Second Echelon

- What it is like in here?
- Key idea analysis
- New key ideas
- Recommendations

---

seem like a contradiction and making clear what is wanted will challenge the CEO's managerial and communication skills.

A further stipulation: The task of the second echelon is not complete until they have prepared and fed back to the senior officer group the results of their deliberations.

The appreciation process will have already touched each officer in different ways and to different degrees. There is no reason to expect that officers leading the several groups will be in the same place regarding the remaking of the company, but the distribution of class ones through sixes will be more favorable to change than the distribution in a periphery-in situation where the executives have not appreciated. But the officers must not be bypassed. Officer support must be assured; it is futile for the CEO to attempt to go on without it. If only one officer does not see the wisdom of remaking the company, he can be carried for a while. If there are several, the CEO must table his plans for the moment.

Leading a second-echelon group through the next step will test each officer's new leadership skills and have an effect on the individual officers. The extent of the officer's commitment to the key ideas will be evident. In most cases, deeper understanding and commitment can be expected.

The discomforts of appreciation will be felt; like the officers, the second-echelon managers are products of life in old-paradigm organizations. A likely outcome is deep understanding and validation of the key ideas. From the point of view of the CEO, the worst case is outright rejection of the key ideas and the thinking behind them. In this event he can refuse to go forward. Without the support of the second-echelon stakeholders, movement is well nigh impossible.

WHAT IS IT LIKE IN HERE?

This essential query takes into account the senior group's answer but is extended and particularized for the area in question. The key managers are positioned somewhat closer to operational activities of the organization and will have some exclusive facts about "what is it now like in here?"

Each second-echelon group will infer the operational paradigm driving structure, processes, and behavior in its area just as the first-echelon group searched out one for the larger organization. Paradigms operative in various functions will differ in some respects because of the nature of the function and the incumbents. Appreciators in the engineering function are likely to make special note of the absence of joint optimization while those in the accounting function will place emphasis elsewhere.

Inferred operative paradigms are then compared with the as yet incomplete goal paradigm established for the larger organization. Some personal paradigm changes (buy-in) will occur in this process and the magnitude of the task ahead of remaking the company will become evident. Clues to personal paradigm change can be seen in the timidity versus boldness of articulation of the operative paradigm within the particular second-echelon group. Those still clinging to the old find it difficult to tell it like it is.

KEY IDEA ANALYSIS

In the initial appreciation, one thought led to another until a coherent body of ideas was formed. One by one these key ideas should be explored, critically tested, validated, extended, and made less abstract. Some action steps will begin to become dimly visible.

Unpredictability Is the Only Certainty of the Future. The senior group has already taken this idea to its logical conclusion—the criticality of attaining an organization capable of rapid and effective response and the relationship of employee commitment to response capability. Several key words will be noted: Having committed people *throughout* the organization means far more than just those on the shop floor and in the nonexempt ranks. All senior executives must rid themselves of the old-paradigm assumption that the degree of commitment felt is somehow directly proportional to one's rank in the organization. Periphery-in's "it is just they who must change" gives way to accepting that none will be exempted from changing. The need for multiple skill proficiency is likewise not limited to those on the shop floor.

It may seem to some at this time that they have just opened a Pandora's box. Once they advance beyond being overwhelmed at the magnitude of the task ahead and the realization that they are deeply involved, they may begin to imagine the potential in an organization in which commitment is deep and widespread.

Commitment Is Conditional on the Work Experience. This idea leads to management accepting the responsibility for creating for everyone a "good" work experience that will result in the highly valued commitment. A need for knowledge becomes evident: What is there about experiencing work that makes it "good" versus that which makes it "bad"? How is an organization to be designed if it is to yield "good" work (the anatomy of self-regulation)? How and from where will this knowledge be obtained? Who in the organization must know what?

Achieving High Commitment Means Organization Change in the Magnitude of a Paradigm Shift. The profound and critically important ideas of paradigm and paradigm shift are explored thoroughly. Once the concepts of paradigm and paradigm shift are understood and accepted, the road to the chosen future can be more safely traveled. The second-echelon groups will validate the senior group's conclusion that modest change and "programs" won't do, and will realize that the prospect of two incompatible and competing paradigms existing simultaneously has far-reaching negative implications. The complexity of the change process will become more visible.

An Operational Paradigm Drives Organizational Structure, Processes, and Behavior. The issue of an operational paradigm has already been addressed by each second-echelon group under "What is it like in here and how did it get this way?" There is more to this reality check than merely supplementing the picture drawn earlier by the senior managers. Opportunities to address the question must be sought for many others in the organization.

The Operational Paradigm Differs from a Professed Management Philosophy. The degree of difference is a root cause of cynicism and the second-echelon managers will be highly skeptical at first. Remembering the way it was when they held lesser positions will underscore for them that broad participation in subsequent appreciation steps can make the difference between success and failure in conveying the genuineness of senior management's new intent.

Existing Controls Must Be Preserved Until They Are No Longer Necessary. The second-echelon groups are sure to agree with the need to preserve controls for some time to come and will be relieved with this assurance of the officers' sense of reality. Interest in the center-out change process will rise: What is it? How will it be done? How will we be involved? At this stage of the deliberations more questions will arise and answers will be elusive.

The Eventual Form of the Functional Areas Can Be Only Partially Known at This Time. Up-front acknowledgment of this reality will upset many in the organization who must give up the comforts of believing in senior management's prescience and omnipotence. The reality itself has potency to create fear in many quarters and unforeseeable complications. These include contemplating unknown changes in roles, potential loss of employment, the redrawing of turf boundaries, and having to wait. The second-echelon groups can begin the planning that is necessary to manage the change process successfully and to cope with the unavoidable negatives sure to arise.

The future for those in manufacturing management is also somewhat unclear. Answers must be found for the question, "What does it take to manage in a state-of-the-art organization?"

Meanwhile, the center-out model begins to take shape.

An Experience Gap Will Constrain the Pace of Change. Confronting senior management's identification of the experience gap can be a bittersweet proceeding, at once ego threatening and comforting. Comfort is derived from the fact of existing organization members being under consideration, mass replacing them is not. Ways must be found to equip them to manage in the new, for a time to contend with absent and underdeveloped infrastructure.

While a constraint, the experience gap needn't mean snail's pace change throughout from this time forward. How to take the experience gap into consideration in strategy formulation may not yet be clear.

Most of Our People Must Undergo a Significant Personal Paradigm Change and This Cannot Be Legislated. This subject was discussed in some detail in Chapter 3.

That managers, supervisors, workers, and union officials cannot be directed to change their way of thinking raises a critical strategic dilemma for those at the center: "I can't order them (subordinates) to change their beliefs. But change them they must because our corporation's *ultimate* survival depends on it."

Attitudes and Relationships with Unions Must Be Reconsidered. The notion that for the long term it is good to reconsider questions of union involvement represents a sea change for most of corporate America.

Those with no labor unions will explore the three-part question "What policies and actions are employed to keep the unions out and how do these policies and actions affect the present, the choice of a goal paradigm, and the change process itself?"

Plant managers of nonunion plants in many companies, dead certain that their careers are seriously jeopardized (if not ended) if their plant becomes unionized, report that their plant is "more union than a unionized plant." The inclusion of plant-level managers in the "What is it like in here" activity will help to bring an honest confrontation of this issue.

The goal paradigm may represent a sincere management concern for the psychological well-being of employees while they are at work. In this case it is neither amoral nor enlightened self-interest. Careful consideration of the extrinsic needs and the role of a labor union in meeting these needs is advised.

In general, the pace and success in redesigning unionized plants in which union cooperation has been gained have outstripped that achieved in their nonunion counterparts. Plant managers in both situations find they have much in common, similar problems and dilemmas. A progressive and involved union can make the difference. Variety, beginning with executive attitudes and relationships with the labor movement, is the hallmark of companies having collective bargaining agreements. The posture regarding QWL and labor-management cooperation varies widely among the many subdivisions within the labor movement.

The second-echelon groups in companies with unions will strive to foresee how to engage with the unions, how to make the most of the situations where the internationals are visibly proactive, and how to overcome the difficulties with those at the international level who favor no collaborative activity. They will be recommending when and how to involve union leaders.

Management must develop a logical counterpart to the union's "We can negotiate hard and represent well. We can cooperate on quality and productivity improvement simultaneously [with the adversarial components of the relationship]."

THE BUY-IN QUESTION
LEADS TO STRATEGY

A report back to the CEO and the senior officers would be gravely insufficient if it omitted consideration of the paramount question, how will we get people to buy-in to these new ideas and the new direction? Endeavoring to answer this question was a major factor leading to development of the center-out model.

Individual paradigm change begins and proceeds in many ways. Marking its beginning is somewhat like trying to establish the origin of a family. For most people, it is a very slow process and tends to proceed unevenly, but occasionally it comes in a flash of insight, like it did for Saul on the road to Damascus. The time it takes and the circumstances vary from person to person, depending on values, experience, and ways of thinking. It is not a question of intelligence or station in life. The only element common to everyone is independent discovery for oneself, in one's own way and when one is ready.

A paradigm change does not result from a written explanation or a presentation in a management meeting or union hall, but rather involves a combination of conditions and events. By far the single most important enabling factor is a dissatisfaction with what one is experiencing, coupled with an inability to explain it satisfactorily. Mentoring by a trusted person such as a boss, consultant, or peer ranks second.

One innovator, who described himself as curious, unencumbered by an MBA from a prestigious university, and dissatisfied with the state of affairs in his work life, referred to his transition as "learning to integrate social psychology concepts with other management disciplines." His working relationship with an external consultant was a key contributing factor.

Events known to have contributed to a paradigm change include visiting an innovative site, taking part in well-designed and skillfully conducted appreciation sessions, attending a conference, being assigned to design a new plant or manage an existing innovative site, participating in an organization of innovators, and reading an article.

Visiting an innovative site can be especially effective. In one dramatic instance, a trio from a new plant design team was being escorted around an innovative site by an hourly worker, as was the custom, along with a team leader. On the fifth floor the hourly worker noticed something and abruptly left the group to confer intensely with two of her team members, who arrived at the same moment. After a short conference, the three workers rushed off in different directions. Meanwhile the visitors waited with the seemingly nonchalant team leader, who did not even bother to explain what was happening. Soon the escort returned to apologize and explain that she had sensed something going wrong in the production process and had rushed to take corrective action. Two other team members had also done so. They quickly decided what was to be done and who would do what, and then they did it. The corrections were made and the process was again under control. In the report the visitors made to their task force, it was clear that this incident, in which they had see multiple skill proficiency and pay-for-knowledge in action, had made converts of them.

Visiting an innovative site outside one's own company often has more persuasive power than visiting an inside one. But paradigm change can be initiated without seeing the new paradigm in action at all. One plant manager in a company noted for its Neanderthal labor relations practices first encountered the phrase "Quality of Working Life" in a conference advertisement. About this time his plant was sold. Given this opportunity to start off on a new footing, he and the president of the local union decided there must be a better way than the trench warfare they had endured for so long. The plant manager attended the conference and immediately took steps to engage a consultant and initiate a QWL effort in his plant.

Another manager charged with staffing and starting up a new plant was put in touch with a network of innovating plant managers. His first meeting with them brought a sudden awakening. He returned with an entirely new plan and a determination to carry it out, and the resulting plant went on to perform better than the Japanese counterparts making the same product.

A seasoned and successful manager, very traditional in his views, was assigned to a new innovative plant in the woes of start-up, to rescue it, as it were. On his arrival, he confessed later, he "thought the organization was designed by the tooth fairy," but his conversion began soon after. Being advised of a malfunction in the production process, he immediately struck out for the control room, as was his style. As he entered, a worker approached and began, "I know why you are here. I am the guilty one, I have explained the screw-up to all members of the team, and it won't happen again." Nonplussed, the manager turned on his heel and returned to his office. Within 18 months, he had become a knowledgeable, ardent, and effective innovator. "Once the plant was running reliably," he said, "I had time to think and to plan, something I had never had before in my plant management experience."

In another case a controller in a traditionally managed plant was reassigned to a new-paradigm plant in the same business unit. He brought with him the hostile feelings toward the new unit held by the people in the old plant, maintaining on his arrival that the cost gap between the two plants was due to freight advantage alone. Three years later his attitude had totally changed and he denied ever making the statement.

Those working with managers who have not made the paradigm change are well advised to note that discoverers are not always the best persuaders. One plant manager who had made the discovery confided to a consultant, "You know, once you learn about this, it is hard to keep from thinking that those who have not are just a little dumb." Jargon can be a barrier. Unfamiliar concepts occasion the use of unfamiliar words, which can trigger a sudden attack or turn-off by someone ashamed of not knowing the word.

The most likely buy-in circumstance to be confronted by the second-echelon groups is widespread dissatisfaction with little awareness of the root causes. Misdiagnosis is rife. Pronouncement is ruled out but not everyone in the organization can go through extensive appreciating sessions—and their doing so is no guarantee of personal paradigm change. Mentors are in especially short supply. Nor can it be arranged for everyone to visit innovative plants or to serve in them. How, then, will this buy-in take place on the scale required? For the answer we turn to the relative successes of properly designed and managed new plants on new sites vis-à-vis the less availing attempts to redesign established plants.

The most common explanation is that in the new plants "special" people were hired, while in the established plants the unic . or the foremen or both were the stumbling blocks. The reasons underlying the differences have to do with discovery. In the established plants it was commonplace for hesitant plant management to make changes cautiously one step at a time. In one form of gradualism, management as a first step declared that groups of people on the shop floor would function as teams. In all cases of timidity, the supervisor was told to expect new worker behavior because there was a team. He, too, was to behave differently but, as always, was held accountable for results and compliance with the rules.

The supervisor soon came up against reality.

I see and deal every day with worker behavior that is counterproductive. I do my best with the inadequate tools I have (rewards and punishments), but counterproductive behavior is still a problem for me. With this team thing my power to coerce is both reduced and not supposed to be exerted. Are we simply going to let this counterproductive behavior go on and get worse? My job is tough enough as it is, and in this new team arrangement I don't see how I can do enough checking on everything.

The dilemma can be brought into sharper focus by asking their bosses three questions:

(1) Should autonomy be given to someone who is not competent?
(2) Should autonomy be given to someone who is not informed?
(3) Should autonomy be given to someone who is not committed?

"No way!" is the inevitable answer.

The supervisors and their immediate bosses were correct. *Gradualism ignores the conditional aspect of commitment and modest change does not produce the conditions for discovery.* Lacking the opportunity to experience a new kind of work and discover that they like it better and that it changes them, people do not respond in the desired and expected way. With the workers behaving in the same ways as before the supervisor is forced to maintain the coercive role of the old paradigm. The discrepancy between the stated desired condition and the actual is clear for all to see. Dramatic bottom-line improvements are not forthcoming and fade-out is not far off.

In the successful new plants the designers took great care to create the conditions—the anatomy of self-regulation—that must be established if the "good" work and the resulting commitment are to be attained. New hires were not special people; for the most part they came from old-paradigm plants in which their jobs were narrow in scope, repetitive, they got too little information, they had no latitude for decision making, all psychological requirements to be met if one is to have an enriching work experience. In the radically different conditions in the new plant an enriching work experience was available at once and, discovering this, the new hires bought-in, took initiatives, and behaved in ways expected of those in a state-of-the-art organization. Commitment was immediately forthcoming. The supervisor, now called something else, could and did behave in a new way because people on the team were committed. The newly hired employees experienced a *discontinuity* in their work life in that they had gone from the "old" in their former employment to the intensely different "new" instantaneously.

A new key idea based on the contrasting experiences in changing an established plant versus starting up a new one emerges. *Intensive change at the worker (or micro) level cannot be brought about in a gradual manner: Microlevel discontinuity is called for.* Team life in the established plants begins only after the necessary psychological conditions of work are established. Extensive preparatory steps are required that include (1) making ready to transfer tasks from management positions, functional areas, and the supervisor to workers comprising self-regulating teams in the core process, (2) arranging for the team's information needs and other elements of the anatomy of self-regulation, and (3) anticipating the necessary adjustments the functional areas will make in their practices so as to accommodate the deep change in the core process. Once workers begin to function as teams autonomy is not "earned"; it is granted with the realization that autonomy is one of the necessary conditions for "good" work. By a "system change" "good" work has been created instantaneously. Workers in the core process are afforded an opportunity to discover that they like the new way and they become committed and more productive, much like the workers in a state-of-the-art new plant. Instead of the dilemma encountered in gradualism, the management person directly associated with the team is enabled to practice new behavior much like his counterpart in a state-of-the-art new plant.

Then the experience gap intervenes. Intensive change suddenly made in the core processes throughout the company or even throughout one plant cannot be supported. With limited experience and resources in mind, one settles for initial intensive change in a small portion of the core production process at one or more

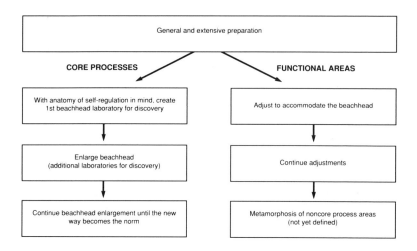

Figure 5.2 The Center-Out Change Process (1)

existing plants. The small area is sufficiently different from its sur-roundings to warrant the label "beachhead." More descriptively, it is a *beachhead laboratory for discovery* in which the indispensable buy-in occurs. Staff and support units are afforded the opportunity to learn to relate to core process teams operating in the new way. They observe workers in the newly created teams going to great lengths to protect their radically different workplace.

Once the beachhead is established, break-outs are planned. The values, beliefs, theories, and techniques are applied to contiguous parts of the core process. As the experience gap is overcome the process will accelerate.

A fundamental plank of the center-out model is therefore: *Requi-site intensive change can be made faster and more successfully with the beachhead-breakout strategy.* Some elements of the center-out model now come into clearer focus (see Figure 5.2).

ENABLING AND SUSTAINING

The second-echelon groups now take up the subject of changing the functional areas. Intensive change in the core process areas cannot be made without adjustments in the functional areas. Within each functional area there are certain components such as project engineering that must quickly modify the way they do business in-order to make possible the beachheads in the core process on the periphery. These components are referred to as *enabling* components. Other components of functional areas, cost accounting being one, are such that actual changes in practices and procedures must await the beachheads. These are referred to as *sustaining* components.

Most functional areas contain both enabling and sustaining components and reside both in headquarters and the plants. Within the human resource function, for example, management development is an enabling component, compensation is a sustaining component. Regardless of dispersion, each component will be of one mind in matters of adjusting the way the function conducts its business and transfers tasks to operating teams in the core process.

As they adjust to the intensive change appearing elsewhere in the organization, the functional areas will anticipate changing "bad" work to "good" work within their own functions. Because they will straddle the old- and new-paradigm parts of the company for some time, and because the adjustments they will ultimately make in response to intensive change elsewhere will not all be clear in advance, changing work within the function from "bad" to "good" must wait until most of the adjustments to change on the periphery have been made. *Success in bringing about intensive change throughout the organization depends on knowing what to change when.*

In time the domains of the functional areas may change significantly. Some may be combined with others. Conceivably, new ones

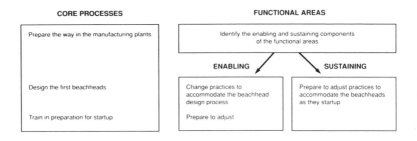

Figure 5.3 The Center-Out Change Process (2)

could be created. Only experience with center-out will reveal the form of the remade company. Yet more of the center-out model becomes better defined (see Figure 5.3).

RECOMMENDATIONS
FOR FURTHER ACTION BY THE CENTER

The second echelon's initial assignment to validate and enhance the appreciation is almost complete.

They have learned some new concepts and have unlearned some old, thus have had firsthand experience with the buy-in process. They have extended the appreciation with their analysis of the key ideas and have added some strategically important ideas as well. A plan for change, though still incomplete, has taken shape. Some parts of the plan are still only dimly visible.

Implications: Policies on Change and Change on Policies. Policies and procedures, created to guide and control actions, exert an ossifying effect on an organization. If change is sought, policies must be examined and changed. The second-echelon groups now endeavor to foresee both how policies and procedures of the respective func-

Key Ideas	Policy/Procedure Analysis	Recommendations
• Unpredictability is the only certainty of the future		
• Commitment is conditional on the work experience		
• Achieving commitment means organization change in the magnitude of a paradigm shift		
• An operational paradigm drives organizational structure, processes and behavior		
• The operational paradigm differs from a professed management philosophy		
• Existing controls must be preserved until they are no longer necessary		
• The eventual form of functional areas can be only partially known at this time		
• An "experience gap" will constrain the pace of change		
• Most of our people must undergo a significant personal paradigm change and this cannot be legislated		
• Attitudes an relationships with unions must be reconsidered		

Figure 5.4

tional areas will encumber the remaking of the company and what policies and procedures must some day become. With several groups involved a structured approach is advantageous (see Figure 5.4).

Changing the Organization Will Require Resources. The threefold benefits of participation—validation and enhancement, personal paradigm change and buy-in, and plan development—are evident to the second-echelon groups. Their report will strongly recommend finding ways to involve many others in this vital process, a task of considerable magnitude requiring resources—people, trainers, and time. Time for retreats, the classroom, and time to visit other sites. People must be on hand to replace those who are temporarily away. General Motors's Tarrytown assembly plant made a substantial up-front investment in hiring extra people so that the requisite training could be accomplished (Guest, 1979).

Time for participation in the change process translates to money in budgets. Money must be forthcoming. When it is not it directly hampers the effort and indirectly sends a strong message that senior management is not serious.

The experience gap is a cause for sound resource planning. Too little, too late makes the change process risky and slow. Once beachheads start up, frequent pauses to assess progress and what has been learned, supported by knowledgeable persons, are essential.

What will it cost? What is the payback time? It is only natural that senior managers will first look for a short-term payback of the investment in participation. A prudent second echelon will make no promises of quick payback. The money spent for participation in the change process should be considered an investment in the future with a long-term payback.

The principal productivity gains should be expected only after self-regulating teams have been put into place and had time to get beyond start-up, much like a new plant. Often earlier returns from investments in participation accrue from the effect noted in the Hawthorne studies; people do become more productive when attention is paid to them, when they receive credible information, when they participate in the important activity of appreciation enhancement. Productivity in plants undergoing participative redesign has increased before self-regulating teams were formed.

Other positive effects have been noted. The plant personnel manager in one plant seemed very patient with a lengthy task force redesign process. Later he revealed that it wasn't patience so much as his satisfaction and relief with the greatly improved labor relations.

Less is known about the early benefits of newly gained commitment in the higher management ranks ensuing from their participation in the early phases of the remaking of the company. Middle managers are not immune to attitude change arising from their involvement in the important matter of the future of the company. The emotion of shame related to a psychologically poor work experience is not restricted to workers. The behavioral manifestations of "bad" work for managers usually include self-interest consistently put ahead of the organization's—personal risk avoidance—decision-making delay—withholding opinion (which way blows the wind?)—intrigue—resigning one's self to mediocrity—getting on the bandwagon. Such behavior makes poor role modeling.

A comprehensive and reliable manufacturing cost data base is essential for estimating and tracking productivity gains and losses in the early periods of the participative change process.

How productivity is calculated is a key factor in how one looks at the potential for temporary productivity losses. Is bottom-line productivity or the more common units-produced-divided-by-direct-labor used? With the latter viewpoint, workers in the classroom are considered nonproductive. Productivity so calculated is sure to fall and managers who persist with this reductionist method of tracking productivity are likely to be hesitant to finance a participative change process. They also run the risk of overlooking the bottom-line benefits of employee commitment—safety, product quality, improved labor relations, reduced risks of environmental contamination, waste reduction, and savings in overhead costs accruing from reduced staffing in the control and support functions.

All sums spent for training need not be incremental increases. Many opportunities will be found when the existing training is examined for its appropriateness to the new direction. Some of this training should be eliminated, freeing up trainers and training money for more apt subject matter.

Recommending a Strategy. The report of the second echelon should recommend an early formulation by the CEO and officers of a strategy for change.

Going Public. Having explored and looked forward, the second-echelon groups will realize that informing the general populace is going to be required. In an immediate sense the deliberations so far are out of character in most companies and much curiosity will have been generated.

The alternative to going public is keeping it secret. To continue in secrecy is to signal lack of commitment; refusal to share with those who must collaborate in bringing about the new reality is to deny the values of the new paradigm whereas going public means commitment to action based on the new ideas.

When, how, how much to say are deeply intertwined. What can be noted is most companies' legacy of narrowly focused programs of short life, advocated and sponsored by a single executive with the CEO only sometimes being informed. Many programs are initiated by less senior executives without the knowledge of the CEO. Managers are known for their short tenure and with new managers, new programs are expected. It is normal for the program to be received with attitudes ranging from enthusiasm and genuine effort to the more common and widespread cynicism. Energy expended on the new program soon wanes as the program is seen to be ineffective or is eclipsed by the next program. In such a climate it is only reasonable to expect that unless new means are employed, an announcement of the new direction will be received in the same fashion.

Going public is neither an all-or-nothing nor a one-time thing. The first step may be no more than a pronouncement of a commitment to move the organization to go in a certain direction. "We will follow through from this value base and will judge all recommendations against this value base."

Inherent uncertainty is associated with a genuinely participative remaking of the company. Even at this juncture the buy-in by the second-echelon executives is uneven and tentative. They are uncertain how their report will be received by the officers and directors. Detailed prescriptions beyond pointing out the need to go public are unwise at this time.

A Proactive Center. The second-echelon groups take note that a "we/they" attitude is a common feature of periphery-in. The innovators on the periphery view those at corporate headquarters as inhibitors. In the center-out model such a division is undesirable and avoidable. Those at the center should be encouraging those at the periphery and monitoring the innovations, seeing to it that they do indeed represent intensive change and that progress is occurring at a reasonable pace, that adequate resources are on hand. In these ways the center fulfills its responsibility to lead.

The second echelon has gone as far as it can. Some parts of the change process have been outlined, however dimly. It is now time for a dialogue with the first-echelon officers and directors.

These deliberations by the separate groups of officers and their key executives will have contributed much to the getting it right at the center.

The center-out model will look something like Figure 5.5.

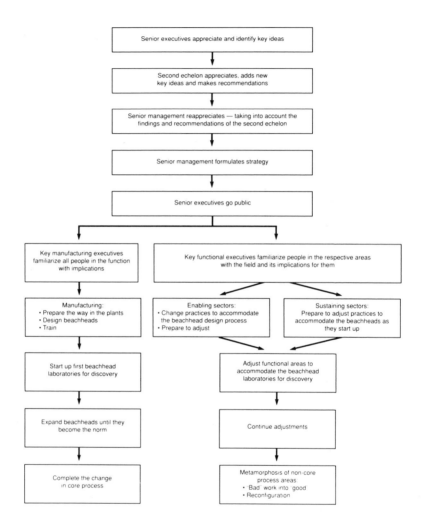

Figure 5.5 The Center-Out Model of Change

Moving the Change Effort
to the Periphery

After employing their unique perspectives and special knowledge, the second-echelon groups have brought back the results of their deliberations to the senior group. These include implications for policy, additional key ideas that will lead to strategy formulation, and recommendations. The experience gap has been identified and acknowledged as natural, not a scourge or sign of weakness.

Considerable dialogue will ensue as the first echelon ascertains that the second understood and internalized the products of the initial appreciation and the second echelon makes an effort to ensure that the recommendations and the thinking behind them are thoroughly understood by the first echelon. Taking note of differences among these several overlapping groups, they work through and find a common ground. To be achieved at this point is a shared understanding of the present and goal states of affairs, magnitude of the task ahead, and elucidation of some principles on which to base a course of action. Things are now more right at the center but much remains to be done.

Early consideration should be given to the second echelon's recommendation to go public, noting that going public is not an all-or-nothing or a one-time thing. The immediate course to follow is dictated partly by the center's degree of readiness. A second condition is the legacy of "programs" and their reception considered in the perspective of the still developing plan to remake the company. Prudence should outweigh haste; there is much from the second echelon to be absorbed, put into perspective, and amplified.

FORMULATING A STRATEGY FOR CHANGE

The next task for the CEO and senior officers is the formulation of a where-to-begin strategy for getting commitment and action in the field units. Which field units will be changed first? How will change be initiated? How will it proceed?

Some fact finding, what-it-is-like-in-here in a new context, should precede the strategy discussions. It is especially important to take note of present and recent past conditions in the manufacturing areas of the company such as managerial policies, labor relations, business conditions, and recent history of the separate manufacturing sites.

In many respects managers in the manufacturing community are much like their counterparts in the larger community Consider where the typical manager in manufacturing is coming from. Most entry points for new managers are in old-paradigm organizations; in recent decades new managers have seldom begun their careers as foremen. Early on, there are too many demands on the new manager's time and energy to permit in-depth questioning of the system's values, structure, and practices. The rare manager inclined to question the organizational paradigm is discouraged from doing so. Therefore, as the manager moves higher in the same or another old-paradigm organization, a cycle of superficial diagnoses and symptomatic treatments is repeated again and again. By the time the manager reaches a position of power, he or she is distant in time, wisdom, and organizational level from the changing shop floor where the action is, associating only with other managers and developing an attitude like that of Kurt Vonnegut's (1952) character Finnerty, a brilliant young engineer, who says in despair, "If only it weren't for the people, the god-damned people . . . always getting tangled up in the machinery. If it weren't for them, earth would be an engineer's paradise" (p. 288). Meanwhile, down where the rubber meets the road, the workers and unpromotable foremen are left to "work it out." When it doesn't work out, the manager's attitude is reinforced. It should be no surprise, then, that most experienced managers have a difficult time making a paradigm change.

Awareness of the general must not lead to dysfunctional stereotyping. Those in the plant manager community who have been encouraged to innovate have responded in a variety of ways. Some have wanted to please their boss but just couldn't get started like the plant manager who made the same "getting started" presentation year after year in network meetings. Another spoke of his desire to do things in his plant but did little, blaming his company's lack of interest, a condition common at that time that was not deterring his colleagues in the network.

Others, when encouraged by senior managers to do something, have become adept at maneuvering, appearing sincere while only seeming to be taking action. Among the sincere are those who believe intensive change to be unnecessary, modest change will solve organization performance problems.

The ranks of those who have not been encouraged to innovate are likewise diverse and include the worn-down-but-undaunted who have been trying hard in the unsupportive conditions of periphery-in. Innovative plant managers operating in periphery-in are often asked, "How do you answer those who want you to prove that your way is better?" One confident and obviously secure manager's feisty reply was, "Let them prove that their way is better!" But security is sometimes fleeting; buyouts, mergers, and spin-offs have taken their toll. One plant manager's efforts at redesign brought outstanding results that were recognized by his immediate boss and those in corporate headquarters. A merger brought new corporate ownership and new players at corporate headquarters who had not heard of the mismatch diagnosis and intensive change; uncertainty suddenly confronted this successful but weary innovator.

"Where there is retirement there is hope" does not always apply. A human resource manager noted that his plant manager's secure near-retirement position gave him the will to stand up for the innovation he had shepherded for several years. Younger newly appointed plant managers seeking rapid advancement are not always enthusiastic about embarking on an uncertain new course.

There will be sincere managers lacking the necessary understanding of the principles and pursuing intensive change with an unavailing strategy of microlevel gradualism.

When the center becomes active those who have been innovating with enthusiasm and determination will say, "It's about time!" After intensive change was achieved at one plant, other plant managers in the company followed. As enthusiasm for intensive change spread these plant managers created their own internal network. They sought to "enroll" the senior managers in the change effort.

Besides incumbency differences, careful attention should be paid to recent history in each manufacturing site. Prudence dictates planning a strategy around what is already there and recent history will lend clues about the likely receptivity of people on each site to senior management's new direction. Some companies will have a thriving innovative greenfield site even though periphery-in with its many pathologies has been practiced. Rarely will a successful redesign be found, but frequently there may be individual plants that have made progress. A previous QWL effort may have failed and the whole idea has a bad name. More numerous are plants where quality circles have been installed but are now foundering and fading out. Just-in-time may have been installed without regard to the need for employee commitment, giving the disaffected in these plants more leverage for the exercise of passive aggression.

Aside from incumbent and recent history variations, each plant manager is faced with a unique set of business conditions. A plant may be about to go out of business, the business may be on the block. The plant may be situated in a populous urban area where property values have soared and the risk of malfunction resulting in emissions is high. Its technology may be obsolete and requires large capital investment to make it viable. The plant may be in a business in which rapidly changing technology with short life is a feature. The product line may have suddenly changed and great energy is required to make the switch. These conditions vary and some make immediate redesign attempts highly risky.

There is an equally great variety of conditions regarding unions and managements' relationships with them. Some plants in the company may be unionized and others not. There may be one or several unions.

WHERE-TO-BEGIN STRATEGY ONE:
A GENERAL CALL FOR PLANS

A bold and comprehensive approach to securing intensive change on the periphery is a general call for plans. In this strategy, the CEO directs each unit on the periphery to develop a plan for redesign steps that will move the unit toward the goal state of affairs.

The substance of the directive calling for the plans is of utmost importance. The directive should contain a statement of the problem and a framework of goal organizational values, beliefs, theories, and models. It should specify a strategy of discontinuity employing beachhead laboratories for discovery. It should acknowledge the experience gap and pledge readiness of the functional areas.

The fact of variations is crucial to the formulation of a call for plans. A lockstep approach to the remaking of the company is not apt to succeed.

Timing of the call for plans is critical. To call for plans before headquarters people have been adequately prepared is premature.

Yet to wait until all of the preparatory activity is completed is to delay improvements to the bottom line unnecessarily.

A general call for plans represents a terrifying shift of philosophy. Land mines are densely planted in a culture of internal competition, gamesmanship, and inability to learn from commission of error.

Under the unfamiliar conditions of intensive change with center-out, all plans are unproven and officers at the center may not be sure that one plan is better than another—and the unpredictable environment always lurks.

It is unwise for senior managers to continue the time-honored custom of fostering competition among subordinates, saying, "Why don't you do it like so-and-so [a competing subordinate]?" ignoring the great variations in existing conditions and causing the destructive reactions of envy and jealousy to set in.

The method of communicating the directive, every bit as important as the directive's substance, conveys a loud and clear message to those long experienced in judging senior managers by what they do rather than what they say. The general call for plans needs creativity, willingly exercised; plant managers are not carrying a sword on a field of battle, doing what they are told. They are being asked to contribute to the higher good under conditions of uncertainty. Under these conditions a seminar with dialogue is advisable.

The CEO's directive to the plant and unit managers must not bypass intermediate levels of line management, as often occurred in periphery-in. Plant managers found themselves presenting plans to very senior levels, and the middle managers were little more than spectators with inadequate understanding and no ownership.

The submitted plans may cover a wide range. There will be units with cogent reasons for doing very little at this time and approval for such plans will be forthcoming. Some unconvinced unit managers will play it safe and recommend modest instead of intensive change. Such plans are candidates for rejection. The unit managers must try again. Some plans will be overly ambitious, failing to give adequate weight to the experience gap and the reality of limited

Table 6.1

- Amenable managers
- Favorable labor-management conditions
- Market opportunity
- Market constraint

resources, and must be returned to the unit managers for further consideration. The lack of a plan will be unacceptable.

The worth of a plan must take into account doing the immediate job while preparing for and making the intensive change.

The subject of relief from profit commitments will arise.

Submitted plans are reviewed by executives at the center who judge them against criteria that have been set forth in the directive. Approval decisions will factor in the time it takes to secure or develop training resources.

WHERE-TO-BEGIN STRATEGY TWO: SELECTIVE DEVELOPMENT

In this less bold, more opportunistic strategy, the executives at the center choose one or more sectors of the corporation in which intensive change is to be first made. With selective development the CEO can feel that he is not betting the company. Part of the corporation may be in crisis instead of the whole being in crisis. Another quite logical rationale for selective development as opposed to a general call for plans has to do with diminishing risk through maximizing the probability of early success in the initial beachheads.

The choice of scope and where to begin after the necessary preparation at the center is dictated by conditions, which may include one or more of those set out in Table 6.1.

Amenable Managers. Much of this book has been devoted to the notion of organization change beginning with the individual and the importance and difficulty of personal paradigm change. By the time the senior officers reach a point of formulating a where-to-begin strategy, they will have experienced and have been coping with individual paradigm change. They will note that skepticism persists and some likely casualties will have been identified. There will be those for whom the key ideas are eminently logical and who take quite naturally to the new behaviors required.

The search for these amenable managers should begin at the center rather than at the plant level. An especially favorable condition: a cluster of amenable managers, for example a plant manager with two or three on his staff along with the plant manager's boss.

Favorable Labor-Management Conditions. Trust between amenable plant management and a local union led by officers strongly believing in the merits of work redesign is the first and most important ingredient of favorable labor management conditions. Even more favorable is international leadership experienced in innovation and actively supporting locals involved in labor/management cooperative projects.

Market Opportunity. Except for the high cost associated with bad attitudes and work practices a plant may be ideally situated with respect to market and raw materials for capacity expansion or adding a new unit to produce a new product. A choice can be offered: continue as they are and get no capital money for expansions and new products, or be granted the capital for expansion or a new product on the condition that they quickly embark on a path to intensive change. In periphery-in this was a dubious strategy and is recommended only for center-out.

Market Constraint. The market for a product is shrinking or has become more competitive. Management is weighing off-shore procurement or withdrawal from the market against becoming competitive via work redesign. The former would result in eliminating all of the jobs while the latter would mean fewer jobs lost. People—workers, supervisors, and middle managers—are often more receptive to change in this condition. Union members often encourage their leadership in their quest to save the plant.

WHERE-TO-BEGIN STRATEGY THREE: CLUSTERING THE INNOVATIONS

Successful intensive change involves the creation of beachheads that for a time will exist as anomalies embedded in a larger system still driven by old-paradigm ideas. The encapsulation complications described at some length in Chapter 2 and further explained in Chapter 3 are certain to arise because deep psychological forces are at work. The practice of center-out with its extensive preparation will reduce but not eliminate the tension that develops across the boundary between an embedded unit and its environment.

In one plant the people in the warehouse receiving product from a redesigned unit upstream suddenly became extraordinarily critical about the product. For the unredesigned units also feeding the warehouse the standards of acceptance were unchanged. In another case a plant engineer cut off maintenance services to one department as soon as a redesign group began the preparatory analysis that would lead to redesign.

People in the different-but-better units act differently once they taste the improved work life. Before redesign of a department in one plant it was customary for the workers to retire to their lunchroom and play cards when the supply of their raw material was interrupted. Their behavior changed significantly once they became a self-regulating group. Upon discovery of an empty receiving bin they quickly dispatched emissaries to the supplying department to inquire what was wrong, why, and when would the material flow be resumed. This "new" behavior, quite out of the norm, evoked antagonistic behavior responses. After a few rebuffs those in the embryonic beachhead withdrew and coalesced around the common danger from people in other units rather than around their mission as was intended. Predictably, they then had less concern for the greater good of the larger system. In turn, doubt about the new way was engendered in the minds of those operating in the un-redesigned parts.

A lone beachhead, whatever its size, is especially fragile in its early life and must not be allowed to twist slowly in the wind. The fragility is diminished when a second beachhead is established in a unit closely related to the first. Succeeding beachheads are developed in contiguous areas and a cluster of innovations is formed.

Three types of clusters can be formed: vertical, administrative and associated. The *vertical* applies only in special situations. Suppose one has three vertically integrated manufacturing plants. The first converts raw materials into some intermediate of higher value for the second plant. The second in turn adds value to the intermediate and supplies a third plant in the chain. A cluster concept would dictate a beachhead in one of the three plants quickly followed by beachheads in the others. An existing well established state-of-the-art greenfield plant would also form the base for a cluster.

The *administrative* cluster looks to spreading the innovation from the first beachhead to other units in a business unit or division. In lieu of selecting one plant in each of several divisions, all manufacturing plants in one are chosen for early redesign.

Associated clustering involves a beachhead in a single plant followed by early redesign in associated functions such as new product development, sales, marketing, finance.

WHERE-TO-BEGIN STRATEGY FOUR: COMBINE INTENSIVE CHANGE WITH OTHER CHANGE THAT WILL OCCUR ANYWAY

Linking the redesign to change that will occur anyway has proved to be an opportunity. Besides new plants on new sites, plant modernizations, expansions, and radical changes in the technology are candidates.

SENIOR MANAGEMENT GOES PUBLIC

Formulating redesign strategy is a precursor to going public confidently.

Going public takes many forms. Involving the second echelon in appreciation is part of going public. Going public requires far more than presentations and written announcements. In planning for going public, all that is known about the dynamics of personal paradigm change, its unevenness, and the need for discovery should be taken into account.

In going public the key executives should express their discomfort with their former approach to the future and articulate their values and beliefs. As a product of their thoughtful microsocial analysis and examination of organizational axioms, they should set forth a few basic models and the theories on which these models are based. Regarding the future, they should indicate that the new state of affairs sought is a *goal* and that they recognize that it does not yet exist. People in business organizations today are better educated and more sophisticated than their predecessors; they have seen managers come and go, and with them policies and the "long-range strategy du jour." By differentiating the goal paradigm from the current operational paradigm, management can substantially reduce the cynicism and the "I've heard that before" response so common in the periphery-in model. And by acknowledging the experience gap, they make it clear that all organization members are learners.

PREPARE THE FUNCTIONAL AREAS:
ENABLING COMPONENTS

Each senior executive in charge of a functional area now begins a new set of preparation activities, educating those not yet involved about the corporation's new direction, the inferred operational paradigm of the functional area, the center-out strategy that has been adopted, and what the remaking of the company will

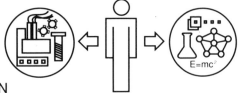

THE PAST QUESTION

What does the technical system (business) require of the person?

NOW-
INCLUDING THE
UNASKED QUESTION

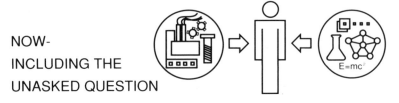

What does the person require of the technology (work)?

Figure 6.1

mean—so far as that can be known at this time—for the function
and its various components.

Familiarizing people in the manufacturing area will proceed simultaneously. Plant-level managers reporting directly to division-
level functions (dotted line relationship to the plant manager) such
as human resource managers, quality assurance managers, and controllers should join their respective functions in the familiarization.

Process and Plant Engineering. The belief that work is an essential
part of life and that commitment to work is conditional on the richness of the work experience has deep implications for the engineering function because the design and arrangement of the
technology can enhance or inhibit the potential for creating good
work. In the old paradigm, the primary question to be asked was,
"What does the technology require of the individual?" In the new
paradigm, a second question is asked simultaneously; "What does
the individual require of the technology?" (See Figure 6.1.)

Engineers have not been trained to ask the second question, and along with middle-level technical experts they have been major impediments to intensive change.

Asking the second question means embracing socio-technical systems theory. As we saw in Chapter 2, in the socio-technical approach, design and operating problems are treated in relation to two different systems that are independent but linked: the technical system and the social system. Designing and managing a socio-technical system therefore requires the integration of widely separated disciplines, the "hard" or natural sciences and the "soft" or social sciences. In the hard sciences, relationships tend to be both quantifiable and predictable. In the social sciences relationships are highly complex and far less quantifiable and predictable; a different kind of thinking is called for.

In either of these systems there is almost always more than one "best" solution or arrangement. But some of the best solutions in a technical system are incompatible with some best solutions in the social system, and vice versa. In the socio-technical approach, therefore, the objective is to deal with the two systems together, seeking out the best solutions in each and finding the best match—those that, taken together, yield the best overall results. This process is called *joint optimization;* it can be diagrammed as in Figure 6.2.

Process and plant design begin simultaneously with organization and work design. Each is tested against the other throughout the analysis and design process, so that the final design represents the joint optimization of the two systems, the best in each that is compatible with the other.

This process is far more than mere theory. One company, making the all too common error of designing the technical system first, was well into the design of a state-of-the-art materials handling system for a high tech plant before beginning organization design. When they belatedly began to analyze the intended social system, it was quickly apparent that the materials handling system and plant layout would thwart their desires for a good QWL. Wisely,

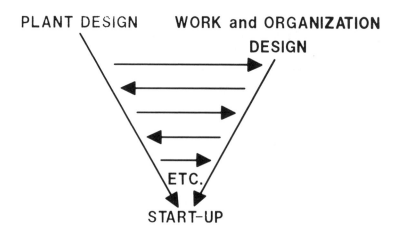

Figure 6.2 Joint Optimization

although there was hell to pay for the plant manager-to-be, the senior managers chose to spend a considerable sum to rectify the problem. From that time on they jointly optimized, and a very successful new unit was brought on stream.

Less successful was a consultant to another company wishing to improve the performance of an existing plant. In the explanation of the socio-technical approach it was indicated that a thorough analysis of the technical system was part of the procedure. This company had recently upgraded the technical system in this plant, and so complete was their misunderstanding of socio-technical theory that the socio-technical approach was rejected.

In most companies new production facilities are being created and old ones are being refurbished or expanded as obsolete technology is replaced and new products require new technology. If the benefits of joint optimization are to be realized in these new and modified units, the changes must be preceded by changes in the philosophy and practice of engineering design. The Lone Ranger approach to design must give way to collaboration across functions, such as production management, accounting, quality control, and laboratories (A. Ketchum, 1987). Criteria for judging designs and designers must also be modified. To overcome the experience gap, training and unlearning will be essential. Not to be overlooked are changes in the way engineering people are rewarded.

Management Selection and Promotion. Manager roles will change in the new-paradigm organization, and criteria for selection must be reexamined and revised. Appointment mistakes of the past must be rectified in the best way available. With periphery-in, more than one plant manager well into redesign has struggled with resistance and sabotage by recent ill-chosen appointees. In center-out, early attention to the selection and promotion process will relieve managers of upcoming innovations of the burden of misfits.

Who is promoted is a powerful signal of senior management's understanding and intention. Problem managers should never be assigned to head up existing successful innovative units for lack of a better place to put them. This step not only places the innovation at risk but signals a lack of seriousness, as does failing to promote successful innovators or worse—getting rid of them, as too often occurred with periphery-in.

Management Training and Development. Helping people develop the skills and understanding needed to manage in the new paradigm is time-consuming and should be given early attention, hence, management training and development is an enabling function. Not all of the managers' skills are suddenly made obsolete but there is unlearning to be done and new concepts to be learned. Those responsible for management development and training should review the underlying philosophy of the training unit and the materials currently in use; many of these materials are likely to be ill suited for movement to the goal paradigm.

In the process of change career paths will change in unforeseeable ways, making the ability to learn the most important attribute of all. The primary responsibility for learning and development should continue to rest with the curious learners; a lack of curiosity may be a sign of a potential casualty.

The subject of training is so important that Chapter 13 is devoted to it.

Recruiting and Hiring. The company will not endeavor to "hire its way into the new paradigm." The few potential casualties will not become evident for some time to come. But the vacancies arising in the usual retirements, quits, and other turnover can be made into an opportunity by well-planned anticipatory coordination. The first intensive change will occur at the periphery. It will be some time before intensive change reaches parts inside this periphery. Besides possessing skills and knowledge appropriate to the positions open, new hires must be suited to aid the change process and function later in a redesigned department.

Vacancies will open in the soon to be redesigned areas on the periphery. The primary criterion for these positions will be the ability to function in a new-paradigm organization.

An early step: Position specifications should be reviewed and changed as needed to bring them in line with expectations.

Once the position attributes are established the recruiting and hiring professionals will examine their methodologies for determining suitability of candidates.

Virtually all applicants will be from old-paradigm backgrounds, a preponderance of them preferring to work in a new setting. With clear, lucid advertising the organization goal can be made known, assuring the hiring organization an ample supply of applicants even in a time of low unemployment. The advertising and subsequent assessment activities must not overpromise by underemphasizing the goal aspect of the sought state of affairs. Recruiters will have to be prepared to be able to field the questions. How does one make uncertainty a plus?

Labor Relations. Preparing this enabling component is done in the context of the key idea regarding the relationships with unions and the union role in the sought future. A radically altered viewpoint will be difficult to explain to the occupants of the labor relations department, especially if the officer responsible for labor relations is only lukewarm to the radically altered position.

The challenge for the labor relations function is to change the union-company relationship—by definition involving a second party—to one conducive to redesign. Buy-in—personal paradigm change—by each party is key to this attainment. It is well accepted that personal paradigm change cannot be legislated, but within the company a manager is free to use the power of his authority to arrange for off-site search conferences, visits to other companies, and other events to open up the subject of how one looks at the world. More directly, this power can be used with subordinates in the areas of management by objectives, performance appraisal, and monetary rewards, deciding how much time and effort to expend on each person as is done with poor performers. Ultimately if all else fails, the manager in charge can reassign or take even more drastic measures to obtain movement in the direction of the goal organizational paradigm. None of these relation changing measures are open to the manager desiring to change the relationship between the company and a labor union.

Another difference lies in the political nature of the union leader's position. However much he might believe in the new ideas, he is not totally free to act, disregarding the opinion of his dues paying members and others in the union who would like to have his position.

In labor relations as everywhere, attitude change is compounded by the catch-22 of discovery. Fortunately at this point in time there are telling examples of the superiority of the new way, thanks to farseeing and risk-taking labor leaders.

It is difficult for a dedicated union leader to acknowledge the role of labor agreements in creating psychologically impoverishing work and their unwitting role as collaborators with scientific managers in making and sustaining the workplace as a psychological slum.

In both management and labor, there may be reluctance to let go the traditional adversarial roles. At a conference on labor-management cooperation, one corporate executive remarked that he enjoyed playing the conflict game. Union officials often have similar feelings; the president of one local confessed that he hated to see contract negotiations end because they were so exciting and satisfying.

Union leaders accustomed to a wholly adversarial relationship are understandably wary of management's new posture. Managers move a lot, union leaders are more stable. The union never knows when new owners will appear and restore an aggressively hostile adversarial relationship.

A big barrier to cooperation exists in companies with both union and nonunion plants. Union leaders see the nonunion plants as a manifestation that the company unwillingly suffers the presence of the union. Keeping union leadership insecure has its costs.

There will be instances of the union leadership inclined far more than their counterparts in management to see the need and benefits of AFL-CIO Donahue's, "We can negotiate hard and represent well. We can cooperate on quality and productivity improvement simultaneously" (1989).

Just as there is an experience gap in management, an experience gap exists in the labor movement. Today's union leaders have never been shop stewards in new-paradigm plants. Once a cooperative relationship has been established the experience gap can be discussed and dealt with.

Company labor relations policies must also be examined for roadblocks. One company following the periphery-in model was pushing its plant and unit managers to start some innovation, while at the same time it had a company policy against acting or appearing to act in a collaborative way with a union.

A study of existing labor contracts and supplementary agreements to uncover clauses inimical to the transition to the new paradigm should be initiated. This will form the base for long-range negotiating strategy in synchronization with the long-range plan to remake the company. Immediately it is an opportunity for education.

PREPARE THE FUNCTIONAL AREAS:
SUSTAINING COMPONENTS

Accounting and Information Systems. The center-out model provides unparalleled opportunity for those in the critically important accounting area at the center proactively to bring about the remaking of the company. Exploitation of this opportunity involves substantial departure from old thinking and acting, including the philosophic, substantive, and role change.

In the realm of ideas, *control* is the central objective of traditional cost accounting. The objective of learning is ignored. Control—knowing after the fact when something has gone wrong—is more important than preventing things from going wrong. According to the new paradigm, real control is creating and sustaining a condition where people do what needs to be done because they are knowledgeable, skilled, informed, and alert, and they want to do it. The primary purpose of information, then, is to prevent things from going wrong and to assure that those in a position to control the process learn to do it better through doing it.

A socio-technical redesign team defines new criteria for information. For example, the criteria developed at one redesigned plant for the level of the self-regulating team were as follows:

- Is the information adequate?
- Is the information readily accessible?
- Is the information timely?
- Does it relate to the team's mission?
- Does it relate to the team's measures of performance?
- Is it an aid to the team's social and technical learning?
- Does it aid the team in relating to its environment?

The change in philosophy itself results in substantive change in who gets information and how it is compiled. Other substantive change is required to accommodate structural change. As we saw earlier, redesigning work according to the new-paradigm shifts to the operating team many functions that formerly were outside its boundaries, requiring modifications in how one keeps track of the costs of maintenance, quality control, hiring, training, and other activities thought of as nonproduction, hence nonvariable. The existing accounting system will make a poor fit with the intensively redesigned units soon to appear on the periphery.

The proactive accounting department in center-out first does the requisite preparatory work—learning about state-of-the-art organizations, what manufacturing accounting will look like in the future when all facilities are designed and operated in the new way, division-level modifications necessary to accommodate anticipated state-of-the-art new plants and redesigned existing plants.

For a considerable period of time, new and changed existing units will coexist with unredesigned units and an essentially old-paradigm larger organization. During this period both new and old must be suitably connected with the still traditional organization. Established plants undergoing redesign present the same problem at another level. Early beachheads and the unredesigned parts must be accommodated. This duality presents a challenge of considerable magnitude that will test the ingenuity of those in the financial function.

Role change is typified by a periphery-in example of new greenfield design. The division controller understood that he was to cooperate with a new-paradigm plant preparing for start-up. To the very busy plant manager trying to get a new-paradigm plant constructed, staffed, and in operation in a mercilessly short time frame he said, "I will exempt you from our regular accounting requirements (a series of manuals built up over several decades) if you will just tell me what you want." That project itself would have required more man-hours than designing the plant organization.

In center-out those in the accounting center will engage with new plant design teams and plant-level managers endeavoring to redesign, providing counsel, expertise, and their findings regarding accounting in the goal state of affairs.

Quality Assurance. Arising in the 1960s, the quality assurance function at first seemed designed to do little more than provide upper-level managers with a warm feeling. Importantly it signaled a shift away from the testing-and-sorting approach to quality. With the onset of Japanese competition, quality took on a different meaning and a greater urgency. Currently there is a diversity of approaches to achieving and maintaining high quality products and services. In general, however, most of the current wisdom about quality is all in the context of the old paradigm. Too little attention is paid to worker commitment and how it can be achieved.

Quality cannot be dealt with in a piecemeal fashion. What managers on the periphery need most from quality assurance at the center is a holistic view of quality and the organization, considering the relations between the parts and the whole. In the new way, quality assurance managers and technicians will seek and be called upon to join redesign teams, effectively to look after the assurance, and contribute their valuable technical knowledge including control charting, sampling frequency, and auditing.

Quality vigilance cannot be relaxed while the organization is redesigned. Consumers demand quality, industrial customers demand that certain quality procedures be followed, and regulatory agencies operating in the old paradigm must be satisfied. Efforts to achieve and maintain high quality must be made in the context of the organization as it exists. Therefore quality assurance is another function that must prepare to keep one foot in the old and one in the new for some time to come.

Compensation and Job Evaluation. About pay one thing can be said with certainty: There is never enough. In the American culture most people's wants tend to be insatiable. Pay influences where and how one lives, with whom one associates, and how one is perceived by family members, friends, and acquaintances. Pay is indeed important to everyone. Deeply ingrained axioms, customs, and practices of pay in private sector organizations are reinforced by laws and regulations. Those who downgrade the importance of pay in their approach to management do so at their peril.

What compensation executives are to do is discontinue their long-standing practice of attending to extrinsic reward factors while viewing intrinsic rewards exclusively as in the province of the human resources department. As they expand their concerns to include the psycho-social factors, they must not create a dichotomy of the intrinsic and extrinsic.

In addition, the compensation executives must realize how the old payment methods are incompatible with the new ways of organizing work. A socio-technically designed organization cannot exist with the old way of paying. In the traditional work system a set of tasks comprises a job. Each job has a value and one is paid for doing the tasks that comprise a given job. If one does other tasks, however temporarily, the pay must change if the temporary tasks are deemed to have a different value. An inevitable feature of paying people for the job being done is rigidity. This pay method together with the work system itself—the two are inseparable—beget many unwanted behaviors and conditions such as " 'S'no' my job," apathy, inattention, unhealthy competition, and a "beat the system" attitude along with the hoarding of information, skills, knowledge, and ideas. Individually based incentive pay schemes make the unwanted behavior even more pronounced.

A new, radically different work system, as yet undesigned, must be created. The method of pay distribution must fit the features of the system; work is designed first and pay system design follows. This being the case, compensation is clearly a sustaining function. As such it will make ready to accommodate self-regulating teams as they appear in small parts of plants on the periphery. Preparation doesn't mean getting all the answers at this time. It is more identifying the key questions.

In the periphery-in approach to change, the units on the periphery came forward with redesign proposals and those in the compensation function asked, "How much will a pay-for-knowledge system cost?" as though there would be an incremental increase while all else was undisturbed. They should have asked, "How much will this pay-for-knowledge method save and why?"

Preparation means becoming ready to assume a collaborative role in multidisciplinary pay and system design groups.

The bureaucratic approach to job evaluation in which conformity and uniformity in job design and job content are sought must be abandoned. In traditional methodology for establishing the monetary value of a job, heavy weight is given to the cost of failure if the tasks are done improperly; little weight is given to discretion. The railway engineer must follow amply supplied signals and thereby has very little discretion. However, the cost of failure if he ignores the signals (malfeasance) is high. A notion that discretion should be highly valued (Jaques, 1956) has made little headway. This formulation calls for relating the level of pay to a span of time beginning at a point when a person receives a directive and extending to the point when the person has carried out the directive and therefore must be given another. With this framework a highly programmed job has less value than one requiring more analysis and judgment.

Traditional job value considerations are often overridden by another principle: The amount of pay for a job must be comparable to that paid for like work in the community, the area, the industry, or a combination of these. Pay professionals have little discretion in their trade; establishing the rate for a job consists mostly of finding comparable jobs, an easy task with scientific management pervasive, and pricing the job competitively. The widely held axiom, "There is only so much that a given job can pay," is reinforced. Those in an anomalous new-paradigm-based organization search in vain for comparable work in organizations around them. The level of work in a core process operating team is clearly higher than the level of work performed by workers in a traditional organization. Higher pay for the higher level of work is justified. One person who left his job as a worker in a state-of-the-art plant to take a job as traditional foreman in a nearby plant in the same industry reported that his latitude for decision making as a worker in the state-of-the-art plant was far greater than as a foreman in the traditional plant.

The need for a new approach to job evaluation was anticipated by a joint labor-management task force that redesigned work in the Rohm and Haas plant in Knoxville, TN. Early in the process, management and the officials of the Aluminum, Brick and Glass Workers Local 90, AFL-CIO-CLC agreed that some day their existing job evaluation methods would need modifications. At that time, however, neither party could say how; only after implementation began were they able to revise the job evaluation methods. To change job evaluation prematurely would have invited disruption and chaos.

Pay and method of pay are important throughout the enterprise and the mismatch between old-paradigm job evaluation and new-paradigm realities is not limited to the shop floor. As more operating areas of the plant are redesigned, the way the plant is managed will change and the question of applying new pay and job evaluation principles to management will arise. The question of new ways to compensate managers will persist as change makes its way inward.

As we noted earlier, career paths will be altered in significant but unknown ways. All the while, compensation and job evaluation practices must stay in tune with the changes being made. For a while the compensation function will be playing two tunes simultaneously, with perhaps some occasional disharmonies. There are many frontiers to explore.

New Product Development. Once the peripheral innovations emerge, things formerly thought to be impossible become feasible. Earlier constraints that could be traced to uncommitted workers and managers are removed. The innovative units excel in more than product costs and quality; they adjust readily to new things, and their production processes are more reliable. Part of getting it right at the center, therefore, is thinking ahead and being ready to exploit the new product opportunities opened up by the improved capabilities in quality and responsiveness.

With things right at the center, the way has been prepared. Much remains to be done at the center but the focus of action now shifts to the plants, new and old.

PART III

New Plant Start-Ups

SEVEN

Planning for the New Plant

New plants led the way in demonstrating the gains to be made from designing work according to socio-technical principles, and they still afford an excellent opportunity to correct problems at once in a significant segment of an enterprise. In center-out, the decision to innovate in a new plant emerges from the appreciation process at the center and is part of an overall scheme. Sanction is coupled with understanding and support. The enabling functions are now ready and the sustaining functions are ready to adjust to the new plant. The way to intensive change on the periphery is eased. The manager responsible for the new plant can confidently go all-out in the innovative sense.

As yet few in corporate America have shifted from periphery-in to center-out. But new plant decisions won't wait and to proceed with a plant in the old traditional mode merely because senior executives have not yet begun or had the time to complete the process of their appreciation and identification of a goal paradigm will mean a lost opportunity. Currently, the more typical situation is one in which an innovative new plant is to be embedded in a larger old-paradigm system practicing periphery-in. Accordingly, this chapter is oriented to the creation of "good" work in a new plant under periphery-in conditions.

Sanction in the periphery-in model will lack understanding and thus the proper kind and degree of support. The manager responsible for the plant may be required to settle for a less intensive innovation.

The decision to innovate in a new plant comes from someone for some reason. Someone is uneasy. He or she may be a line manufacturing executive or a human resources executive. Occasionally an internal consultant will wield considerable influence. One bad combination: a desire on the part of one senior in the organization to emulate, combined with short-range expectations and too little lead time. Doing it for the wrong reason endangers the effort.

INITIAL ANALYSIS

A number of matters are settled before a plant manager is named. These include location of the plant, size of the plant, labor union involvement, technology to be used, lead time and start-up date, expected unit cost, and anticipated volume in the first few years. Overly optimistic expectations are the norm.

The operational organizational paradigm will determine the attitude toward involving a union. There is no question but that the majority of managers in the United States will, when building a new plant, seek to keep it "union free." These same managers see some areas more prone to unions than others. Local Chambers of Commerce and others wishing to attract industry will tout this characteristic of their community.

Without doubt, the labor unions still have far to go in seeking a modified role wherein they are effectively active in seeing to the psychological well-being of their members while they are at work. It is also true that virtually every new socio-technically designed new plant in the United States in the last two decades, regardless of location, has remained nonunion (as have, of course, a number of plants not a product of socio-technical thinking). The unions should heed this, and probably do, but have not yet figured out what to do and how to go about it. In a few innovative plants where management has attempted to keep out the union but the union has prevailed, all vestiges of new-paradigm thinking and application have been wiped out. Regrettably, these instances contribute to the general attitude that the union is the primary cause of psychological impoverishment in the workplace. Only without a union, it is said, can one design really good work for people.

In fact it is becoming more and more feasible to seek the collaboration of the more progressive unions. Of special note is the Shell plant in Sarnia, Ontario, where the union was involved from the inception. The manner in which General Motors is working with the UAW in the Saturn project is also worth watching.

Where to locate the plant analysis begins with consideration of basic costs fixed by its position relative to markets and raw materials. Energy-intensive products and technologies differ from those that are not heavy energy users. Water supplies and waste treatment factors also get primary consideration. Local and state taxes must be considered, along with land costs, land development, drainage, fire protection, and ease of access by rail, truck, and automobile.

Analyzing a prospective location in socio-technical terms involves considering the richness of the environment in supplies and services. This richness will determine the degree of self-sufficiency to be built into the new plant.

For example, the first author undertook a World Bank-sponsored socio-technical design of a diesel locomotive repair shop in the Sudan, an underdeveloped country. First a small shop in the state of Florida was studied. Purchase orders over a two-year period were analyzed to determine the amount and kind of supplies and services used by this shop in the rich environment of a developed country where low-cost transport is readily available. This information was then used to ascertain the "boundaries" of the shop. In the Florida environment, when the motor on the crane malfunctioned, an electrical shop was called and the trouble soon fixed. In the Sudan, shop self-sufficiency was critical; the electrical shop had to be part of the enterprise.

Richness in human support and services is also important. However important a job is, it is only part of living. Opportunities for people to extend their formal education are important, especially for workers in new-paradigm plants, where the richness of the work experience stimulates the desire for future growth. Locating a plant in a community without facilities for higher education diminishes the ability of the enterprise to attract the best people.

The availability of training services from state-funded training and local community colleges is also a plus. The value goes beyond saving money in the training of those hired first. Important to the continuing success of the new plant is the ethic of individual responsibility-taking engendered in the community educational resources.

Of growing importance are family-related opportunities. Around plant managers' spouses at social gatherings the subject of being banished to an unacceptable living area is certain to be raised. It is not just shopping and social opportunities; spouses also seek educational and career opportunities. The quality of public schools is a key factor.

Area unemployment should be considered, but whatever the level of unemployment at the time of the survey, it may change. It is more important to assure that the QWL in the new plant is good enough so that people in the area will want to work there.

One large employer announced plans to locate a new plant in a sunbelt area, paying "Northern" wages. A few months later a smaller company announced plans for a new-paradigm plant, paying "local community" wages, in the same area. The manager of an existing plant in the area, an old-paradigm plant also paying local community wages, was concerned that when the company paying Northern wages began to hire he would lose many good employees. As it turned out, the existing plant lost none to the high-wage plant but did lose some to the new-paradigm plant.

Local employment practices should be taken into consideration. What are considered customary working hours? Do other plants work fixed or rotating shifts? Again, one should not necessarily do as others do. More employers and unions should heed what has been attempted at the Shell plant in Sarnia, where the work that must be performed at night has been minimized and the necessary night work is shared.

The operational organization paradigm will come into the site location decision in another way. Some people still believe a state-of-the-art plant will function successfully only if special people (read "compliant") are employed; these managers will place strong emphasis on finding a location where such people are available. More knowledgeable managers will realize that it has been demonstrated that new-paradigm organizations can successfully function in many environments.

Plant size is a relative matter. The size of a new plant can be expressed in several dimensions: investment, number of employees, capacity, scope of the transformation made to input materials (value added).

As part of their strategy to remain union free some companies place a limit on the size of their new plants, limiting the size to no more than 500 people.

One very successful company practices decentralization for other reasons. It has a large number of products that compete in an equally large number of relatively small markets.

With the experience gap in mind a policy of initial smallness is wise but should not prevail to the detriment of other factors dictating a larger size.

Several key questions regarding the product and the technological process need to be asked and the implications of the answers considered. What is the product? Is it a new product that will be linked to costly introductory advertising? Or is the plant being built to increase capacity to make an existing product? Will the plant be furnishing components to a larger system? Is it to be the sole supplier? The cost of failure of any kind will vary substantially from one situation to another. The greater the cost of failure, the more lead time should be devoted to the project.

Probing the technology is also important. Is it tried and true, known to you or will some of it be tried and true and some of it never before have been used by you? An inventory of technical resource people should be undertaken. It may be that some or all of the technical process has never been tried before on a production scale by anyone. For each case, what of the expected life of the present technology? Will it quickly be obsolete or is the expected life a decade or more?

If the new plant represents an increase in capacity to produce existing products and employs similar technology, one should take advantage of opportunities to interview workers and supervisors in the existing facilities.

Beginning late extracts its penalties. Planning for an innovative new plant should begin before the need for a plant has arisen. In the periphery-in model this is not practiced. When a capital investment for a new plant is being considered many questions must be asked and most of them have uncertain answers so decisions are delayed by deliberation, the quest for certainty and waiting for the arrival of "perfect information." As a rule operating people don't have sufficient lead time for thorough analysis, planning and execution.

A late beginning takes a toll in a number of ways. Crucially important preparatory activities are incomplete and inadequate, and start-up costs are higher than they need to be. A late beginning thus adds failure factors that would otherwise not exist.

Late beginnings mean losing an opportunity for joint optimization of the social and technical systems. With periphery-in plant design will separately begin long before the analysis and planning for the organization. The center-out strategy will correct this.

A late beginning exacts a painful toll of the new organization members. When the time is too short any new plant start-up is unusually stressful and frustrating. Most new plant start-ups can scarcely be described as affording a good quality of working life. But the start-up is temporary and most will willingly endure the stress because for them the new-paradigm plant offers a once-in-a-lifetime opportunity to be involved in a really creative endeavor.

Appointment delays are inevitable and exacerbate the consequences of insufficient lead time. In no other area are large organizations so slow and processes so cumbersome as on the urgent matter of hiring people or appointing them from within. When someone is hired from outside, there is the time required for the executive search, the wait for the applicant to accept, to give notice to the current employer, and often to relocate. Appointing from within may take even longer as a manager resists letting a good person go.

In one company where things had not been made right at the center, the responsible executive was told that he must select as project leader someone well below the rank of plant manager in the company. The reasoning was that the project leader would be required to stay with the new plant for some time and would grow into the plant manager rank. It would be unfair to appoint a person already at the plant manager level, who would have to remain a plant manager for three or more years while seeing to the success of the new plant. For the responsible executive, this was an issue worth fighting for and in the end he prevailed, but the price of delay was paid in full.

THE PROJECT TEAM

Most new plant project teams are made up of people who will manage the new plant. This practice is particularly advantageous when the experience gap is prevalent. While it is by no means unfailing, the joint optimization process of designing a new plant has proved to be an excellent means of bringing about personal paradigm change.

The choice of the project leader is a critical one. Mixing state-of-the-art intentions with rigidly old-paradigm managers brings failure. The successful candidate should have the golden rule as a personal value, and be undogmatic, personally secure with little self-doubt, and willing and able to function in a collaborative system with low structure. He or she must be creative, something of a risk-taker, a teacher, a learner, and an unlearner. A tolerance for ambiguity is essential, as is a willingness to challenge and confront when honest differences become apparent. Some understanding of the dynamics of human groups is needed.

The person named should have the potential to regard manufacturing as a set of processes and the role of the manager to observe the functioning of these processes and to intervene in appropriate and effective ways when any process becomes dysfunctional. This approach requires systems thinking; problems and issues must be related to a framework of fundamental principles.

A broad perspective beyond the usual functional outlook is needed. Other generic attributes of the good manager should not be overlooked. Intelligence, honesty, good communication skills, and a good technical background are critically important. The job of project leader is not for a lazy person. A good track record is essential, especially when the new plant is the first attempt at intensive innovation in the company.

These make good specifications for all managers in the new plant.

Not everyone on the project team must ultimately be a part of the plant management. A link with engineers is critical and can be established by including one or more on the team. As we have seen in earlier chapters, the physical plant design can enhance the opportunities to create good work or it can make the creation of good work almost impossible. The key to success is joint optimization, described in Chapter 4.

The substance of the project team's charter will depend on the change model being employed. A charter given in center-out will emphasize the long-range importance of the project to the company, include a goal paradigm, and describe the meaning of "having-it-right" at the center of the new plant and direct the team to make it so. Being given a goal paradigm does not, however, make introspection unnecessary. Personal paradigms are a way of thinking, and the goal paradigm must be internalized by the project team. The experiences of the last two decades have demonstrated that success is closely linked to the time and effort that the project team spends on ideas. Devoting attention to ideas will run counter to the team members' previous experience, however, so the charter should clearly spell out that it is expected and sanctioned.

When the new plant is the company's first attempt at intensive change, the chartering executives should give some consideration to the questions of how many wheels, and which ones, to reinvent. The basic new plant design methodology need not be completely reinvented. Criteria against which the design will be tested in the approval process should be spelled out. The team should be admonished to have a sound reason for every aspect of the design.

If the innovative new plant is not the company's first it is important to make clear that this project cannot begin at the point that an earlier project has reached. Any new social system is embryonic and must go through its own stages of learning and development. It is like a newly born second child; experience with the first child has taught the parents much about guiding and nurturing a child's growth, but the new baby must still go through his or her own growth and learning process.

An important principle in new plant design is to make all parts fit. Harmony is sought and this first principle brings on a second: A good fit among the parts of a system can be achieved only with an iterative design process. Individual parts are not final until the whole is complete. Once these two principles are accepted it easily follows that design by sequestered functional areas will not yield this vital harmony. The charter should include taking the necessary steps to involve and integrate all the relevant disciplines and constituencies. In the center-out model the project leader's charter includes this provision, which is also made known to those in the relevant disciplines and constituencies. In periphery-in, the burden of getting others to cooperate will fall on the project leader.

Planning a new plant is a series of interrelated decisions. The project team can make only a fraction of these as a group; most must be made by individuals. How, then, can one expect a coherent and harmonious design? The answer is to create a framework within which these separate decisions are to be made. Ideally, this framework is the goal paradigm that the senior management has established during their appreciation process. If such an explicit paradigm does not exist, the project team must create one. Even so, frequent validation of the design by the project team is required.

Key functional executives should be involved. In the center-out model, they are brought into the change process by the senior managers at the center. In the periphery-in, this step is missing. In the latter, the project team should endeavor to create a group of interested key functional executives who will stay abreast of the new plant project and the policy exceptions that will be required for the plant to function.

Policy exceptions come hard and take time. The project and the key functional executives should jointly endeavor to become familiar with the complications that accompany intensive change. Once these complications are understood as a natural part of an organizational paradigm shift, coping comes easier. If the problems are thought to be unique to the project and people are labeled good guys and bad guys, even more severe complications develop.

When the unit-to-be is the first innovation in the organization, someone senior to the project leader should undertake to assure that the organization learns from the experience of creating it. This is not easily done in an old-paradigm organization. People are proud of what they have done, and the pride may be justified. But real learning comes from correcting error, which involves admission of error, and in an old-paradigm organization one never admits error. The difference in the treatment of error is an absolutely major difference between old and new.

If the new plant project is not the first, the project team should make use of the earlier experience but not just copy what the others have done. Old habits are likely to persist, however; the not-invented-here attitude is widespread. In one plant-in-transition the first joint labor-management redesign team was called "core group." After they had made their recommendation but before it was implemented, a second redesign team was named. This second group would have nothing to do with the recommendation of the first and even insisted that they call themselves a task force, not a core group. The name, so long as it was different, didn't matter.

At first the new plant project team is overwhelmed and unable to decide where to begin. It is usually their first new plant experience and each will be mindful of career prospects. Important decision makers who have sanctioned the innovation will be watching. Is this the first new-paradigm venture in the company or has a successful beachhead already been established? Being second after a successful first has an important implication. To succeed in the second when others have been successful before you is expected. Recognition is limited; it has all been done before. But to fail in an endeavor in which others before you have succeeded can be devastating. Special problems of second timers should be part of the deliberations at higher levels.

The project team members have not forgotten their functional experience and working in a team is strange and inefficient. Each will have ideas about some functional tasks that need to be done. Learning how to work in a team is often unhappy learning. Doing familiar functional tasks is more comfortable so team members often reach out and work on things before the time has come. They are somewhat like carpenters told to build a house but given no plan. Digging the foundation is different from their craft and is hard work, so they try to saw and hammer before they are certain of the dimensions needed.

One way out of this situation is to begin by listing on the right-hand side of a page everything that needs to be in place by start-up

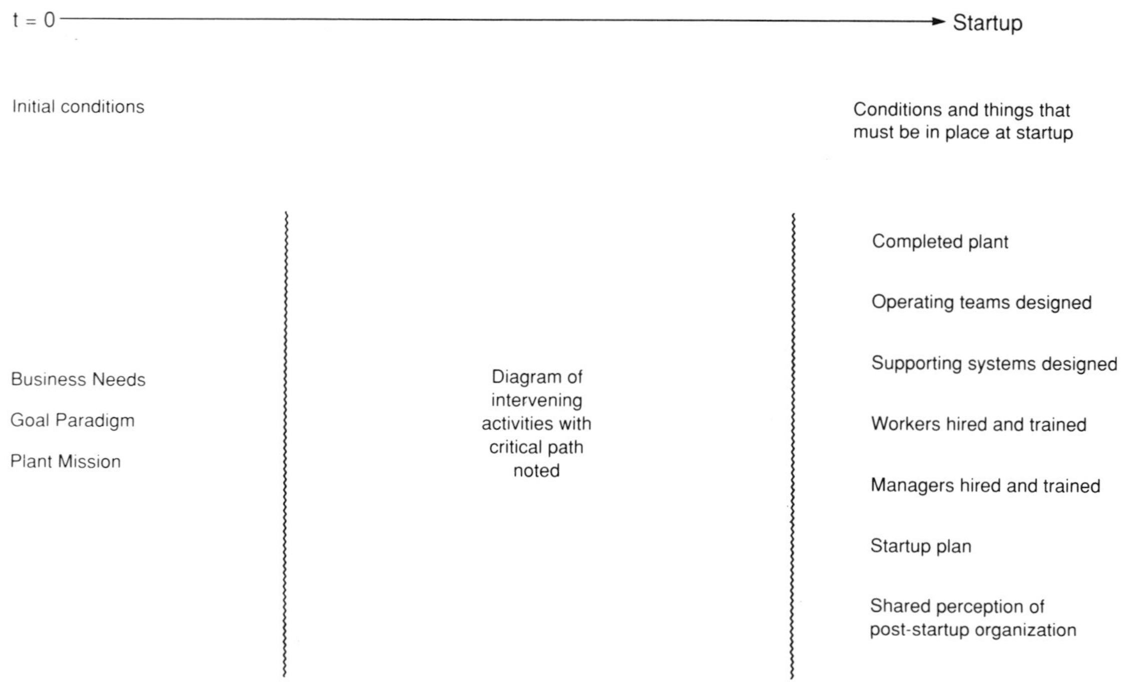

t = 0 ——————————▶ Startup

Initial conditions

Conditions and things that
must be in place at startup

Completed plant

Operating teams designed

Supporting systems designed

Workers hired and trained

Managers hired and trained

Startup plan

Shared perception of
post-startup organization

Diagram of
intervening
activities with
critical path
noted

Business Needs

Goal Paradigm

Plant Mission

Figure 7.1 Activity Mapping for a New Plant

(see Figure 7.1). On the left side is the project beginning, t = 0; the business needs, goal organization paradigm, and plant mission. In the center an activity network is laid out much as a critical path diagram is constructed for new construction or a turnaround. Noted on the activity network is who decides what, who needs to approve what, who must be informed about what. Additional notations are made regarding which activities must be done by the entire team in concert and which can be divided among members. When this process is carried out the planning and design go forward expeditiously.

Those in the project team should find out as much as they can about the state of affairs in division and corporation management, especially with periphery-in. Merely finding out is not enough; active reaching out is required. A technique for this is to draw a small circle to represent the project team people. The project team then scan their environment, making note of those with whom they will have relations during the life of the project. Referring to the six classes in the chapter on the center-out strategy, where does each person and group in this environment fall? In some cases project managers find this a depressing exercise. But these people must be influenced and it is best to know what they are like as regards their relationship to the new plant and the new paradigm.

In Chapters 8 and 9 we will take up the activity that follows, design and start-up of the new plant, respectively.

How Not to Bring a New Plant on Stream

This example, not atypical of the past, was a form of periphery-in. It was a company in which the influence of the Japanese was clearly present, especially at corporate headquarters. The recession was on but one division was authorized to build a new plant. For this corporation at that time, this new plant was the only new game in town. An important and powerful corporate executive was troubled by the product quality and productivity state of affairs but had not yet reached the point of the third-order diagnosis. This troubled corporate executive directed the general manager of the division building the new plant to bring forth a state-of-the-art facility in both a technical and organizational sense. The division general manager's response to the senior executive was that expected of an ambitious comer in a Fortune 500 company. He assumed that he was expected to know what a state-of-the-art organization was. Naturally, he did not ask.

This large company was a many layered bureaucracy and the powerful corporate executive levelwise was quite distant from plant management. The mandate from the corporate executive came late. This division general manager had already directed the old-paradigm division engineering group to begin the design of the plant. Like those in corporate headquarters, he, too, was heavily into quality circles but he was innocent of socio-technical theory.

In due time the general manager made the appointments for the managing staff of the new plant-to-be. In doing so he cloned the larger old-paradigm organization, appointing a plant manager, a plant personnel manager, a plant controller, a plant manufacturing manager, a plant quality assurance manager, and a plant materials control manager. No special appointment criteria were established to assure that these managers were most likely to be successful with a state-of-the-art organizational approach. Some of them were anything but "naturals." The appointment created instant stakeholders who were directed to bring forth a state-of-the-art organization to operate the state-of-the-art technology that, although it was not said, they would inherit from the engineers.

Soon after the management group began its deliberations, they avowed that they did not have time to be involved in the plant organization design so they created a design team at the next two levels in the new plant organization.

People in this organization pride themselves on being results oriented. So, a plan was immediately drawn up to specify the dates when various aspects of the design would be separately reviewed and approved by counterpart functional executives in the division and the corporation. For example, the date was set for an employee manual to be completed, for recruiting plans to be established, for a compensation and benefit package to be completed, for plant policy formulation, for an organization chart, for training plans, for quality assurance plans, and the like. It was fractionated, segmented planning.

Once the plant manager got the plan approved, he set out to learn what a state-of-the-art organization really was and how to create one. (Typical of periphery-in, he later was vainly to attempt to educate his superiors on the subject.) As always, the time was short, but soon he began to realize what the design team already knew, that a holistic approach was required and that individual parts of the design could not be final until the whole was complete. For example, one should not devise a pay scheme until one understands what people are expected to do. The along-the-way due dates for separately conceived plans could not be met. Sensible logic calls for explaining to division and corporation line and staff people the concept of a state-of-the-art organization and its interactive design process. But in this most traditional of traditional divisions, resetting a due date was tantamount to missing a due date; and missing a due date could threaten one's career. So, the upper levels were kept innocent.

As time went on the due dates approached and the plant manager and staff demanded the piecemeal plans. Naturally, they were not forthcoming. When the compensation plan was called for the design team could only say, "It is not ready." Naturally, the manager and his staff intervened. The form this intervention took began with the plant manager and his staff visiting a new-paradigm plant with an excellent pay-for-knowledge system. They liked it, and there it was, ready. The due date for the compensation plan could now be met! They adopted it, directed the design team to use it, and began preparation of the presentation. Predictably, this "copied" pay system did not fit their plant. Also predictably, the design team, by now knowledgeable about and committed to a new paradigm, was furious! Conflict and chaos of crisis proportions resulted. Fortunately, the corporate compensation functionary discovered a scheduling conflict and postponed the review. Serendipity saved the day and the design team was permitted to complete the total design, including a pay system that did fit. But, stress on all of these people undertaking start-up and operation of the plant became almost intolerable. Needless to say, the outcome was a new paradigm in operation at the shop floor and the old paradigm in operation at the level of the plant manager, his direct reports, and the balance of the division and corporation.

EIGHT

Designing the New Plant

Critical to good design is knowing what is good work, how it differs from bad work, and how to put this knowledge to practical use, that is, how to design a socio-technical system that will yield this good work. Old habits that must be broken include the top-down design that begins with cloning of the larger organization by establishing the manager and staff positions. In the new paradigm, one follows the principle, "First, design (make things right on) the shop floor where the work is done (the core process) and then design support and managing groups to keep this production process going smoothly." In doing so one identifies clearly the needs of the shop floor operating teams.

Designers make the operating team the basic building block of the organization (Davis, 1983; Emery, 1966) and design follows this general sequence: First the team's size, location and characteristics are considered. Next follows a bundling of tasks within the team into assignments, the counterpart to jobs in the old way. Then comes attending to the balance of the organization. This is done by focusing on the needs of operating teams—what must be supplied to the operating teams if they are to be successful. This leads to information system design followed by design of the team manager role. Finally, comes design of the managing and support teams to supply the needs of the operating teams. The "anatomy of self-regulation" is thus established.

LAYING THE GROUNDWORK

Why People Work: Choosing Between Extrinsic and Intrinsic Motivation. Like senior management at the center in its appreciation, the project team must engage in an essential microsocial analysis that leads off with the question, "Why do people work, anyway?" A person performs tasks for one or a combination of three reasons: Task performance satisfies an intrinsic need; task performance brings extrinsic reward; nonperformance of the task brings undesirable consequences. This leads to the basic question for the design team: "On which of the two sources of motivation—extrinsic and intrinsic—will you place major reliance for shaping behavior in the new plant?" The answer affects the design process, the design itself, and the way of managing. It is not a question of choosing one source of motivation and ignoring the other but of deciding on which to place the major emphasis. Those holding the view that performance problems stem from bad work will put major reliance on the intrinsic. Their goal becomes to get everyone to do what needs to be done because they want to do it.

Continuing the microsocial analysis leads to consideration of variance control, a variance being the occasion when some attribute of the material being processed does not meet the specifications or is otherwise unsatisfactory. If people are to be trusted to make the right decisions to control their technical system effectively, certain conditions must be met. One is that they understand the technical process: its chemistry, its thermodynamics, its electrical and mechanical aspects, and so on, as well as the interrelationships among these factors. Another is that they must have up-to-the-minute information about what is going on throughout the system, not merely in the section to which they happen to be assigned. What is steady? What is rising? What is falling? This information is in rates, quantities, temperature, product attributes, and the like. They also require current information about the mechanical and electrical state of the technical system, such as worn cams, failing sensing devices, pumps, levers.

Some in the project team will usually point out the old saw about people not wanting to make decisions, an attitude arising out of their experiences in a traditional work system where, sure enough, many are found who don't want to and won't make decisions. A project team is well advised to consider the factors that discourage worker decisions in a system that relies on extrinsic rewards for motivation. Some of these are lack of interest, the fear of doing something wrong because of limited knowledge, the fear of doing something wrong because of inadequate information, a "not paid to do it" attitude. Sometimes people don't realize what decision needs to be made; more often, the boss discourages decision making. The boss's past reactions to operator errors are also a contributing factor. The list goes on, including the lack of opportunity to learn from decision making, no information on the total outcome, and the lack of a forum in which to share experiences.

An extended period in this kind of a system doing "bad"—psychologically impoverishing—work leads to personality changes. The worker forgets that he needs to learn, to decide. Faculties atrophy. But atrophied faculties, like muscles that shrink when the limb is placed in a cast for an extended time, do come back when the proper stimulus is provided.

Why Teams? The Making of Good Work. Having decided to place primary reliance on intrinsic motivation, the project team now must provide a psychologically enriching work experience for those who will one day be joining the new plant organization. Bad work must go and with it the inordinate reliance on extrinsic motivation, especially coercive supervision. Good work requires increasing the

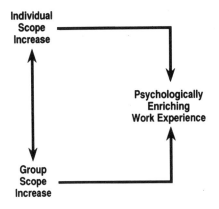

Figure 8.1 Making Good Work (1)

scope and variety of each person's work far beyond that normal to the old way. Generally, overcoming the limitation of scope and variety means putting workers into teams. Teams, as units, can be given a very broad scope of responsibility and thus greatly expand the scope and variety for each person. For this reason the team becomes the basic building block of the new organization (see Figure 8.1).

Although organizing people into teams goes a long way toward the desired expanded scope and variety, more is needed. The additional *mechanism* for final attainment of the psychologically enriching work is multiple skill proficiency—the condition in which each person has "extra" relevant skills, more than he or she is using at a particular time. Fred Emery (1976) called this condition "redundancy of the functions" (as distinct from parts) (see Figure 8.2).

Multiple skill proficiency is not merely flexibility, the authority to assign people where the manager wants them. This is a familiar battle ground for management and the union, and for several decades all of the skirmishes have been won by the union. The absence of the prerogative of flexibility is indeed costly and it is being

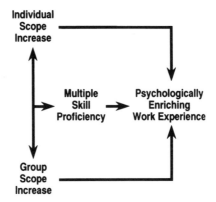

Figure 8.2 Making Good Work (2)

changed in some back-against-the-wall situations. Unfortunately, today some senior managers will direct their subordinates to "go to teams" in the expectation that the prerogative of flexibility will be recovered.

Multiple skill proficiency is not just job rotation! The uninitiated too often believe that rotating a person from one psychologically impoverishing job to another is a viable technique. Neither flexibility nor job rotation changes the psychologically impoverishing job content and it is psychologically enriching work that brings about worker commitment to the enterprise. Multiple skill proficiency is essential to that end.

The commitment itself means that the production process is more in control. Two positive feedback loops are then at work (see Figure 8.3). Doing a good job (controlling variances, hence the production process) reinforces commitment. And as people learn by doing, their competence increases. Rising commitment and competence mean ever better control of variances, all as a result of paying attention to the work life of the individual and placing primary reliance on intrinsic motivation.

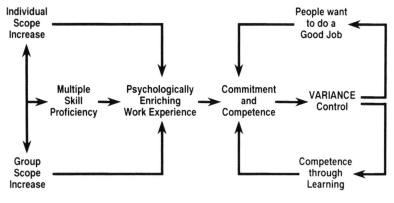

Figure 8.3 Making Good Work (3)

A Technical Analysis. It is not only the social system that is analyzed at the micro level. A thorough, rigorous, and detailed analysis of each step in the production processes is also required; the sooner begun, the better. The technical analysis follows the material being processed through all the various steps to the finished product. For each step there are questions to be answered. What goes in? What is it supposed to be like here, and why? How is the material changed in this step? What goes out? What is it then supposed to be like, and why? The availability and timeliness of information is examined.

Variances that may occur are then analyzed. A list of possible variances is prepared and a matrix showing the interrelationships of the processing equipment and things that go wrong is then constructed. An analysis of the control (prevention or correction) of the most serious variances follows. In which step does the variance occur? In which step is it observed? In which step is it controlled? What tasks are performed in its control? What information is required by the person controlling the variance and what are the sources of this information?

The technical analysis identifies the information that must be available at all points, who must have it, and where it can be generated. The analysis also shows what information is generated at each point and who needs this information. This analysis enables the design of a usable information system that does not overlook the needs of the people on the shop floor, who in the end really control the process—that is to say, make it work.

The completed technical analysis is the information base for the tasks that are to be performed and it thus enables the designing of assignments.

The technical analysis has other uses. It is a check on the completeness of the physical design. As the technical analysis proceeds, the issues that must be decided and the questions that must be answered are revealed. One manager noted, "As you do the technical analysis you are constantly reminded of decisions that need to be made." In one case, one raw material was both critical and unique. There were few suppliers and their products were not interchangeable. The vendor had not been chosen, even though the choice affected the design of the process. In another case, the project team uncovered the need for an additional processing step that otherwise would have been omitted. These issues are frequently unrecognized. Without the technical analysis, one is condemned to encountering the omitted and undecided in start-up—usually in the wee hours of the morning! Fixing those mistakes during start-up incurs unnecessary costs and human stress of great proportions. The value of a thorough and early technical analysis in creating a new plant is further illustrated by these comments by managers: "It brings out details that might have gotten lost." "It is iterative and allows you to refine your system." "I found changes I had to make in my software specifications to vendors."

The technical analysis is of immense help in making decisions about automation. Should a step be automated or left manual? What level of automation should be applied, both in general and at particular points?

The technical analysis is a base from which present and future members of the organization can gain a detailed understanding of the production process. The operation can be dissected, making it possible to give each person complete data on how to operate his or her assignment. "What if" games can be played and from these people learn as much as can be learned without the technical system actually operating. The variance matrix enables managers and workers alike to understand the relationships among the various parts of the technical system and the people who operate it. With it workers and others can easily learn about the impact they have on people and things in other parts of the operation. All share a common map.

The doing of the technical analysis affords vitally important project team building. As one busy manager noted, "It gets people together for two days to talk about the technical system when they otherwise would not find the time to do so."

In addition to its extensive utility in design and start-up, the technical analysis is of great value in other ways for a long time to come. It is kept up to date and becomes the repository of learning.

DESIGNING CORE PRODUCTION PROCESS OPERATING TEAMS

Fixing the Technical Boundary. Making good use of the completed technical analysis, designers fix the extent of the technical system over which the team will have jurisdiction. This is best done in concert with the design engineers in the process of joint optimization. Where possible, a team's technical boundary should begin where there is a discontinuity in the material transformation process. Likewise, it is best when the team's technical boundary ends in a discontinuity. In setting the end point of the team's boundary the significance of the material transformation is taken into account. An insignificant transformation forecloses the inclusion of important decisions in the province of the team's responsibility.

Writing the Team Mission. For each team a statement of mission—the purpose or reason for the team's being—is required. Mission accomplishment is what all team members share. It is another of the forces that both brings them together and makes them a distinctive group apart. Thus the mission is another form of boundary. If there is no shared task, the appropriateness of the team makeup must be reconsidered. Great care should be taken in the preparation of the mission statement to make it clear, concise, and comprehensive while reflecting the values in the goal paradigm.

Establishing Scope of Team Responsibility: Team Processes. At the heart of a state-of-the-art organization is the concept of self-regulation. Self-regulation goes beyond self-management. The core idea in self-regulation is learning from experience. Managing in the old paradigm way is woefully short of learning from experience; the label "self-managing" applied to a self-regulating team therefore misses the mark.

To make learning-from-functioning operational in the new plant, designers apply the concept of *team processes.* A team process entails a transformation of some inputs into some outputs coupled with a pause for learning and making plans to do it better the next time. The process is cyclical, has a beginning and an end, and extends through time.

A team process consists of several steps: Step one is *action,* the transforming of inputs into outputs (experiencing, doing, doing it right, doing it wrong). After the action step comes step two, a *pause for learning* that consists of generating information on the outcomes followed by review and evaluation. How did we do? Is this better or worse than before? Why is it better or worse? Is the performance better or worse than we expected?

A new question follows: What can we learn from all this? Group discussions such as this in a culture in which error recognition is built in make the team meeting into a powerful learning forum. Important learning should be recorded. There will be new mem-

Action

- Experience

Pause for Learning

- Generate information
- Review information
- Evaluate information
- Make note: "What can we learn?"

Plan for Action

- How we will proceed in the next cycle

Figure 8.4 A Cycle in a Team Process

bers coming into the team and they shouldn't have to reinvent every wheel or recommit every error. (One plant has as its motto: "We will make only new mistakes!")

Now comes step three, *planning for action in the next cycle*. In this step they are given relevant new information and with the new information and the learning acquired in this and earlier cycles the team plans how to do it better the next time. They are now ready to begin the next cycle (see Figure 8.4).

As the designers set forth the processes for the self-regulating operating teams, habits learned in the old paradigm of scientific management will intrude. Deciding the scope of team involvement is a stern test of the project team's commitment to the new paradigm. A bold and committed new plant project team with its eye on the future instead of just the first six months of start-up will include team processes as shown in Table 8.1.

The most obvious of the operating team's processes is carrying out the transformations to their material and information inputs— that is, making in-specification products. In this process the action is the carrying out of individual assignments on the shop floor during the week. The pause for learning and planning for the next cycle, however, is done weekly in a face-to-face setting, the team

Table 8.1 Team Processes

- Making in-specification products
- Avoiding accidents
- Maintaining the technical system
- Maintaining good relationships with other teams
- Administering the pay-for-knowledge system
- Obtaining needed replacements
- Assimilating new members
- Exiting members
- Developing individual team members
- Developing and maintaining the team

---

meeting. In practice, information gathering overlaps action; as they do their assignments team members make mental and written notes, thus preparing for an efficient sharing of data in the team meeting.

Overall, people learn from errors made in the transformation. They learn to do it right. They learn to cope with variations in inputs to their technical system and variations in other matters. They also learn to cope with variations in the nature of their technical system, that is, cams, sensing devices, voltage variations, and the like. They learn about their own and others' idiosyncracies.

Transforming material inputs into in-specification products or outputs is but one team process. Others, though less obvious, are equally vital and follow a similar pattern. An accident avoidance process will comprise training, goal setting, and review. Such a process makes safety every minute, every hour a shared responsibility. Each team member becomes an expert in the field of safety.

Another test of the designer's commitment is deciding the extent of maintenance to be performed by operating teams. When the operating teams do most of the maintenance, maintenance department resources become smaller in number, broader in function and more demanding in skills. Maintenance people are both teachers and doers—doing when the needed skills are not present in the core process operating team.

Maintaining good relationships with other units is also a team process. No team is an island. Self-regulation is the exercise of responsible autonomy, not selfishness. A well-designed self-regulating team will develop an intense dedication to its mission. With this strong cohesion around the mission comes a tendency to forget the importance of the larger unit's mission and the importance of collaboration between the team and other individuals and units. Including the external relationships process will preserve the desirable intrateam cohesion and secure the vital collaboration among teams.

Administering the pay-for-knowledge system should be included in the list of processes. It puts individual capability assessment in the hands of the experts—team members who know very well who can do what.

The process of obtaining replacement members when needed will vary in scope from examining candidates supplied by someone else to a more comprehensive process beginning with the placing of help-wanted ads and extending through hiring.

A separate but related process is the assimilation of new individuals, making them into productive members while preserving the team and larger organization values.

The process of exiting members fairly and lawfully becomes especially important in a new plant start-up because selection does not end with hiring.

The important team member proficiency process has many parts. Once a new member is assimilated, he or she must acquire and maintain many skills. Team members need knowledge and skills used in material transformations, the practice of safety, and teaching. They must learn to be effective in group meetings and how to learn from outside resources. They must learn technical troubleshooting, social problem solving, evaluation of team member skill proficiency, communication skills, interpersonal skills, statistical process control methods, and how to hire and terminate fairly and lawfully. This variety of skills to be developed in the team member is tangible evidence that a person in the new organization is to be treated as a resource to be developed rather than as an extension of a machine and a replaceable spare part. The growth potential for team members is substantial.

Ensuring that attention and energy are devoted to the development and maintenance of the team as a unit is a process. As a beginning the designers should specify categories of team health, including effective meetings, group problem solving, goal setting and planning, and proficiency in regulating team processes. A healthy, productive team exists only when team processes are healthy.

The cycle time varies from process to process. In their post-startup life, teams will pause weekly to review and learn about making the product. Other cycles will run into months. One must gain some experience before the pause for learning. For example, a team would not learn much about how they are doing in assimilating new members if they paused weekly to do so. The time it takes to gain sufficient experience is the key factor determining cycle time.

With team processes specified, team responsibilities are understood; unnecessary ambiguity about what a team is to do is eliminated.

The Team Meeting. A meeting of the entire team should take place weekly. A format that has proved highly successful is as follows:

> *Mission statement review.* This is a "Why are we here?" reminder, so vital to effective functioning of any group.
> *Team performance review.* In this "How are we doing?" segment, the team is furnished information on each category of performance.
> *What have we learned?*
> About our raw materials and supplies?

> About our process machinery and equipment?
> About the way we do our tasks and work with each other?
> About the way we work with those outside our boundary.
> *What is to be done?*
> *How can we use this meeting time more effectively?*

The meeting format takes into account the team's existence in three frames of reference (see Figure 8.5).

The primary frame of reference is the team on the shop floor. When they meet, they step out of the primary frame into another, a vantage point from which they can view themselves in the first. In this way they get ever-better at what they do on the shop floor.

The final step of the meeting is the third frame of reference, from which they view themselves in the second, thus continuously improving themselves in the second frame of reference. Essentially the final step of the meeting is a self-critique and employs well-known techniques of group dynamics.

In some meetings the team will allocate time for review of one or more processes that have cycle times longer than one week.

Designing Assignments on the Operating Team. Another critical distinction between the new and the old paradigms lies in people thinking of their work life in terms of carrying out "assignments" on a team to which they belong instead of owning a fixed "job," narrow in scope and invariably repetitive. In the new, each person is multiskilled and competent to do many things required by the team's functioning. The project team must never lose sight of the reality that commitment is a bargain, dependent on a psychologically enriching work experience. Therefore, assignments are carefully designed to maximize intrinsic motivation (while not overlooking the extrinsic).

Coordination in the Operating Team. Certain team matters are best handled by one person on the team. The "everyone responsible for everything, and no one responsible for anything" condition is

TEAM ON SHOP FLOOR

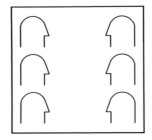

TEAM MEETING

CRITIQUE

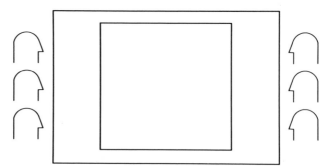

Figure 8.5 Team Frames of Reference

paralyzing and must be avoided. Some tasks are therefore not included in the assignments. Things more appropriately looked after by one individual include safety coordination, maintenance coordination, information securing, and scheduling. Several team members (as many as needed) are designated as coordinators; in addition to their assignments they will perform the better-done-by-one specialized duties. Coordinators "serve" for an extended period—nine months, for example—and then relinquish the coordinating role so that others may learn and grow. Elitism is minimized without a sacrifice of excellence.

Coordinating roles are different from establishing power of authority differentials within the team. The designers must resist a tendency to transfer much of the traditional foreman's power to direct and discipline to a team member, making one person on the team a de facto traditional foreman.

PAY AND ITS DISTRIBUTION

With elements of the new plant design such as teams, assignments, and coordinator roles in place, the next challenge for the design team is to devise a pay method that is consistent with the key ideas and the design of the new plant insofar as it has been developed.

Under conditions of the center-out model the design team can begin with the key ideas set forth by senior management at the center and derivatives of these key ideas developed in the deliberations directed to preparing the sustaining functions of compensation and job evaluation. Lacking these the design team must think the issues through from the beginning.

Two critical issues: perceived fairness of compensation and tailoring the pay system so that other elements of the design can become and remain operative.

With any payment method there is a direct correlation between one's perceptions of the fairness of pay and one's attitude toward the job and the employer. Designers should strive to attain a condition in which pay distribution is deemed fair and equitable by all employees.

The fairness of monetary rewards is never evaluated in a vacuum. The following comparisons are the minimum that need to be made:

- Me and the company. (Workers tend to believe that company profits are excessive.)
- Me and others in the company—senior executives, the boss, the boss's boss, close associates with whose work I am familiar, those holding positions subordinate to mine, others with fewer years' service with the company, others with more years' service with the company, others with COLA (cost of living adjustment) pay arrangements, others belonging to a powerful labor union.
- Me and others outside the company; those close to me—relatives, friends, acquaintances; those not close to me—corporate executives, others in my field, plumbers, electricians, and other tradesmen. (Seldom do we choose to compare ourselves with the lowest paid workers.)

The "me"s are different. Other factors are age, the generation to which one belongs, inflation, and the fear of inflation.

The comparisons can be invidious, tending to cause discontent, animosity, or envy. Not many people today assume a count-your-blessings stance when they think about their pay.

Participation in matters of pay and its method of distribution is one key to achieving perceptions of fairness. For management to attempt to impose and administer a system that will be deemed fair and equitable by all employees is to invite disappointment.

A second necessary condition is a well designed work system. Early indications of these relationships were seen when Ed Lawler and his group from the University of Michigan found that satisfaction with pay in the Topeka Gaines plant was the highest they had ever encountered. That same survey showed something about intrinsic motivation: "62.6 % agreed that their team 'tries to do a good job because it is the right thing to do.' Only 2.3% disagreed." Furthermore, "64.5% agreed that 'money shouldn't motivate them to do something (they) ought to be doing anyhow.' Less than 10% disagreed."

The hallmark of a successful state-of-the-art plant is widespread and continuing development of commitment and competence, a condition highly dependent on extensive multiple skill proficiency. An inappropriate pay method, the long established pay for the work being done at a particular time, easily defeats the critically needed multiple skill proficiency. A proven and attainable alternative is paying workers for knowledge, for what they can do when it is required.

Being multiskilled and deployable does not mean that the end point is jacks-of-all-trades-masters-of-none nor that deployment is unlimited. Allowance for a considerable range of preferences as regards multiskilling and assignment interchange is desirable. The less venturesome and more modestly endowed can then find suitable niches. Individual preferences, however, must not encroach on the rights of others to develop their skills and get more pay. Nor should these unique, individual preferences take precedence over the need to make the enterprise secure.

The speed and extent of advancement in a pay-for-knowledge application, to be practicable, should depend on the desire and capability of the individual. The pay system should include a provision for ensuring that the person learns an assignment thoroughly before moving on to another. Some minimum tenure times may be specified. Designers should also recognize that knowledge and skills must be maintained and kept up to date as products and technology change.

BRINGING THE DESIGN TO COMPLETION

With the design of the basic building blocks complete, the designers now turn to the remainder of the plant organization. The first step is a question: What do the core process operating teams require in order to carry out their processes effectively? In general terms a team needs in-specification material inputs, supplies, utilities, payroll, benefits, maintenance assistance, and timely and relevant information. Good information for operating team members who are treated as business partners is critically important. Information requirements might include orders and schedules, state of the production process from the off-going shift, company and plant policies, the plant organizational paradigm, relevant laws and regulations, state of the business (market, customers, suppliers, competition, etc.), plant performance, team performance, new technical developments (maintenance techniques, instrumentation, controllers, computers, and so forth).

Operating teams also need access to people with sufficient technical expertise and to others with sufficient social and problem-solving skills. They need facilitation, especially in the start-up period. They need intervention by management. Intervention is the act of using one's power of authority to question or overturn a decision made by an operating team. Another form of intervention is making a decision when the team is unable or unwilling to make it. Expressing intervention as a need reinforces the reality that teams are conditionally autonomous, not free to go where they want and do what they want without regard to the larger organization. The design team will get into considerable detail on each of these requirements.

Connecting Operating Teams with Management. Team needs must be met and the team connected with management. With acknowledgment of semantic shortcomings, we shall call this role the team leader, one who is a part of management and "responsible" for one or more teams. Harmony between the role of the team leader and the features of the core process operating teams is critically important and the features and underlying theories that led to them must be kept in mind every step of the way.

System change is again evident; the role of the foreman in a traditional organization is not revamped nor does the design team simply reassign to others part or all of the tasks comprising the foreman role—some to the team leader, some to certain members in the team.

Some tasks of the foreman are made unnecessary, others must be preserved. Most of those to be preserved are reallocated to the team. For design purposes the foreman role may be used as a starting point (see Table 8.2).

Foremen estimate that most of their time is spent doing the tasks listed in Table 8.2. In a company conference presentation, Louie Keeling, team leader in the Rohm and Haas, Knoxville plant exclaimed, "Before, all I had time to do was take care of things, things, things. Now [after redesign] I have time to train my people," and he went on to outline other more creative and productive uses of his time and talents.

A reallocation of tasks to the team leader takes place. The sources of these tasks are specialist groups, notably safety and human resources, and plant middle management. The team leader's time horizon extends far beyond the short horizon of the foreman.

The team leader does "new" activities required by the "different" organization. Just as teams are the basic building blocks of the organization, team processes become the basic building blocks of the team leader role. The team leader's primary function is assisting the team in its efforts to become ever more proficient in regulating its processes. Calling on unique skills, he or she will be active with the team in varying ways—observer, facilitator, participant and intervener—always relying sparingly on the power of his or her authority. By now the designers will understand that team-leader behavior is a function of the team's stage of development at a given point in time.

The team leader is a custodian of the design; the anatomy of self-regulation must be made right and kept right.

Table 8.2 Disposition of Foreman Tasks

Tasks Having to Do with Making Product

Doing the tasks

> Old: Foremen in unionized plants are neither expected nor
>   permitted to perform tasks construed as production. When for
>   some reason they do a production task it is a serious matter
>   and causes much tension between the foreman and workers
>   accustomed to saying, "That's not my job."

> New: The team leader is not expected to do tasks but is not
>   restricted from doing them. If he finds himself doing tasks
>   too frequently, he will ask himself and the team why.

Directing others to do tasks

> Old: Exclusively in the province of the foreman. His is to
>   organize, plan, direct and control, with sharp focus on the
>   activity of individual workers.

> New: Directing at the task level is a team responsibility. Self-
>   regulation is "A system so organized that everyone does
>   what needs to be done because they want to do it."

Seeing to it that others do, have done tasks

> Old: The foreman does

> New: The team does.

Relaying information from one worker to another

> Old: Officially for the foreman to do.

> New: The team does. Multiple skill proficiency and other features
>   of the team design facilitate information transfer.

Readjusting (move people around) when some are absent or late

> Old: Solely the foreman's responsibility

> New: A team responsibility in a work system that minimizes
>   lateness and absenteeism

Table 8.2 (continued)

Tasks Having to Do with Rule Enforcement

Tell worker when not in compliance with rule

Old:	Solely the foreman's responsibility.
New:	A team responsibility in a work system where many of the rules are made by the team members.

Keeping records of rule infractions

Old:	The foreman keeps a "little black book"
New:	A team responsibility that includes cognizance of laws and regulations and the keeping of proper records.

Verbal reprimanding

Old:	Solely the foreman's responsibility.
New:	Changing behavior is a team responsibility.

Written reprimanding

Old:	Solely the foreman's responsibility.
New:	Changing behavior is a team responsibility.

Appearing in grievance meetings

Old:	An ex officio foreman responsibility
New:	An ex officio team leader responsibility in a system where the look of discipline is different, and grievances tend to almost disappear. In the matter of formal grievances in a state-of-the-art system, much remains to be learned.

Supplying Information to Others Outside the Team

Maintenance work orders

Old:	Solely the foreman's responsibility.
New:	Team responsibility

Table 8.2 (continued)

Time cards

    Old: Solely the foreman's responsibility.

    New: Team responsibility

Scheduling vacations

    Old: Solely the foreman's responsibility.

    New: Team responsibility

Disciplining activity and records

    Old: Solely the foreman's responsibility.

    New: Team responsibility

Scheduling (what is finished, etc.)

    Old: Solely the foreman's responsibility.

    New: Team responsibility

Accidents

    Old: Solely the foreman's responsibility.

    New: Team responsibility

Requisitions for supplies

    Old: Solely the foreman's responsibility.

    New: Team responsibility

Other information for boss

    Old: Bosses in the old paradigm often have an insatiable need for reassurance. Requiring detailed information at extremely short intervals contributes to many undesirable things in a traditional organization including a poor work experience for the foreman and conflict between the foreman and the workers.

    New: Information for bosses is significantly reduced in quantity and the time interval is extended. The quality of the information improves.

Table 8.2 (continued)

Tasks Required At Shift Change
Supplying oncoming foreman with detailed information
Old:　　　　Solely the foreman's responsibility.
New:　　　　Information transfer at shift change is a team to team affair.

Another point of departure for designing the team leader role is the list of team needs. The design team spells out which of these needs will be supplied wholly or in part by the team leader. Additionally, the team leader will act as an expediter when the team's requirements are unmet.

Variations in the team leader role and team functioning arise from laws and regulations pertaining to who may be responsible for what. An old-paradigm mentality undergirds our law making processes; decisions an hourly paid worker may make in one industry must in other industries be made by a management person. In a hearing on a terminated employee's right to unemployment benefits, the examiner was momentarily stunned when she asked, "Will the person who terminated this employee please come forward?" and the entire team rose to comply.

Support and Management. Design is almost complete. What remains are support for the operating teams and the proper connecting of the plant with its environment. These two must make a good fit with the core process operating teams and with each other.

It is wise at this time to reappreciate the plant environment. In the case of our chosen example of a single division company, the most important domain in the plant's environment is management at the corporate center.

The state of affairs at the center is not static. How far along the road of personal paradigm change have those at the center traveled? Which change model is now being practiced? Next to the practice of center-out with its proactive center, the most desirable state of affairs is one in which a group of interested functional executives at the corporate center stayed abreast of the new plant project, paved the way for policy exceptions, frequently validated the design as it unfolded, and became educated in the process. They and the design team became familiar with the complications that accompany intensive change made in a periphery-in manner.

A less desirable and more common state of affairs: One or more of the sanctioning managers has moved on and the replacements lack ownership.

Other old-paradigm aspects of the environment are not to be overlooked. Customers may not understand what is being attempted, especially in start-up.

Schools may be curious about how the plant is managed but they are not likely to be interested in modifying their practices to better equip their graduates for a new kind of workplace.

Resources for the Operating Teams. Before going too far one must step back and see what is involved. The enablement of high performing core process operating teams is a major consideration. Many in the plant who serve as resources to teams are also important intermediaries between the new-paradigm plant and the old-paradigm organization. Consequently, the state of affairs in the functional areas at the corporate center takes on prime importance in design deliberations.

For the moment, the designers focus on the ongoing post-start-up organization with its lean staff requirements. Once the design is complete, attention turns to the special situation of start-up with its sizeable requirements for resources, resources that must disappear as the people in the plant develop.

The same socio-technical principles applied in the design of core process teams are valid for resource teams. Commitment is conditional on a satisfactory work experience. People should be placed in teams only when they share a common task. The anatomy of self-regulation must be supplied. This is does not mean that a support team will look exactly like a core process operating team.

Plant Management. To say that the plant must fit its environment is not to say that it must conform. Going forward from the third-order diagnosis, the designers have made a break with the past but for the time being their object remains enmeshed in the world of that past. Thus is defined in part a role for plant management; acting at the point of discontinuity between two paradigms, they connect the plant as a unit to the company. They maintain a two-way flow of information on policy, strategy, goals, performance, problems, needs, and capabilities.

Connecting the plant to other parts of the environment is no less important and will be no less challenging, until more of our industrial society takes up the new paradigm. Regulatory requirements or more stringent self-imposed standards must be met. In the old way, failure is shrugged off with attribution to human error. A glitch in a new-way plant will be seen as a failure of the system.

Primary responsibility for establishing and maintaining good relations with the community falls in the province of plant senior management and takes on special importance with the commitment to a good quality of working life for those employed. Here, too, the operative paradigm must not be allowed to stray from the expressed paradigm.

Plant management's focus on the internal, although much less and much different from the old way, is not to be neglected. They continually assess the health of the plant organization and take corrective action when the following questions are answered negatively: Is the plant mission being accomplished? Are processes effective? Is behavior consistent with the plant operational paradigm, remembering that in this case the plant operational paradigm is the new paradigm. Are capabilities developing and being maintained? Is the organization adapting itself to changing conditions?

As they carry out their connecting and inward functioning they manage by principles, and they must continuously revisit these principles—their paradigm—to make certain that decision making and behavior stay consistent with these principles.

Their most recent appreciations of the state of affairs in the corporation will lead them to definition of the role of the plant vis-à-vis the changing of the corporation. They may be showing the way or, if others have gone before them, confirming the more general validity of the ideas. Either is a challenging assignment.

Much remains to be done to make the plant into a highly effective operating unit, take it from ideas to concrete accomplishment of significant bottom-line contributions—prove their pudding.

In Chapter 9 we will discuss the next phase of the design team's stewardship; who will be employed, how will they be obtained, how trained, how will the plant start up and operate.

NINE

Making the New Plant into an Operating Reality

ATTRACTING AND HIRING THE RIGHT PEOPLE

Although good design ranks in relative importance ahead of staffing and deserves the emphasis it has received, selecting good people does contribute to success and those having stewardship for the new plant should endeavor to get the best people available.

The hiring process should be designed to give the successful applicants some understanding of the plant, its raw materials, its technology, mission, and customers, and what the plant must do well in order to thrive.

Of special importance is candidate awareness of the multiple skill proficiency principle and its related pay-for-knowledge, why these techniques are employed, how their use benefits the individual, and what this will require of him or her in day-to-day work life. Utmost care must be exercised to get the new employee to understand and accept that the first and most important emphasis in start-up must be on in-depth learning and proficiency of each individual in a small part of the technical system, a single assignment within a team. Only when the plant has begun to run reliably should energy be devoted to developing multiple skills and advancing in the pay-for-knowledge scheme. It should be made clear how a team must grow into a fully participative state; that the early phase of start-up, while much different from their previous organizational experience, will not be fully participative and will be stressful. Too much autonomy in the early stages of start-up will result in chaos, early intervention, frustration, and a perception that the participative philosophy is a promise that will not be fulfilled.

Attracting and Screening. Selection begins with advertising worded to enable potential job seekers to sense the innovative nature of the new plant. Criteria against which to measure applicants should be written before ads are composed and the copy should present a balanced emphasis on the privileges and responsibilities of employees in the new plant.

Relevant information on wages, hours, shifts, and benefits should be included. This practice was followed by team leaders in the Gaines pet food plant in the initial hiring before start-up in 1971 (see Figure 9.1).

As a rule, far more people apply than are needed so a fair and lawful screening is needed to reduce the numbers and raise the quality of applicants. It is a common practice to utilize state employment services for the initial screen.

The ratio of those passing the screen to the number of openings must be estimated in the context of attrition expected in subsequent selection steps and early start-up. Too often new plant start-up managers have been so concerned over layoffs that they made no allowance for casualties and voluntary withdrawals after hiring. When some of those hired did not work out, replacements were sought but there was no longer an extensive hiring process in place.

After the Initial Screen. The next task is the choosing of the best from those who passed the screen. Good people are wanted but the concept of goodness must be examined in the context of the new

GENERAL FOODS — TOPEKA PLANT
NEEDS
PRODUCTION PEOPLE

Work in a new, modern Gaines Pet Food plant with an exciting new organization concept which will allow you to participate in all phases of plant operations.

Qualifications: • Mechanical Aptitude
• Willing to Accept Greater Responsibility
• Willing to Work Rotating Shifts
• Desire to Learn Multiple Jobs & New Skills

If you would like to work with an organization that emphasizes individual potential, learning and responsibility, with excellent earnings and benefits, job interviews will be conducted beginning Sept. 16th through Oct. 5th, between the hours of 8:30 A.M. and 3:30 P.M. (or call 235-0023 for a convenient time)

APPLY AT: KANSAS STATE EMPLOYMENT SERVICE
1309 TOPEKA BLVD.
TOPEKA, KANSAS

Figure 9.1

plant's uniqueness that goes beyond factors of location, technology, ownership, customers, and market. The uniqueness will be reflected in what is considered good in the people sought even though all of the staffing criteria are not new.

A key difference between staffing for a new old-way plant and a new innovative plant lies in caring about what people *are* in the former and a strong emphasis on a person's *potential to become* in the latter. The managers of one new plant sought people

> with a potential to be comfortable taking responsibility for self, being neither "uncooperatively individualistic" nor "always a herd follower"—able and willing to think critically and analytically—comfortable expressing his or her opinion before a small group—a good listener—aware of tendencies in self and others to stereotype thinking—aware of the difference between opinion and fact—skilled in giving and receiving feedback.

A second key difference; new-way plant staffers seek people who share the embodied values and *want* the quality of work experience to be found in the new plant. In this respect major emphasis is placed on the choosing by the applicants, less on being selected or rejected by the employer.

A third key difference rests in the notion that variety in life experiences and skills is desirable, not merely tolerable.

At first glance the hiring process for a state-of-the-art new plant seems in principle little different from a thoughtfully designed three-part hiring process for a new old-way plant: (1) identify the characteristics wanted (capabilities, skills, credentials, habits, values), (2) devise a process enabling the hirers to distinguish applicants who possess the desired characteristics from those who do not, and (3) execute the process and make the selection from those who "pass." All of this must be done in the context of existing laws.

Looking deeper one sees that the additional dimensions inherent in staffing a state-of-the-art plant—the potential to become and people who want—introduce new requirements to the hiring process. A four-way focus must be maintained; the supply of potential applicants, the segment of that supply you want to begin with, what you want successful candidates to be at the end of the selection process (when hiring is complete and pre-start-up training begins), and what you want those hired to be when the plant starts up. The starting point is a community of people, employed and otherwise, who may choose to seek employment in the new plant. Although the numbers of socio-technical applications have grown, for some time to come virtually everyone seeking employment in the new plant will be from old-paradigm institutions and will bring only old-paradigm experience and expectations. The first consequence of the lack of experience in a new way work setting is the inability of the applicants to know if they want the different work experience the new plant will provide. Discovery being the instrument for knowing, those who must make the selection decisions can't find out if the new work experience is sought by merely asking.

Old selection processes do not enable hirers to gauge the applicants' potential to become. There are severe limits to testing in this regard, even if the legality of testing methods were not a consideration.

Fortunately the solution of one inadequacy of the old process becomes the solution of the other. The potential to become is best assessed by observing the experience of becoming. New selection methodology includes means for the applicants to experience some aspects of life in a new-paradigm organization. Through personal discovery applicants are enabled to make informed decisions regarding their desire for the quality of work experience the new plant affords. Meanwhile, observing this process affords those responsible for accept/reject decisions an opportunity to judge the applicants' suitability to attain the behavioral requirements. An added benefit: As the applicants experience life in a self-regulating team some modest personal paradigm change will take place.

A reality-based process is effective. With the core process operating team design as a base, the plant staff forms the applicants into self-regulating learning teams of 12-16 each. Each team is given a fourfold mission.

(1) Gain understanding of specifics drawn up by management representatives, that is, plant technology, system design, history, company strategy and goals, schedules and product requirements, and so forth.

(2) Provide its applicant members with some experience that will enable them to decide between pressing on or opting out.

(3) With the design of the new plant in mind, write specifications to be met by successful applicants. (It is made clear that hiring decisions will be made by company representatives working with already drawn specifications.)

(4) Sort themselves into (a) self-determined opt-outs, (b) those most like the applicant generated specifications, and(c) those least like the applicant generated specifications.

With assistance, each team writes its measures of performance, conducts pause-for-learning meetings, and self-regulates its activities. To be sure, the mission is a difficult task because the inescapable reality of any hiring process is that applicants are in competition with each other. There are more applicants than openings and many will be unsuccessful.

The power to decide is divided between applicants and organization representatives, the latter making the final choices only from applicants that the applicant teams identified as being most like the specifications the former drew up.

Even at this time the strength of the design team members' convictions about participation and self-regulating teams may vary widely. There have been many additions to the staff and some of the additions have clung firmly to their initial positions while others have been edging along toward a less conventional position. For them, the reality-based hiring process is a challenge and a discovery opportunity. Inexperienced with embryonic self-regulating teams and early stages of team life, they must take responsibility for team formation and for making observations of candidate suitability, all the while conveying information about the technology and other matters. Much assistance will be needed and it is a good place to begin the practice of internal (or external) experts teaching instead of doing. Some wheel reinventing is both necessary and desirable.

Some division of labor should be practiced. In the Gaines pet food plant the original design team of four, with expert assistance, designed and conducted a hiring process for the team leaders. When it became time to hire team members, the design team became less active and the team leaders, with expert assistance and the benefit of their experience in the selection process along with newly gained in-depth knowledge of the plant, designed and conducted the hiring process for team members. Besides freeing up the very busy more senior managers, the team leaders gained deeper understanding of the principles and goals while developing much needed skills.

TRAINING:
AFTER HIRING, BEFORE START-UP

Plant managers preparing for, in, and beyond start-up frequently discuss "Is it better to give the newly hired employees 'social' or 'technical' training?" The answers vary but a pattern can be discerned. Those who have placed strong emphasis on technical training have been heard to exclaim in the 9- to 18-month period after beginning operations, "If I had it to do over again I would certainly put the emphasis on the social training!" Conversely, those who favored social training will say, "If I had it to do over again I would certainly put the emphasis on technical training." Seldom, most will agree, has there been enough training.

Sometimes the "which" question is the wrong question. Faulty organization design is often the cause of difficulty. Where the requisite anatomy of self-regulation has not been adequately established, difficulties naturally ensue and persist.

Sometimes people weren't trained in the right things; "standard" training designed to prepare people for an old-paradigm organization was employed. Much of this training is off-target for people expected to start up a state-of-the-art organization.

Pre-Start-Up Training Strategy. Because time and resources are finite and usually in short supply, a strategy for pre-start-up training should be carefully devised. We shall discuss two. One is the let-nothing-go-wrong strategy. The other, the welcome-Murphy-since-you-are-coming-anyway strategy, is founded on experiences with Murphy's inexorable law and the vagaries of a brand new technical system.

Once the new plant is erected only the technical system exists. The social system is like a living organism and cannot be suddenly created as a fully functioning unit. It must grow and develop from an initial, embryonic state. Nor is the completeness of the technical system assured. Important realities about the technical system should not be ignored. It may be new technology, in which case it, too, is far from complete in the sense that all about its operation that is needed to be known is not known. The same is true when familiar technology is highly automated. Newly constructed "low" known technology also will never be without problems because Murphy's Law—Whatever can go wrong, will—inevitably pre-vails. What does go wrong in this technical system can be minor or major. It may be closely related to one or more of the following: calibration, material flow and handling, electronic circuitry, mech-anization, or computer program. Other factors are product changes and out-of-specification raw materials. Sometimes it is the physical environment, that is, temperature and humidity. Correc-tive action can range from mere adjustment to extensive changes in design.

The absence of joint optimization in the design process can haunt a start-up. Engineers in one company practicing periphery-in designed a highly automated and totally integrated state-of-the-art technical system with an extensive scope of transformation (value added). The social system was designed separately. That, too, was state-of-the-art. The magnitude of the investment and the state-of-the-art intentions brought high expectations by the senior levels and a spotlight effect. Malfunctions and mistakes, to be ex-pected in the early stages of start-up, continued for a seemingly interminable time. The failing of one sensor or the entry of one wrong number anyplace in the extended system caused the entire plant to shut down. The equipment ran so little that learning, which comes through the experience of error correction, was not taking place. Workers, managers, and highly qualified technical people could not learn. For a long time the plant made very little product. Gradually, painfully, and at great cost over a period of several years the automation was decoupled. Finally, people could and did learn. Today the plant is a high producer and has become a showcase of a state-of-the-art organization operating a state-of-the-art technology, albeit to a large extent still uncoupled.

Murphy's law is not restricted to technology! Marketing is replete with environmental and other uncertainties. Shortly after the second plant on General Foods's Gaines Topeka site began producing a high meat content canned dog food for which the plant was designed, meat prices rose dramatically. Under the new conditions the product concept was deemed economically unviable. With another new low-in-meat-content product waiting in the wings, new marketing plans were executed. However, the plant could not make this product until extensive revamping of the raw material unloading, handling, and storage systems was completed. Fortunately in this case, many in the start-up organization came from the first plant on the site and were equipped with multiple skill proficiency. Their skills were put to good use in the revamping.

In another case a new plant was to produce a line of products with which the management was technically unfamiliar. Besides allowing too little time, they chose a prototype unit for the production process. The unit could not be made to function; the vendor was called in but it took some time to remedy the problems. Meanwhile, the sales department, making the assumption that the plant would soon produce at the capacity rate, kept taking orders. The start-up organization was then swamped with the monumental task of making quantities of product with malfunctioning equipment. There was no time for training of any kind. Hours were long and stress was high. The QWL was abominable for all concerned. Dollar losses were heavy. Heads rolled and the innovation itself was a casualty.

New plant start-up teams who dedicate all available resources and energies to assuring that nothing in the technical system can or will go wrong are destined to be disappointed. Wiser managers will reject the let-nothing-go-wrong strategy in favor of one deploying the bulk of resources and energy to prepare the start-up organization to competently cope with the unexpected.

PREPARING THE START-UP ORGANIZATION

A new plant start-up is a condition in which an extraordinary amount of adult human learning must take place in a very short time. The project team, now expanded by the filling of new positions in the new plant organization, will study adult learning and how it is facilitated—how individuals learn psychomotor skills, cognitive skills, and interpersonal skills. We learn parts. We assess what we have learned. We integrate what we have learned in order to grasp a whole. Maximum learning in a new plant start-up requires a common set of terms, some record keeping, and frequent sharing and assessment of experiences. The team meeting format described earlier in this chapter contains good ideas on how to achieve the organized sharing. The learning power of properly formatted team meetings is easily underestimated.

There are other important points to consider in planning the training activity. What is the role of experience; can one gain useful learning without making mistakes? What is the role and the limit of classroom training? (There is a limit to what one can learn in the classroom about riding a bicycle.) What is the role of a "What have we learned" segment in team meetings? What is the best mix and timing of experience, classroom and team meetings? In the new plant there will be experts and learners. Some of the experts will be temporary and others permanent. Good relationships among them are vital to success. It is healthy when the experts can acknowledge to themselves and others the limits of their initial knowledge of an untried system with its many yet-to-be-revealed idiosyncrasies. In this sense the experts, too, are learners. It is healthy when the experts sense "where the learners are coming from," that is, their limitations, yet their potential to learn when intrinsically motivated to do so. It is healthy when the experts respect the observing capability of motivated learners and how these observations, when employed by experts in conjunction with learners, can enhance learning by both. These qualities are not usually found in experts with old-paradigm backgrounds.

The interdependent relationship between experts and learners should be molded early in the pre-start-up training. Time for team building must be taken. The relationship will change as the start-up proceeds. Provisions for monitoring and maintaining the relationship must be devised. The concept of team processes is especially useful here.

Making full use of the technical analysis, pre-start-up training should be designed to enable learning about variances that can occur and their consequences, how to control (prevent/correct) them, information required in order to perform properly the tasks in each assignment, and where to get this information. On the related information generation side, the training should cover the information generated at each assignment and what to do with it, that is, Who needs it? Where are they located? And how is it to be conveyed?

START-UP AND THE FIRST SIX MONTHS

Besides early mastering and motivated application of the required perceptual and psychomotor skills at all points, one should strive for early identification of trouble spots coupled with quick, accurate diagnosis and early corrective action—not patching and Band-Aids. Besides intensive training in a small part of the system, all people need familiarization with the entire system, that is, how various parts fit into the whole.

The technical system must be debugged and integrated while the human system learns and develops. As described earlier, the first can interfere with the second.

Tracking Development of the Operating Teams. Appropriate means to assess start-up progress, especially for the early stages, should be agreed upon by key people in the plant and in division or corporate headquarters. Linear increases in units produced is not to be expected, thus units of product produced in week one, week two, week three, and so forth, will not accurately reflect start-up progress. One sixth of the expected first six months' production is not achieved in the first month and realistic learning curves should be drawn. Too often the curve of expectations in units produced is a reflection of needs and desires of marketing and finance people and has little connection with reality.

One may be lucky in the early stages; with experts on hand and no technical system malfunctioning, units produced will look good for a short time. After the experts withdraw, production can plummet because the permanent organization has learned little.

When technical problems are encountered, the experts, under much pressure, may fail to involve the learners, rendering them unable to learn or be a resource to the experts. The experts ultimately withdraw and chaos is created.

Team processes are the key indicators of team development. The teams must not be overwhelmed and in the early stages need much support from resource people who understand how to assist an embryonic living system in its efforts to develop. Several questions arise: Will the team immediately engage in all of its processes or will it begin with just a few? If only a few, which? Some team processes require a degree of sophistication the team will not possess in the early stages. Some processes have little or no relevance in the early life of the team. One approach: initial limiting of the number of processes. As the team develops, processes are added. When this course is chosen it is to be remembered that what the team doesn't do must be done by someone else.

Another choice: Get the team to engage in all processes from the beginning. Invariably the team will emphasize some over others but they will not lose sight of the comprehensiveness of their mission. In either case, team development is monitored by judging the growth of team effectiveness in their processes.

DIVISION/CORPORATE MANAGEMENT IN THE EARLY DAYS

All of the factors leading to start-up success or failure do not reside in the plant. Executives far from the local scene play an important part. The inadequacies of the periphery-in model will be manifest. Besides the handicaps inherent in the experience gap, senior management have themselves not engaged in the necessary microsocial analysis. Communications between plant people and senior line and staff executives will be difficult; the latter will tend to make excessive demands for detailed information and explanations in the early stages, especially the first month. They will misjudge the results. Unnecessary information and explanations dilute the time and energy of plant people.

Ideally the immediate boss of the plant manager will take steps to assure confidence in the plant manager's analysis, design, comprehensive and well-thought-out start-up philosophy, strategy, and plan. Further assurances that the on-site permanent personnel and the start-up resource people have become a cohesive, well-functioning team should be sought.

Once these steps have been taken, this key executive can establish the conditions that will trigger an intervention, the earliest that this intervention might be made, and its purpose: Replace the plant manager? Serve as a resource? Give directions? Other? Thought should be given to the information required for a decision to intervene. What is the source of this information? When will the communications begin? And what will be the time interval between communications? Working out these points with the plant manager well in advance of start-up will go a long way toward assuring successful start-up under periphery-in conditions.

Plant managers with innovative new plant start-up experience under periphery-in conditions urge others to reach an understanding with more senior executives about start-up, its beginning and its end. As one plant manager negotiated it,

Start-up is to be considered complete when the following four-phase program has been accomplished:

1. Quality shall be demonstrated by the production of a product that meets all current specifications.

2. Quality shall be produced at batch cycle times and instantaneous rates consistent with the process engineering design basis.

3. Quality shall be produced by the start-up organization in a four-day test to confirm rates, yields, and efficiencies in accordance with the overall plant design basis.

4. Quality shall be produced by the plant steady state organization in a five-day test to confirm all engineering and plant organizational design criteria.

None of the above will be as effective as the adoption of the center-out model of change in which lies unrealized potential of unknown magnitude.

OPERATING THE PLANT:
THE POST-START-UP PERIOD

Despite endless variety in the state of affairs in corporate managements, some advice for the key managers in new plants is universally applicable. Continuance of a frame of mind that they are learners and acceptance of the experience gap being real for them for some time to come are essential. The key managers in the plant will repeatedly go back to the guiding principles—the paradigm—for guidance in decision making and for decision testing. They vigilantly strive to avoid becoming ensnared in professing one paradigm while employing another, an operational paradigm that is inconsistent with the paradigm they worked so hard to establish. They refine their paradigm as they gain deeper understanding of it.

As long as a periphery-in change model remains prevalent, key managers in the new plant embedded in a larger, unprepared system, should become well schooled in the enduring phenomena associated with the creation of something radically different, substantially better. Seasoned innovators with aging innovations still struggle with counterproductive actions by misunderstanding or conformity seeking senior managers. These actions have appeared in many forms and are often well intended. One frequent occurrence: a senior manager wanting to "improve" the new plant. A common form of improvement is the imposition of an incentive pay scheme disguised as management's desire to "share" productivity gains with those in the plant.

More commonplace: a conjecture by a senior manager, born of his personal paradigm, that "top-out"—workers in the plant one day reaching the maximum rate of pay and thereby becoming demoralized—is a problem sure to be encountered and one that needs immediate attention. This position involves a static view of the plant organization, quite contrary to the basic principles of adaptive organization design.

Other tendencies exhibited by unprepared senior management include

> forcing a system change when the plant gets into regulatory trouble instead of intervening to find out which process has gone awry and what must be done to fix it;
>
> imposing programs across the board without regard to the uniqueness of the various plants;

naming ill-suited replacements when vacancies occur in the management ranks of the new plant;

wanting to expand the new plant quickly without the basic preparatory
steps, because the new plant is so good.

Under periphery-in conditions the manager of an innovative
new plant can scarcely be too paranoid.

Managing the new plant under conditions of center-out is vastly
different. The new plant is part of an overall strategy set forth by
an active center that has done its homework down to the microsocial analysis, has set forth basic key ideas and has had these validated, thus establishing a consistent paradigm. Theirs is not to
seek conformity but to show the way by creating new plants on the
periphery as learning laboratories for all, not merely those in the
plant. Mistakes are made, but they are new mistakes.

PART IV

Redesigning Established Plants

TEN

Readying the Launch Pad:
Getting It Right
at the Plant Center

Next to the potential that lies in making those at the center committed and strategically active, the greatest potential for more effective use of people and other resources lies in redesigning existing facilities. Frequently an existing plant is where the first intensive change in the corporation is to be effected. When it is to be the beachhead of intensive change in the corporation and not just an isolated innovation in periphery-in, the importance of the undertaking far outweighs the importance of the change in the plant.

As with new plants, how one proceeds in existing plant redesign depends on what has taken place in division and corporate management. Overall at the corporate centers, the current state of affairs is still old paradigm whereas the ranks of plant management are filled with people of every hue.

Most companies in which intensive change is attempted still operate with a periphery-in model. Nevertheless, center-out model principles can be applied to the redesign of manufacturing plants and their counterparts in the service industries. In this case the center is the plant manager and staff and the periphery is the shop floor in the core process where work is done. This chapter is largely directed to those in the plants and follows—and strongly advocates—the center-out model.

APPRECIATION BY PLANT MANAGEMENT

In a very important sense, the first steps to take at the plant level are little different from those taken first in the corporate-wide center-out model. It is vitally important for plant management to know why change is required and what they must endeavor to become. Getting it right at the center therefore begins with appreciation. Plant managers will do well to consider the greenfield edge traceable to the breadth and depth of preliminary analysis undertaken by the design team soon to manage the new plant. They conducted a microsocial analysis. The values, concepts, theories, and models were well understood, owned, and implanted from the very beginning, giving the greenfield plants great staying power even under attack from division and corporate staffs. Plant managers must undertake a similar expenditure of time and energy to establish a sound foundation for the road to the future.

Like appreciation at the corporate level, the plant center's appreciating process has an internal and an external component and with each they look at the past, the present, and the future. The established plant lies within the larger organization, situated on its periphery. The division and corporation are a portion of the plant's environment. The time frame under consideration is, in some ways, shorter and much of the substance is different; for example, there is little reason at the plant level to contemplate what business one should be in. Yet in some dimensions the time frame is fully as long as at the corporate center. At the plant level one must be equally interested in the kind of people available for hiring in that long-range future.

A look at the present:

> What is it like in division and corporate management? (finding out where you stand)
>
> What is it like out there? (the plant's wider environment)
>
> What is it like in this plant and how did it get that way? (the operational paradigm)
>
> Is there a good fit among all of these or is there some mismatch?
>
> Could we do better than we are now doing? (what is possible)

A look at the future:

> If we were free to choose, what would we want things to be like in this plant?
>
> What is the environment likely to become?

The final question:

> How must we modify our preferred future "in here" if we are to accommodate the expected future "out there"?

These steps are enumerated as separate and distinct, but in an open system it is seldom that only one step is being performed. Like so much in intensive organizational change, iteration is called for.

A more detailed discussion of several of the steps in the appreciation process in an existing plant follows.

FIND OUT WHERE YOU STAND

The appreciation process at the plant level should reveal the state of things in the division and corporation. In those cases—as yet rare—where things have been made right at the corporate and division centers, the plant manager and his staff may begin with validation of the key ideas taking care not to shortcut the experience of appreciation.

More common are senior managers with a short planning horizon. To them, long-range is no more than two or perhaps three years out, and all goals are stated in line item terms—that is, unit costs, number of people, number of levels, ratio of workers to first-line supervisors, and so on. This view makes the assumption that business as usual will go on indefinitely and that all one has to do is put numbers on the early signposts of a relatively straight road. A small number of these managements are practicing periphery-in. More of them are contemplating only modest change—a stretching of the old paradigm.

"Crowd-out" threatens redesign that is underway in established plants and deters plant managers from embarking. Creating the beachhead and breaking out is an extensive undertaking. Meanwhile, well-meaning senior managers who have not experienced the appreciation process do not understand that the socio-technical approach—fundamental, broad, and systemic—gains control of the production process so that quality, yields, and other economic objectives are attained. Lacking this understanding they look to solve problems by bringing in programs and techniques—the latest hula hoops—that promise fast returns and require nothing of themselves. Long accustomed to segmented planning and fragmented execution, they will appoint a vice president for quality, for example, with instructions to get some programs going. The new appointee must show results, and demands fast implementation of the programs in every plant without exception, regardless of the state of redesign achieved. One resigned plant manager, referring to a widely sold program on quality based on a belief that if one does enough training in the techniques of process control operators on the shop floor will be automatically committed, remarked, "We are going to get it whether we like it or not."

These programs absorb all the available development time and energy of the lower levels. Much-needed activity in the area of team development, team manager development, information system refinement, and other aspects of self-regulation is delayed or omitted. The result is that development of individual supervisors and workers is stunted and teams do not develop to their full potential. Moreover, in initiating these programs senior managers who see the world differently send a message about their beliefs and their lack of understanding of, hence commitment to, the redesign.

Senior-line manufacturing executives rarely have endeavored to protect their socio-technical practicing units from the crowd-out.

In one plant a very successful beachhead laboratory for discovery was created; within six weeks every previous product quality and productivity index had been surpassed. Separately, the division president decided that a campaign for quality was needed and appointed a division-level manager of quality who bought a "program" founded on dubious motivational theory. The program was decreed, and compliance by all plant managers was demanded. The plant manager with the very successful beachhead and his consultant successfully persuaded the division quality manager that the new program was unnecessary in the beachhead, but the decreed quality program crowded out all diffusion activities, thus contributed to another fade-out.

In another plant, redesign of the first beachheads was very successful, product quality and yields were at record levels and continuing to improve. In the next redesigned areas, team development was lagging. Appropriate training of team leaders and their bosses was arranged and a team development effort enthusiastically launched. Suddenly a corporate-directed, technique-driven program was imposed. Everyone was to be taught various techniques of technical problem solving. Lost in this lockstep approach was the logic of analyzing the unique development needs of each team and doing with each what made sense at that point in time. The imposed training, sapping the energy of the teams and the lower and middle managers, crowded out the fundamental and lasting team development activity.

Premature thin-out is a condition plant managers must reckon with in these days of "downsizing," "restructuring," and other euphemisms meaning getting rid of people. In most cases the reduction reflects the failure of past senior managements to read the signs. They waited until their backs were against the wall and force reductions are a matter of survival. The threat of shutdown is apparent to those in the plant and the motivation arising in the fear of extinction sometimes deceives the management into believing that they have done all that is necessary.

There are other motives behind force reductions. One argument holds that worker involvement can be forced by the reductions in the number of supervisors, the supervisors left will have so much ground to cover that they will *have* to get the worker to take over. In another view, it is seen that state-of-the-art organizations have fewer managers and fewer levels; therefore, if we first reduce the number of supervisors, middle managers, and the number of management levels, a state-of-the-art organization will naturally follow.

A new-paradigm organization surely requires fewer people than an old-paradigm organization. When and how to thin out, however, especially in the plants, is a subject of prime importance. There are stresses inherent in an organizational paradigm shift. When staffing is arbitrarily reduced simultaneously with asking people to participate in or accept organization redesign, anger, resentment, cynicism, and mistrust are sure to arise in the ranks of workers and lower-level managers. The situation is exacerbated when the force reduction is accompanied by a demand for more product.

In an old plant there are never enough supervisors, never enough managers, and the nature of things demands that they be on the job all the time. Intensive redesign requires many hours for the activities outlined in this chapter. Under the best conditions, there is a shortage of time for training and "working through." Getting middle and lower-level managers off to the training room puts a severe burden on those who must cover for the absent trainees. The entire change process takes longer and increases the risk of failure.

The functional areas at division and corporate levels should be carefully studied. Unless the center-out model is being practiced, the concept of reimporting tasks from the functional areas to those in the core process will be alien to those at the center uncommitted to intensive change.

An especially important question for the plant manager undertaking intensive change in an established plant is, "What is your boss like?" A recent survey of bosses to whom managers of significantly different greenfield or redesigned plants reported showed several types. The list is by no means exhaustive.

- The boss had not heard of QWL, socio-technical concepts, and related subjects. Not every boss fitting this description is like one division-level manufacturing vice president who, in his end-of-the-day summary of a socio-technical familiarizing session for his key plant people, confessed that the entire day had been a humbling experience for him.

- The boss was in a corporation with a general-call-for-plans strategy, even though things had not been made right at the center.

- The boss was a silent supporter who, besides trying to get other plant managers to innovate, endeavored to protect his one innovative unit from the "measurers" and those who had suddenly discovered quality and gotten attention and resources.

- The boss, earlier when a plant manager, had successfully created an outstanding greenfield site. He had very traditional (noninnovative) plants reporting to him and his thrust was to get something started in them. (Having successfully initiated a greenfield site is no guarantee that one knows how to proceed in an old established plant.)

- The boss was one who, though not the originator of the plant-level innovation, liked the idea, gave heavy support to his innovators, and made serious attempts to bring about diffusion of the ideas and methodologies into the corporate center.

- The boss had come into manufacturing from another function and suddenly found himself in charge of a greenfield innovation.

In all but the center-out condition, the innovation-minded plant manager should proceed with caution and ingenuity. One innovative plant manager maintained one organization chart for review with his boss and the personnel people at headquarters and privately maintained another representing what he had in his plant. Another plant manager prudently accepted senior management's mischaracterized long-range plan with its goals stated in line items. Privately, he thought of the handed down goals as "intermediate" and set forth his long-range goal for the plant as a state of affairs in which his plant would be maximally effective because of "highly developed work teams throughout the plant, offices, and management."

WHAT IS IT NOW LIKE
IN THE WIDER ENVIRONMENT?

Asking only about the division and corporation is insufficient. The key managers in the plant can begin with "What does it take for us to thrive in this business and in this environment?" This leads to assessments of schools, laws, competition, regulatory agencies, customers, and transportation. This aspect of appreciation follows patterns described in earlier chapters.

WHAT IS IT LIKE IN THIS PLANT
AND HOW DID IT GET THIS WAY?

Answering "What is it like in here?" demands an earnest effort to look reality square in the face. Old-paradigm organizations have many faults and managers, all too human, are very adept at keeping this information from themselves. In this, just as in the senior management group when they faced the realities of what it is like in the organization, Bierce's (1911) cynics are valued assets.

One manager of a small chemical plant took his staff into retreat and explored the appreciation questions. "What is it like up there?" revealed that the vice president of operations was actively supporting socio-technically based redesign in another plant in the company. The company president supported the socio-technical efforts of this vice president. In short, things "up there" were pretty good, although far short of establishing the necessary conditions in the functional areas. The innovation was hostage to the continuance of the president and the vice president in their jobs.

After "What does it take for us to thrive in this business and in this environment?" came "How good are we today?" in which they summarized the present level of variances, breakdowns, and service shortcomings. The extent of mismatch between the plant and the existing environment became clear.

Sobered by this analysis, they then began exploring the social system by asking:

How is the plant management perceived by the various groups in the plant (foremen, clerical nonexempts, technicians, maintenance people, operators and others)?
What are our (plant management's) perceptions of each of these groups in our plant?

This assessment, too, was sobering. By now a clear picture of "What it is like in here now" had emerged along with awareness of how the old paradigm had contributed to this state of affairs.

The Traditional Model exercise is a more extensive, thorough, and demanding technique for "looking squarely into the face of reality." In addition to drawing a picture of what it is now like in here the exercise enables people to understand how organizations are shaped by underlying tacit assumptions. For most people it shows that the basic problem is a mismatch between the people and the nature of the organization, the third-order diagnosis. Because it is experiential and raises fundamental value questions, it often generates hostile feeling in the participants, especially when insufficient time is allowed for discussion and reflection. Sufficient time means inclusion of the exercise in the content of a three-day meeting in which the participants' work system is explored in depth. Although the exercise is provocative and unavoidably iconoclastic, it has been successfully applied at managerial levels ranging from president to foreman. It has also proved useful in preparing workers, shop stewards, and foremen for participation in the work-redesign process. It has been used with mixed groups such as shop stewards and first-line supervisors. The size of the group should not exceed 15, and the spread of management levels is best kept to a minimum.

At the start of the exercise participants are asked to imagine that a being from outer space came to earth and for some time has observed, unseen, our industrial establishments. Initially knowing nothing of our customs, traditions, or ways of behaving and unable to communicate with the members of the organizations, the observer took note of our behavior, organization structure and compartmentation, policies and their implementation, management development, selection process, decision-making processes, union-management relations, labor negotiations, labor agreements, recruiting, hiring, firing, machine design, process design, new plant design, and project engineering. It observed how information systems are designed and how information is handled—who gets it, who does not get it, and how those with information use it. The observer also reviewed business and engineering school curricula, texts, and literature. From these observations over a period of time, the extra-terrestrial being inferred that people in our industrial society make several fundamental assumptions. A list was drawn up and the trainer purports to have gained possession of the list.

The participants are asked to test the aptness of each inferred assumption by choosing between two propositions:

> According to the structure, processes, and behavior here, we too seem to be making this assumption; OR
> According to the structure, processes and behavior here, we don't make this assumption.

Table 10.1

The human being is an extension of the machine, useful only for doing things the machine cannot do.

People are unreliable and require control.

There are two classes of people:

Employer	Employee
Thinker	Doer
Decision Maker	Follower

Job fractionization is a way to reduce costs by reducing the skill contribution of the person.

Primary attention to the technical system leads to lower product costs.

Satisfying the requirements of interrelated social systems increases costs.

Managers possess unique skills and leadership.

There is a correlation between rank-ability-power.

Once everything is known and planned for, then fully effective control, applied by management, leads to good outcomes.

The cautious trainer will define *here* and *we* as the larger industrial society, while the confident will specify *we* as the participants and *here* as their organization.

Two ground rules are given:

- You may agree or disagree with the aptness of an assumption if you tell your colleagues why, citing personal experiences.
- Don't make value judgments. You are not to determine if the assumption is good or bad, appropriate or inappropriate. The question before you is limited to "Is this assumption operative here?"

The nine assumptions used by the trainer were garnered from Davis (1971) and Driggers (1967) are shown in Table 10.1.

After three hours of intensive discussion, most participants agree that however dysfunctional these assumptions are, they

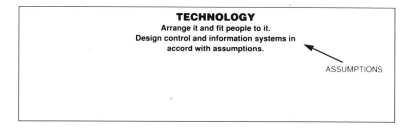

Figure 10.1

TECHNOLOGY
Arrange it and fit people to it.
Design control and information systems in
accord with assumptions.

ASSUMPTIONS

TECHNOLOGY

JOB DESIGN
Simplest possible jobs — fractionation.
Hierarchy of Jobs.
People are interchangeable spare parts.
Minimum skill contribution.   ◀—— ASSUMPTIONS
Machine pacing where possible.
Minimum interdependence.
Minimum need to communicate.

Figure 10.2

indeed are the ideas that drive their organization. It is not an easy process; the telling-it-like-it-is comes slowly and for most it is intensely unhappy learning. Submerged organizational issues surface as the operational paradigm is revealed.

Having made these points and created this awareness, the focus of the exercise now shifts from a validation of the assumptions to some detailing of outcomes inextricably interwoven with the now revealed assumptions. The trainer employs a visual build-up technique to demonstrate and make clear the complex interrelationships of ideas, things, and people that we call the organization. Consistent with the technological imperative, the trainer first turns to the outcomes in technology (see Figure 10.1).

Job design follows (see Figure 10.2).

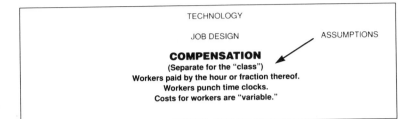

Figure 10.3

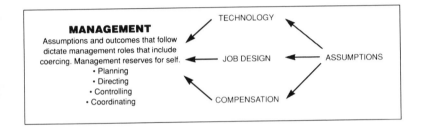

Figure 10.4

Compensation is next (see Figure 10.3). Generally, the participants are supplementing the trainer's characterizing of the outcomes. Almost invariably, pay incentives are mentioned.

When management is described (see Figure 10.4), managers are often glum while union officials are downright gleeful.

The trainer moves to the subject of worker behavior, noting that the characteristics of the work system relegate the worker to a position of low status. The feelings of low status are but one key determinant of behavior (see Figure 10.5).

Unless considerations of the environment from which the workers come are included, a discussion of the behavior of workers is

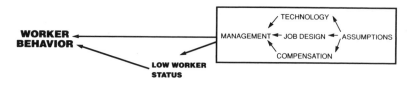

Figure 10.5

unfruitful. The concepts of socialization and adaptive behavior are introduced. The participants, ordinarily not inclined to be receptive to a trainer's abstract notions, are remarkably alert and eager at this juncture.

To understand behavior in the workplace the concept of adaptation is essential. Otherwise one is forever shackled to the notion that unchangeable character traits are the primary sources of motivation, little else matters—a notion leading into the blind alley that solving the problems of counterproductive behavior requires getting rid of the people with the undesirable character traits and hiring new people with the desirable traits.

Any living thing must adapt to its environment if it is to survive and thrive. Applied specifically to the workplace, this principle has it that a worker (or any employee) must adapt—make peace with that which cannot be changed—or not survive—leave the workplace and vainly seek a more hospitable one, drop out, or develop a neurosis. Making peace is not as benign as it sounds and can range from being cheerful to sullen to actively angry.

The adaptive behavior one chooses is heavily influenced by the environment existing during one's formative years. Thus it is related to the time of a person's birth and therefore generational. Changes in the environment result in changes in the characteristics of people who come into the workplace (see Table 10.2).

Acknowledging that the discourse is unidimensional and an oversimplification, the trainer separates people into three groups

Table 10.2 Societal Trends

Rising levels

    Wealth
    Security
    Education

Decreased emphasis-obedience

    Churches
    Schools
    Families

Decline in achievement motivation

Rising expectations

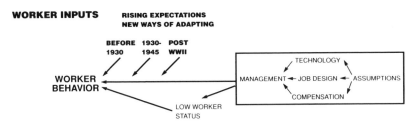

Figure 10.6

by dates of birth: pre-1930, 1930-1945, and post-1945[1] (see Figure 10.6).

The conditions of socialization for those born before 1930 are described along with the reasons workers in this group tend to adapt with *responsible* behavior in the workplace. "Responsible" is doing what the supervisor wants done, when it is wanted done, and in the specified manner.

A similar discourse is given on those born in the period 1930 to 1945. The most common choice by workers in this group is *apathy*.

Table 10.3

Born Prior to 1930

Experienced hard times
Appreciates a job
"Ego" needs are gratified off job
Provided better for family
More education for children
See "job" as "means" to away-from-job "ends"
Adapt with "responsible" behavior on job

Born Between 1930 and 1945

Less affected by Depression
Higher education level
Reduced fears of unemployment
Rise of welfare programs
Influence of TV—rising expectations
Adapt with "apathetic" behavior

Born After 1945

Still higher educational level
More social welfare programs
Major influence by TV
"Here and now" expectations
Fought in increasingly unpopular wars
Changing values:
   Obedience
   Achievement
Adapt by seeking ways in job to satisfy ego needs—"Militant" behavior

---

It is noted that the post-World War II group, of which the number is rising, tends to adapt *militantly* (see Table 10.3).

Militant behavior takes many forms. Often it is playing games with supervision. The underground knows where the supervisor is at all times. Horseplay is common. Overstaying breaks is common. Sometimes they control process rates for their own gratification instead of supplying the next department at the rate it requires. Slowdowns when the supervisor cracks down are another form of

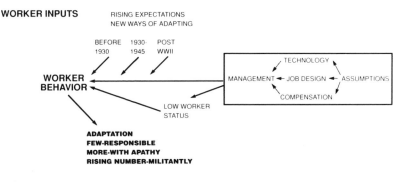

Figure 10.7

ego gratification, and most of us are familiar with intimidation of achievers.

The trainer's discourse holds few surprises for the participants who have been deeply engaged in describing the characteristics of their work system as they validated the aptness of the inferred assumptions. Invariably participants offer examples from their experience that reinforce and extend the trainer's line of reasoning. Managers and union officials, now distant from the shop floor, supplement the reinforcements with descriptions of how it was when they lived as first-line supervisors and workers. Most generally their evidence is of widespread absenteeism, errors, apathy (passive aggression), and sometimes active aggression in the form of sabotage or making the supervisor's work life difficult. Occasionally one will approach the trainer in privacy and marvel at what he and his colleagues did, how bizarre it was, and wonder how they could have behaved like animals (see Figure 10.7).

Additional consequences ensue. The behavior leads to having more workers than are needed, a consequence with both economic and psychological ramifications. Participants continue citing their own examples, especially when it is a group comprised of workers, shop stewards or supervisors.

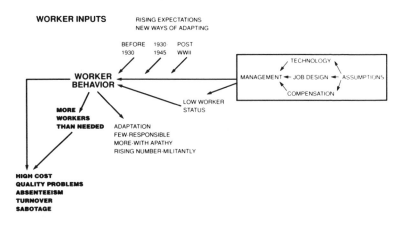

Figure 10.8

Behavior also leads to system performance, that is, high costs, quality problems, absenteeism, turnover, and sabotage (see Figure 10.8).

The buildup continues with the trainer making the point that if the management system is one of coercion, the only solution to system performance problems is making more rules. Each rule must be accompanied by a punishment (see Figure 10.9).

Another facet of adaptive behavior is formation of or an affiliation with a labor union. Unions generally are present because people want them, not because unions possess superior organizing skills.

Sources of counterproductive clauses and practices in labor agreements are shown as job insecurity, income insecurity, and low self-esteem.

Due process (see Figure 10.10) is a benefit of union membership, hence a union responsibility. But due process requires laws! And

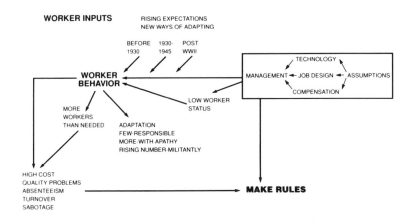

Figure 10.9

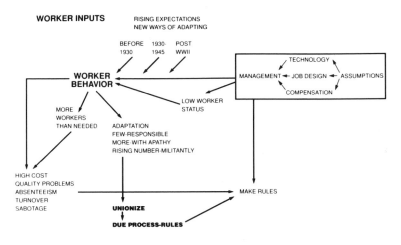

Figure 10.10

when a law or rule doesn't satisfy needs for due process, new rules are created. As time goes on, the body of laws or rules grows, extending far beyond what managers feel is required. Everyone must be treated alike so rule enforcement becomes legalistic. The penalty system becomes ever more elaborate and rigid. More staff to administer these penalties are required and overhead costs grow.

Rules must be posted, continually reminding workers that they are not treated maturely.

Work simplification—managers began it, the union takes it further. In pay rate bargaining, simple and rigid job content is easier to argue about than flexible systems. Methods and the stopwatch become the tool of the union as well as the management.

It is much the same with craft distinctions. Scarce skills are the most valuable skills. Management begins with demarcations it believes to be to its benefit and the union takes demarcations further. Restrictions are placed on the tasks workers are allowed to perform, thereby limiting worker skill development. Rigid demarcation means more jobs.

Scientific management assumptions lead to a hierarchy of jobs. But job security, to most workers, uninformed by management and therefore unbelieving, means being as far from the bottom of the seniority list as possible. Having seniority within a classification further enhances job security. Over-crewing makes one's job seem more secure. So, the job hierarchy, originally created by management, becomes more elaborate, categories proliferate, and restrictions on the scope of tasks a person is permitted to perform multiply. Foremen know all too well the it's-not-my-job behavior that these factors produce.

The implications of the need for the union to maintain power are many and far reaching. Without power, the union cannot deliver on its reason for being. Union power comes from two sources: security clauses in the labor agreement and worker discontent and mistrust of management. Management, in its effort to reduce or contain the power of the union, seeks to gain the loyalty of the worker, and to protect and maintain management "rights." In these circumstances, union officials must look to worker distrust and discontent as the source of power. The more insecure the union, the more apt it is to place reliance for power on worker discontent. One must be a union person or a company person.

The unintended products of these processes include:

- Workers having less variety, less opportunity to develop and contribute skills;
- Workers seldom understanding the whole, hence not feeling a part of that "whole";
- Psychological impoverishment, already created by scientific management, is exacerbated by the union.

As the union responds to member needs for job security, it locks the enterprise into an over-crewed condition.

Finally, one is tempted to say, the union decreases the coercive power of the foreman (see Figure 10.11).

The story is far from over.

The foreman is a part of management. It is the foreman's responsibility to get results. He must also deal with the many overstaffed departments telling him the obvious things to get workers to do with none telling him how to get them to do it.

The foreman must enforce the rules, "helped" in this endeavor by labor relations department procedures requiring him to keep records of employee behavior, that is to say, rule breaking, so they can "back him up." So, known to all, he keeps a little black book.

His job is not whole. Someone else checks his quality, does his hiring, his firing. Someone else settles his grievances. His maintenance and repairs are performed by a separate department. Because maintenance is always a scarce resource, he must compete with his peers to get what is needed.

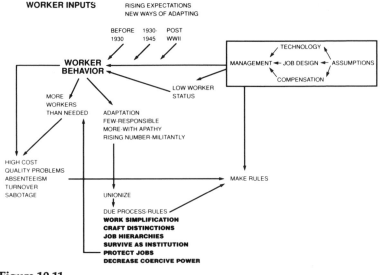

Figure 10.11

Process conditions he is to maintain are set by process engineers on the assumption that there are no variances in his raw materials.

Engineers do not consult him in equipment selection, installation, or rearrangement. Foremen complain that they "inherit" the technical system and then they must "fix it so that it will work."

He gets most of his performance information on an exception basis, that is to say, only when it is bad.

He is chosen because he is conscientious, yet he is not permitted to perform any tasks even when he sees a small thing to be done and can't find or get someone to do it.

The quantity of pay for those who report to the foreman is determined by the collective power of the workers. The foreman's pay is set by a so-called merit procedure.

Promotion of those who report to the foreman is decided on the basis of length of service. The foreman's promotion will be decided by qualifications.

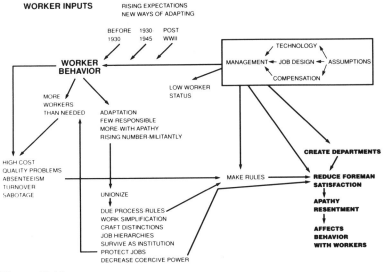

Figure 10.12

The foreman's tools are the rules, rewards, punishments. But long ago he lost the power to reward and the union persistently reduces his power to punish.

All of these contradictions and catch-22s understandably dismay the foreman who, being human, reacts with apathy and resentment (see Figure 10.12). At times under these conditions his behavior with workers becomes abominable.

The foreman's behavior demands a response and, understandably, the workers oblige with greater apathy or more militant behavior. In either case, it is dysfunctional and leads to even worse system performance. Management's response, the only one possible in a coercive system, is to create even more rules, put more pressure on the first-line foreman. Abominable behavior intensifies. Then the union's power increases and this power is focused to reduce the coercive power of the foreman. There is a never-ending circle (see Figure 10.13).

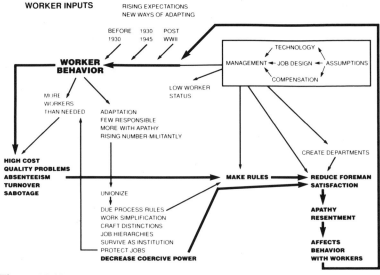

Figure 10.13

As every engineer knows, positive feedback means that a system is out of control.

When the exercise reaches this point the participants are largely silent. Clearly, some are undergoing a paradigm change. After a period of silence, the most common comment is, "I knew all of this was happening but I never before saw it laid out like this."

The trainer then carries the presentation to its conclusion. What is happening in management? Only managers coordinate, so the many departments require many managers for coordination. More departments mean more coordinators and more coordination requires more managers. More managers mean higher costs. Because the organization is pyramidal, more levels are created; feeding back into low worker status while blocking and filtering information flow.

Rigid compartmentation of the organization ensures that few managers have whole jobs. Conflicting objectives and measures of

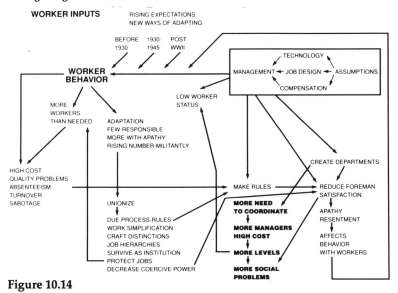

Figure 10.14

performance result in dysfunctional competitiveness and adversarial relationships. The production manager's performance is judged on costs, quality, labor relations—elements requiring a steady supply of in-specification raw material. The purchasing manager is judged on money tied up in inventory and purchase price. He risks running out of material as he pursues his objectives. Quality assurance polices quality control, quality control people police production people. Departments compete with each other for scarce resources. These are but a few examples well-known to middle managers in corporate America. These and many more result in conflict or social problems in management (see Figure 10.14).

Three areas are of concern: Organization performance, workers and the union, and social problems in management.

The trainer now presents an exposition of old-paradigm "solutions" (see Table 10.4). These, as the participants have experienced, are but Band-Aids applied in a disjointed manner. Quality programs,

Table 10.4

Reduce Hours
Vacations
Higher Wages
Benefits
Recreation
Communications (to Employees)

Supervisor Training
Work Planning and Control of Worker

Human Relations (Learn how to treat worker in ways that will cause him or her better to accept your direction and control)

Hire
   Seek the best
   When they adapt militantly. . .
Fire

---

energy saving programs, training programs, human relations snake oil, higher pay, and more vacations bring little permanent improvement.

Hiring the best and, when they adapt with militant behavior, firing them is equally ineffectual.

None of these solutions change for the better the work experience of the individual. Thus they do not begin to cope with the basic problem, the mismatch between the organization and the people employed by it. The real solution is a fundamental change in our way of thinking about people and organizations—a paradigm shift.

At the conclusion of the Traditional Model exercise, most managers, some grudgingly, will agree that there is a serious mismatch. The warts are visible. The partial picture of the present includes how it all came about.

WHAT IS POSSIBLE?

The partial picture of the present must be extended. An assessment of profitability improvement if the warts were removed—if there were no variances, no undue turnover, no absenteeism, if machinery ran at capacity and did not break down—is in order. Intensive change is not accomplished without cost and the opportunity costs of not making the change should be estimated.

A LOOK AT THE FUTURE

Whatever the processes used to uncover the operational paradigm, the misfit, and its associated costs, the next step deals with the future. In this regard there is an important distinction between the center-out model and some commonly employed long-range planning practices that seem to assume a stable, nonchanging environment. With the latter, problem identification is immediately followed by a visioning of a desired future in which these problems will not exist. Then attention is directed to the remedies— "how-shall-we-go-about-getting-there"—an effort that will extend over a considerable time period. By the time these remedies are put into place, new environmental conditions will have emerged and a misfit persists, one still must play catch-up.

In contrast, those following the center-out change model imagine an ideal organization but postpone formulating action plans until the crucially important step of conjecturing the future environment has been taken. Conjecturing the future brings forth the key idea of uncertainty and modifies how managers think about practical issues. For example, a plant engineer using the older approach would have sought ways to make his instrument people ever better at maintaining instruments in a technology of pneumatics.

By contrast, a plant engineering manager using the new approach and aware of the uncertain future would have sought a state of affairs in which the instrument people were good and ever better learners. They would be taught fundamentals of physics and general science and when electronics came along to replace pneumatics the learners would have easily made the transition. The plant engineering manager using the old approach might have discharged the pneumatic experts and hired new experts in electronics.

After pondering the future "out there," they ask what their organization must be like to thrive in that environment, thus arriving at a position to consider the adjustments needed to their desired "in here" to accommodate the expected "out there." The product includes a goal paradigm—the ideas that will drive the plant organization in the future. For example, the idea that the quality of the work experience is not a valid consideration has now been discarded for a position that lies between a view holding that enlightened self-interest justifies efforts to provide a good work experience, and a new-paradigm value that management ought to enable work experience of good quality.

While the process of appreciation at the plant level may have begun because the plant manager's boss wanted it done, because it was the thing to do in the corporation, or some other externally initiated motivation, earnest appreciation has brought to the plant manager and his staff a clear and in-depth understanding of the necessity of intensive change, that modest change will not do. Many conditions in which the plant management must operate in attempting to make intensive change are visible—some of the terrain has been mapped. The key managers in the plant are ready to pursue other necessary preparatory steps.

NOTE

1. The Traditional Model exercise was developed in the early seventies when the first author agreed with the conventional wisdom that it was people that had changed that brought about the malaise in the workplace. As he continued his work in the field a larger truth became evident. The problem of mismatch has existed for a considerable period of time. Even with the outmoded wisdom, the exercise still succeeds in helping the participants acknowledge what they have today.

ELEVEN

After the Assessment

Changing an established manufacturing plant is a political process involving competition between interest groups or individuals competing for power and leadership, in both the formal and the not to be underestimated informal modes. All power is not derived from the authority that goes with one's position in the organization and in the real world there are limits to power derived from authority. One deals with what is rather than what ought to be.

Stakeholders—those who may perceive potential gain or loss if things are changed and who have power to constrain or prevent change—are numerous. Initially a stakeholder thinks: How might I gain, how might I lose, and how can I know? The uncertainty factor initially makes most stakeholders barriers to change.

With so many businesses under pressure and many with backs to the wall there is a tendency to think that redesign is driven only by short-term economic necessity—survival. Fear is a well-known motivator, but alone it will not induce and sustain buy-in to the scale of change needed. Plant managements are well advised to place a balanced emphasis on the company's welfare and the right of the employees to a good work experience. Skeptics who expect old-paradigm values emphasizing business results to the exclusion of the psychological welfare of employees are plentiful, and it will take time and events for management's new values to show through.

An inescapable reality of the change process in an established plant is an ever-changing setting. Things won't stand still while the organization and its technology are redesigned, and short-term results must be maintained. Product demand changes, and layoffs occur. Products and technologies change. Raw materials change. Macro economics—interest rates, taxes, consumption, and the business cycle—change. Companies merge or are taken over; segments of companies are spun off. People retire, quit, are promoted or reassigned, or they are not reelected. Replacements from the outside come in with incompatible personal paradigms.

What works in one plant does not necessarily work in another. Especially unhelpful is a flow chart of a change process that someone from another plant has retrospectively drawn. A well-intentioned question at conferences goes like this: "If you had it all to do over again how would you go about it?" The speaker is then expected to lay out the cookbook for the world to follow. Some inexperienced presenters will, indeed, lay out a cookbook, generalizing on limited experience. Those who won't are criticized for being vague.

The process is somewhat like being atop a high hill (the present); another high place you want to reach (the desired future organization matched with the conjectured future environment) is in view. Between the two hilltops there is a dense fog. Visibility is limited to about 10 feet. Your map is incomplete. You cannot buy a map at the book store. Maps supplied by others who have gone before you are of limited value. Uncertainty is unavoidable. As you progress in this milieu of limited visibility, you trip over logs. You find a ravine and must construct a bridge. You find you are at the end of a canyon and the only way out is to retrace your steps. With compass and knowing the direction you want to go, you chart the terrain as you experience it.

Not all of the problems ahead can be clearly seen. William Wilkins, president of the Aluminum, Brick and Glass Workers, AFL-CIO-CLC, and Joseph Foster, assistant plant manager, acted insightfully and courageously early in the joint effort in the Rohm and Haas, Knoxville, plant that began with the objective of overcoming technological obsolescence. They agreed that they could not foresee and solve all the problems up front. They then agreed to "handle problems as they come up." Besides courage, this required high trust. Many of the anticipated problems did not materialize and some unforeseen ones did arise.

SEEKING BUY-IN TO THE ASSESSMENT

The assessment has yielded a picture of the past, present, and future and has led the key managers in the plant to resolve that changes in the way things are done are in order. The next vital task is to obtain the maximum possible buy-in to the chosen course of action and its supporting rationale, a task that goes well beyond senior site management merely communicating their vision to the others in the plant. To ask that the others accept plans unilaterally developed by the key managers in the plant is to continue to live in the tradition of the old paradigm in which management reserves for itself the right to plan and direct.

An alternative to mere communication is participatory validation in which others are asked to confirm the appreciation that led management to decide that change is needed, what the change is, and how to go about making it. It is not that validation is simply to begin. Even before the deliberate formal appreciation started an initiating manager began with a picture, however dim and incomplete, drawn from data seen by a lone pair of eyes. Unsatisfied, the initiating manager began validation by including others, ranging from a pair to several, to examine, test, clarify, extend, and add detail to the innately incomplete picture. A crucial component of the picture, an inset as it were, is the rationale for changing from the current state of affairs. One's reasons for wanting to change are necessarily highly subjective, involving personal values, perceptions of the consequences of doing nothing, the discomfort being experienced, and the effort required to exist in the present. As buy-in is personal, validation is part persuasion and part discovery. If persuasion is to occur the initiator must expose others to the rationale and thus permit comparisons of, "What's in it for me?" "What's in it for him or her?"

Participatory validation requires that plant management's assessment, especially the conjecture of the future, be clear, cogent, and communicable, virtues often absent in past efforts to redesign established plants.

Because many will be asked to validate, a structured process of participatory validation must be devised and the help of professionals is recommended.

By its very nature, participative validation involves feedback to the senior managers on the site with potential modifications of their original assessment. The success of what comes after depends upon how well the validation is accomplished. One can validate downward in a cascade fashion or by department. If by department, the department manager should assume responsibility for the validation process. Several diagonal slices can be employed.

There is danger in too slow a pace. Validation should proceed at a quick pace and not unduly delay other change process activities.

ORGANIZING FOR THE TASK AHEAD

Getting things right at the center has been a large task requiring extra effort on the part of senior plant management. Much remains to be done.

Preparing the plant to enter the future is the responsibility of all key managers, not merely those in the production department. While some extra structure may be indicated, one should guard against the tendency for parallel structure to permit reluctant managers to absolve themselves of their responsibility for change. Leaving reluctant key managers behind is inadvisable. It may be better to ask, "Are we ready for the journey?"

Steering committees are popular and deemed essential by some, yet the Rohm and Haas Tennessee plant never had a steering committee and their redesign success is unparalleled. Another plant initially formed a joint labor-management steering committee. It worked well at first but broke down after a union election put three "pro's" and three "anti's" on the committee. Suddenly the union president was being asked to break ties at every turn. The tone of steering committee meetings reverted back to the adversarial and the mere existence of the steering committee was a drag on everything in the plant. After some struggle, the steering committee was disbanded. At once the plant began breaking productivity records.

Before deciding about the structure needed in the plant from this time forward, one is well advised to review what experience in established plants has taught us about making the deep, far-reaching system change (we have characterized it as intensive) that is required if commitment is to be forthcoming. Because modest change does not suffice, gradualism fails; intensive change must be introduced at once. The experience gap prevents introducing and sustaining system change over a wide area. Relatively small beachhead laboratories for discovery are created. Worker commitment is forthcoming and management roles and behavior in the beachhead area can change. It is a *planned discontinuity*.

Unavoidably, the greater number of people in the plant for some time to come will live under the old conditions. There it is business as usual and controls must be preserved. Typical of plants operating in the old paradigm, fires will still break out and must be extinguished. In the unaltered, old-paradigm part, it is management's lot to keep things glued together. Management and the union must become adept at keeping one foot in the old-paradigm parts and one foot in the new. As the new expands, the old shrinks.

All the while, the entire plant must be connected to its environment, mostly by the plant manager and staff.

With the beachhead-breakout strategy, change will be accomplished in stages, sector by sector, more step-like than continuous. The best managing structure for one stage may not be the best for the next stage when new conditions are encountered. One must ask, "What has the management functioning been and what must the functioning become?" (See Table 11.1.)

MAKING SUFFICIENT RESOURCES AVAILABLE

Success in plant redesign is dependent on having people with skills and knowledge not ordinarily extant in a manufacturing plant today. One can't learn from experience one hasn't had. People who are competent and experienced in intensive organization change, paradigm shift, and its accompanying phenomena are in short supply and are likely to be for some time. An early assessment of resource needs and existing inventory is advisable, taking into account the shortcomings of the usual credentials, levels, and titles. If the project is begun with outside help and a strategy to encourage development within, competent people are sure to emerge as did Charles Volk of Local 56, Meat Cutters, AFL-CIO, in the Maxwell House coffee plant in Hoboken; Irwin Hopson of Local 90, Aluminum, Brick and Glass workers, AFL-CIO-CLC, in the Rohm and Haas plant in Knoxville; Gary Cook of General Electric's Specialty Chemical plant in Morgantown, WV; and Ron Grover of Colgate-Palmolive, Kansas City, KS.

The more successful insiders will search for the narrow middle ground between being too dependent on outside consulting help and outright counter-dependency.

WHEN THERE IS A UNION

A plant manager who is committed to participation in the change process will naturally look to the union and its members.

Table 11.1 Stages of Change in the Redesign of an Established Plant

Stage 1: Initiating change

Prepare the center
Connect the plant to its environment
Manage the as yet unaltered parts
Validate management's assessment

Stage 2: Preparing first beachhead

Design first laboratory for discovery
Prepare the center
Connect the plant to its environment
Manage the as yet unaltered parts

Stage 3: Making first change in core process

Start first beachhead laboratory for discovery
Adapt the plant to the beachhead
Prepare to break out—redesign second sector of the core process
Prepare the center
Connect the plant to its environment
Manage the as yet unaltered parts

Stage 4: Expanding change in the core process

Develop first beachhead laboratory for discovery
Breakout—start second laboratory for discovery
Adapt plant to second redesigned sector
Redesign more sectors
Continue center preparation
Connect the plant to its environment
Manage the as yet unaltered parts

Stages 5, 6, 7, etc.: Toward critical mass

Continue development in redesigned sectors
Adapt plant to expanded redesigned areas
Further enlarge breakout
Start new laboratories for discovery
Continue center preparation
Connect the plant to its environment
Manage the as yet unaltered parts

Stage X: After critical mass

Continuing evaluation and learning

The role of the labor agreement in intensifying and sustaining psychological impoverishment of the union members will have been made clear in the appreciation step "What is it now like in here and how did it get that way?" If the work experience is to be changed, change in the labor agreement is essential. Union leaders can block these changes or they can energetically search for a modified role that ensures preservation of the union while aiding the change to a better way. Importantly, union officials can sustain the change effort when managers flag or move on to other positions in the company. A joint arrangement for the pursuit of intensive change is an important ingredient of success. Owning is better than going along.

Local union officers, like managers, come in all shapes and sizes. The variety is endless. Additionally, some are unable to visualize a modified role in the new-paradigm scheme of things and sincerely fear that proliferation of new-paradigm organizations will damage not only their union but unions and the labor movement in general.

Some local union officials sincerely believe that workers do not want the new kind of jobs that the new paradigm promises or that many in their bargaining unit cannot adapt to this new job content.

Experience has taught all union officials to be wary and untrusting.

Some officials are simply not comfortable with anything but a wholly adversarial relationship. "You (management) act and we (union) will react," is their motto.

Some union officials mistrust their counterparts in management on principle and not on the evidence of their behavior.

Most difficult of all for the plant manager aspiring to move toward the new paradigm is the union official with another agenda such as communism. Although difficult to do, managers should ask themselves what it is about their workplace that causes the disaffected to turn to radical figures and give power to them. It has been said that "management gets the kind of unions they deserve and they deserve the kind they get."

Hostaging is a reality to be taken into consideration. Some union leaders succumb to the temptation to use the redesign process as a hostage to get what they want. The temptation is great because hostaging is so like the adversarial game that has been played for so long. One form of hostaging occurs in the very early stages of engagement. The local union officials will have conditions that must be met before they will engage. Some use these conditions as a cop-out; deep inside, they do not want to get involved. Some are meeting realities of their positions. Often the conditions are based on earned mistrust of management.

Late starting managements also have conditions for entry. With their backs to the wall, they have painful decisions to make and want to make these decisions in the context of a joint effort. Some in the past have used the survival crisis to exact concessions from unwilling union officials even as they profess to enter into a joint effort to improve things.

These conditions of entry should be brought into the open early. When unresolved they continue to plague decision in the redesign process. Under some conditions it may be better not to proceed in a unionized plant. Another form of hostaging can arise later in the game.

When Hostaging Failed

In one case a joint labor-management design team had set up two teams on each shift in a sector of a food manufacturing plant. Each team had its mission, measures of performance, and some other enablers to self-regulation. Unionized laboratory workers administratively reporting up through another channel were included on the team. The beachhead was established and many things in that part of the plant were getting better. Clearly, those involved liked what was happening to their work experience. Then the chief steward of the union having jurisdiction over the laboratory wanted something from management that was unrelated to the new way of working. He did not get it, so he began to use the QWL as a hostage. Going to a team member from the laboratory he ordered the member not to attend any more weekly meetings until he gave the okay. Whereupon he got the surprise of his life. The young and obviously courageous worker had made a discovery. He became defiant. In clear, earthy language he responded that he would continue to attend these meetings.

The second form of hostaging is sometimes played by managers. A middle manager in one plant, possessing far greater power to influence matters than could be attributed to his position, was highly proficient in subtly blocking the movement toward labor-management goals for the plant. In one case he attempted via a redesign task force to gain an important change in a contractual matter that should have been done through negotiations with the union. Fearing a past-practice trap, the union perceived him hostaging the entire task force proposal with one issue.

A third form of hostaging is making the redesign into a bargaining chip in contract negotiations.

Hostaging, the potential for it, and its effects when it emerges at a critical time, should be discussed in the early stages of engagement. This up-front activity takes time and an impatient manager may view it as not worthy of the delay incurred. Impatient newcomers need only to look about them, see how long some have been at it and have so little to show for their time and effort, all because the potential for hostaging was not confronted by both parties early on.

There is an extensive variety of circumstances in which union officers find themselves. The union may be prosperous or in decline. They may have their backs against the wall, a not uncommon condition in these times. The plant may be a prosperous unit in a prosperous company, a prosperous unit in an unprosperous company, or an unprosperous unit in a prosperous company. Nowadays few in union leadership positions are complacent. The events and trends of the past two decades have not gone unnoticed.

Some local unions are more autonomous than others. The attitudes that senior officials in the internationals hold toward work redesign run the gamut from negative to strongly positive. Some at both local and international levels are advocates of participation but only of a modest character.

There is a great difference between being appointed and being elected. Any union official involved in the uncharted waters of intensive change must cope with great uncertainty and the attendant political risks. Intensive change leads to changes in how seniority is applied and to changes in thinking about pay and methods of payment. It leads to new methods of job evaluation. Fewer workers are required. Other unknowns are the tenure of the present plant manager and what the replacement's attitude and behavior will be toward the joint effort for which the union leader has put so much on the line.

The nature of individual paradigm change and the slowness of the change process combine to produce significant risks for the proactive union official. In the early phases of intensive change, few union members have had the opportunity to discover the new work experience.

In one plant five years after the union first engaged with management in an intensive change effort, one of the last redesign task forces convened for a three-day orientation. At the end of the second day, two workers who until this time had had no direct contact or experience with intensive change, took the union trainer aside to tell him, "We couldn't imagine what would be discussed for three days in an orientation. We didn't realize the extent of the union's involvement. We thought it was a management trick, and we have been automatically against it. Until now, we thought the union had sold out to the company. And we have been talking about you union officials in a demeaning way. We didn't realize the extent of the socio-technical program. We now have a better appreciation for the union's involvement." The union, in this instance, all along had made a heroic effort to communicate. In a number of other unionized plants, candidates for shop steward and other union offices have run on an anti-change platform. Sometimes they have won.

Whatever the situation, the plant manager must endeavor to develop and preserve a trusting relationship. The existing relationship is a product of the past, and the relatively short tenure of managers makes trust development difficult.

THE TIMING OF UNION INVOLVEMENT

When to involve the union has proved to be a dilemma. In one case, plant management involved the local and international union officers early. The initial discussions were very much like bargaining. The union officials saw two problems, the ubiquitous and imprecise "lack of communications," and shop stewards' strong feelings of neglect and low status. The solution they offered was for plant management to require each building superintendent to have daily coffee with his building's shop steward.

Management's agenda was to get the union involved in a joint QWL effort. Although mention of productivity was taboo, the omission did not concern this plant manager who was convinced that if they could move out of the old way into a new, productivity gains would follow. Earlier, this plant manager and his staff had made extensive use of the Traditional Model exercise in their appreciation activity.

After considerable discussion, the local and international officials present were given a short review of the Traditional Model. The first meeting ended without a decision, but the second meeting a few weeks later showed that valuable insights had been gained. The union dropped the demand for required coffee klatches and announced their willingness to take part in a multidisciplinary redesign task force. The discussion then turned to the perceived disadvantage the modestly educated shop stewards would have in a forum that included management people mostly with undergraduate degrees. Union officials then readily took to a proposal that union shop stewards be given an opportunity to become familiar with socio-technical concepts and the stewards' role in a redesign task force.

A two-day-long training session with the shop stewards and local officers followed. At the close they were asked for recommendations. They had only one, that they be given a third day. Obviously some discovery had occurred. When at the end of the additional day they again were asked for a recommendation, they strongly recommended that every foreman in the plant be given a similar familiarization opportunity. Not atypically, the foremen and middle management were furious. The union had been familiarized first and on top of that the stewards had made a recommendation for and about them. Weren't foremen a part of management? These feelings were later overcome, but for some time it was a serious problem. Dealing with these feelings took much time and energy. On the other hand, if the entire management group including the foremen had gone through the familiarization before the union was approached, the union would have said, "This is joint? You have already decided!" Furthermore, had this sequence been followed, the middle managers and foremen would have had a convenient path of retreat from confronting their personal paradigms. The claim that "the union will never buy this" would have taken up most of the time and energy in the familiarizing sessions. In the matter of timing the union's involvement, it may be partly a case of deciding which problems one would rather encounter.

FIRST-LINE SUPERVISORS
DESERVE SPECIAL ATTENTION

Development of team leader skills is one of the most important issues in the whole arena of change and it is critically important to work intensively and patiently with the foremen from the time of the first signaling of the intent to remake the organization to the time when teams are functioning. The foremen must be trained in the new way if they are successfully to assume a new role.

When they first hear that there is a new way coming, their instincts will tell them it is just another program. Most of them are experienced with being admonished by managers and trainers to learn and to use human relations skills to change worker behavior, when in fact worker commitment is conditional on the work experience over which the foreman has almost no control. They will not understand socio-technical concepts, what a team is, and especially how teams develop. Meanwhile, life for the foreman and those being supervised will go on in the old paradigm, with all of the difficulties that motivated management to seek a new way in the first place. It is only natural that the foremen will be troubled by uncertainty, apprehensive, and anxious. "Will I like it?" "Can I ever do it?" "Will my job disappear?" The foreman's concerns are both real and imagined.

- *How will my status be affected?* Status is important to most foremen. They never seem to have enough, and there are forces in the plant that continually erode their status. In one plant, status was so highly valued that a key issue with the foremen was the kind of material their uniforms were made of. It had to be better than the material used in the uniforms of the unionized hourly workers. It is not uncommon for union members to taunt the foremen about the relationship between foreman salary, raises, and benefits and the gains achieved for union members in the most recent bargaining. Invariably, foremen initially see work redesign as further erosion of their status and there is no one around with credible experience to say it won't happen.

- *Can this new way be done in this plant?* In the foreman's paradigm, worker behavior is a matter of character traits and nothing in his career so far supports the notion that commitment is conditional on the work experience. Workers with faulty behavior traits "should never have been hired in the first place." But they were, and those with these faulty behavior traits must be coerced into submissive behavior or fired. "But management won't fire them!" This feeling, with some justification, will persist for an extended period of time.

- *What about my job security?* Many foremen fall into the over-40 age group. Usually having modest educations, they are terrified at the prospect of losing their jobs, considering themselves virtually unemployable elsewhere. They think of their employability only in terms of the same technology. "But this is the only paper plant (or steel mill, glass factory, etc.) in town. Besides, the pay in our factory is above anything else in the area." First-line supervisors will seek repeated reassurances for some time to come.

- *Perhaps it can be done, but can I do it and who will show me?* Being without the knowledge and the experience, the foreman's boss can neither teach nor show the foreman-become-team leader how to do it. In old plants well into change, managers usually cannot write out, much less explain, the new role for their first-line supervisors who have lately become responsible for connecting a self-regulating team to management.

Two factors govern what is to be done to develop the present foremen into the new role. The first has to do with their anxieties. If their concerns are ignored, training them to function in the new way is ineffectual. They need immediate assistance in their old-paradigm situation and if that help is not forthcoming, they turn off at any mention of change to a better way.

The second point relates to a sound principle of adult learning—the best learning takes place when the learner is ready for it and can relate to it. It is impractical to train a foreman in how to develop a team when there is no team to develop. One plant manager learned of a five-day Systems Workshop and sent virtually all foremen and managers in his plant to it. But two or more years elapsed before most of these people were involved in the new paradigm. By then they had forgotten the entire experience.

Preparing the existing staff of foremen, paradoxically, is best done by combining the training to help them function better in the old-paradigm surroundings with training in the concepts that underlie a state-of-the-art organization. The training is set up as a cyclical learning process.

Certain preparatory steps are taken with groups of foremen from a given area and the second-line manager to whom they report. Together they explore two questions: What are the factors that diminish the quality of your work life here? What are the biggest obstacles to getting your here-and-now job done? Preparatory work includes ordering and selecting the most important diminishing factors and obstacles.

The cycle consists of five steps:

(1) *Experience.* Everyday life at work in which the participant tries new things, makes mental and written notes on outcomes in previously specified categories. The participant observes the scene with awareness that change is occurring as a result of his or her actions

and the actions of others making up the group. The participant organizes the observed data so that subsequent sharing will be efficient.

(2) *Experience review.* Participants meet with their boss and a consulting resource. Observations from the experience step are made public. There will be successes, failures, dilemmas, paradoxes, and mysteries.

(3) *Interpretation.* As a group the participants interpret the shared data, noting similarities, differences, themes, trends, and possible cause and effect relationships. Explanations are posed, and tentative connections are made with the models in the organizational paradigm. Models are tested and modified if experience shows that the models are inadequate explanations. If models are absent, things have not been made right at the plant center.

(4) *Conclusions.* From the interpretations the group draws written conclusions, tentative and otherwise. From time to time the consulting resource uses this step for minilectures on relevant behavioral and organization theories. This information helps in the here-and-now and also prepares the participants for the future.

(5) *Planning.* The participants discuss how this new, clarified, or reinforced learning will be applied in the workplace during the next cycle. Much of the planning covers how they can use their power of authority more wisely. The cycle then begins anew. Throughout the meeting and in the next experience period on the shop floor, each participant is a resource to the others.

The group begins the learning cycle and continues it until the time when redesign comes to their department and they go into intensive training appropriate for those about to take responsibility for the developing of a self-regulating team.

Carefully and thoroughly preparing the way in the plant will pay dividends for a long time to come. Neglecting to do so has high business and social costs. The next chapter deals with what comes after preparation.

TWELVE

Making the New Values Operational

The strategy of microlevel discontinuity calls for setting up a beachhead laboratory for learning in the core manufacturing process. This is done at the earliest possible moment commensurate with the sufficiency of preparatory steps taken to enable intensive change and ensure its successful start-up and continuance.

Seldom will the best location for the first beachhead be immediately obvious. Success has several dimensions; discovery by those in the beachhead is important. So also is the beachhead's positive influence on the people around it even though the better mouse trap theory is not to be relied on. The time it will take to design and start up the beachhead is a factor. Success in an ill-chosen site may not be best for success of the overall redesign.

Performance improvement is important. It must be evident that the job being done in the beachhead is better than it was before. Confident managers tend to place the first beachhead where variances most affect the plant while the less confident tend to choose a very small unit, often a new and atypical area.

Requisite discovery in the beachhead depends on the intensity of the change attained. Without intensive change there will be little discovery. The anatomy of self-regulation must be sufficient and authentic.

> Not comprehending the factors that contribute to success, one plant manager chose the introduction of a new product as an opportunity to introduce intensive change. Existing equipment employed to make the new product spanned three departments and was shared by existing products. Workers from two different unions operated the units.
>
> The beachhead was doomed from the start by jurisdictional considerations. In this case the product failed in the marketplace so the redesign was abandoned before it had failed. From the experience the manager gained confidence. He went on to choose for the beachhead an important section of his production process but valuable time had been lost.

Success is more assured when the first unit is headed up by an amenable manager. The posture of the area shop steward is important.

THE REDESIGN TASK FORCE

Not to be overlooked in the success equation is who is to redesign the area and how they will proceed. Participation is called for but it is not possible to involve each and every person directly so a new structure in the form of a multidisciplinary redesign task force is created to analyze a sector of the plant and develop a proposal for its redesign. Theirs is to find how to get it right on the shop floor. Implementation of the proposal becomes the first beachhead laboratory for discovery.

The task force serves other larger purposes. Its presence becomes credible evidence that there is a new and different way of going about important matters and that management is serious about establishing this new way. It is participative, involving people in the lower levels of the organization. Being multidisciplinary, it breaks down barriers of compartmentation, and gets more inputs into the decision-making process.

The task force serves to develop and reinforce new organizational values such as:

> Every person here ought to be responsible for his or her behavior;
> We ought to be collaborative here and not so competitive;
> We ought to follow the golden rule;
> We ought to be sharing more of the good and the bad.

Serving on a redesign task force gives its members an opportunity to sample and experience team life. For most of them it is a first, although they may have been touched by the validation process. They see firsthand in a real, not contrived, situation how a group develops. They learn that groups can accomplish projects and that a group can function well in new-paradigm conditions. In these respects the task force is literally the first laboratory for discovery.

In a unionized plant, the redesign task force involves the union, thereby demonstrating the union's support for redesign, reducing a source of intimidation that otherwise prevents workers from joining in. The fear of intimidation does not immediately abate, even when a key local union person is a member. In the first two meetings of a task force in one plant much time was spent to overcome some union members' fear of "being called down to the union hall."

The task force must not be so large that it is unwieldy, but it must not be too small. Three important conditions are to be met. *Knowledge*—lore—of the underlying principles of the technology, cost accounting, quality assurance and socio-technical discipline, must reside in the task force. So, too, must *information*—how things really are in various parts of the organization, especially in and around the area of the task force's concern. The final consideration in constituting the task force has to do with *politics*. Important constituencies must be represented. These include not only the union but foremen and those responsible for quality assurance. The size of the task force usually becomes a matter of compromise. Task forces as large as 20 have been successful.

The union will insist that they select the bargaining unit members. This is as it should be. Who they will chose for the first task force is unpredictable; local officers will be on unsure ground. One local union president selected his officers. Another selected only workers but chose some for their "anti" tendencies and some for their "pro" tendencies. Another chose shop stewards and included a trusted officer who also served in the plant as the QWL coordinator. In one small unionized plant, informal leaders, determined to sabotage the efforts to change, placed their least competent member on the task force.

In plants without a union, workers in the affected area should choose the worker task force members.

The participation principle should be followed in the naming of management members, especially the foremen.

A charter for the task force is essential and its importance for the first redesign task force goes far beyond the task force itself. Much thought and effort should go into its preparation because the charter communicates intent and values. No matter what has been propounded, the charter reveals the goal operational paradigm. If the charter is promulgated by management only, it says a great deal about management, the union, and the relationship.

The charter enables the task force to know the scope of inquiry and specifies that analysis and recommendation is wanted. It must be made clear that the task force only recommends; it does not decide.

A "blue sky" approach is best. The blue sky approach requires the task force to develop first a "low constraint" proposal, keeping in mind that it only recommends. The task force is instructed that once it has completed the analysis leading to the low constraint proposal, it is then to "back off" to some level of "do-ability." The business and social costs of the backing off are to be noted and, where possible, quantified. What are the implications for product quality? What are the implications for product cost (not limited to variable labor costs)? On the social side, what psychological impoverishment will result because the task force has bowed to restraints imposed by custom, the labor agreement, salaried stake-holders, division and corporate staff policies, and the like. After exploring what is possible, considering the backing-off costs can make management, the union, and other stakeholders aware of the economic and social sacrifices that the old way imposes on every-one. The task force will then formulate its final proposal for rede-sign of the selected area, including the back-off costs. Management and the union will then decide.

It takes special effort to avoid misunderstandings regarding the task force and the labor agreement. The task force changes no pro-visions in the labor agreement but this is not to say that contract changes are impossible. To say that is tantamount to charging them to change nothing.

The charter should point out that the task force has a finite life, which ends once the recommendation is accepted. Organizations have a way of trying to perpetuate themselves, and a task force is no different.

Task forces are unaccustomed to such a sweeping analysis, and they will tend to want to make piecemeal recommendations as they go along. Good ideas emerge early, but some turn out to be not so good once a larger whole is considered. Clarifying in the charter what is wanted and what is not wanted will overcome this tendency toward piecemeal reporting.

The charter is a test for managers. Their commitment to partici-pation and their faith in people is tested in the writing of the char-ter. Some interesting dynamics emerge when management insists on a blue sky approach as far as the labor agreement is concerned and at the same time writes into the charter various "you musts," such as crewing maximums, performance minimums and the like. Usually, managers strive for hourly crew reductions but are quite averse to any challenges to the numbers or levels of management. This is sometimes a source of friction between the union and management.

In the matter of finding someone to "take" a task force, it is well to consider the territory that the task force members will encoun-ter. They must:

(1) take flack from their nonunderstanding fellow workers;

(2) examine their axioms and go through painful unlearning;

(3) learn to take responsibility for things within the task force. (This is a hallmark of new work systems. "Forces you quickly to grow up and take responsibility." [Kiefhaber & Cochren, 1990].);

(4) keep the basics in mind as they deliberate and devise alternatives;

(5) take into account realities of all kinds;

(6) establish their own values such as the golden rule, the "right" to a good quality of working life;

(7) cost out both the social and economic costs of insufficient innovation;

(8) lengthen their planning horizon;

(9) expand their universe;

(10) learn concepts;

(11) learn to tell it like it is.

Qualifications for the "taker" include knowing how and being able to do a social analysis that often surfaces unpleasant truths, do a technical analysis that reveals the members' ignorance of the technical process and deal with the emotions this exposure evokes, sense when the group is adrift versus being anchored to the values and concepts, make them aware when they are adrift and draw them back to the fundamentals.

The taker pilots the task force past the reefs, acts in multiple roles including being the leader, guru, mentor, developer, trainer, sensor, skill developer, holder of the mirror. Other descriptive terms: escort, conductor, usher, shepherd, convoy, guide, scout, groom, pilot, navigator, lightning rod, conscience, shamer, judge, trainer, sphinx, role model, captain (taking charge in a crisis), energizer.

This person of many talents must endure hostility and wrath inherent in the process, must tolerate the suspicions—"you already have the answer" and "management already has the answer"—sense when they are copying instead of doing something because they have a reason, and ever remain aware of the tradeoff between group development and getting an immediate task accomplished.

It is easy to see why so many plant and human resource managers underestimate the skills needed by the person serving in such a vital role.

A charter alone, even the best-written one, will not ensure that the redesign task force will be effective and productive. They need some help in getting started with their work. An up-front three-day orientation and training session is recommended. One had best be flexible in design and expectations, ever alert to surprises because the task force is an arena where feelings, hostile and otherwise, from the shop floor are brought up and must be worked through. The trainer, our designation for the person taking the task force, must devote the necessary time and energy to the necessary working through. Even under the best conditions, three days is not enough; subsequent training is required because there is a limit to what can be learned in the classroom at one time.

First in the orientation comes a review of the charter and testing of its acceptability. Then task force members are exposed to theories of motivation, open systems, adult learning, good work versus bad work, and the conditional aspect of worker commitment. They must also be taught business concepts such as financial investment and pay-back. Trainers assist the members in structuring the task force as a self-regulating team and in understanding the anatomy of self-regulation. The members must be helped to develop their skills of listening, telling, giving and receiving constructive feedback, analytical problem solving, logic, and writing. They must learn and motivate themselves to be free of stereotypical thinking. Finally, they must learn the how-to's of socio-technical analysis.

The training/learning process should aim for heightened individual awareness of self and others in stereotyping, of fact versus opinion, of the effect of assumptions on one's thought process and behavior, of leadership and power and their sources and limits, and of what is going on elsewhere in the innovative world of work and intensive change. The list goes on with social objectives, the performance gap in the present operation, and the gap's relationship to the job security of all.

After orientation the task force studies the plant and the plant environment, that is, the area itself, the suppliers, users, support systems, and competition. It performs a thorough and rigorous technical analysis (see Chapter 8 on new plants). Existing jobs in the unit under analysis are rated against psychological criteria. Task force data are supplemented by carefully structured open-ended interviews with workers in and around the unit. The data from all the activities are brought together in a variance control analysis. Twenty to 30 full-day sessions are usually required to reach a recommendation.

Task forces and their resources should prepare a thorough, comprehensive, and cogent document, especially the first time around. The document serves as a communicating and educational tool, especially when the plant management and union officials have not done sufficient homework by the time the recommendation is submitted.

Some task forces produce amazingly good recommendations and documentation; others do not. In those not measuring up it is usually found that absenteeism is high and absentees give their proxy to one person, members take a "change anything except my situation" attitude, the task force makes decisions without iteration, they accept constraints that are really not constraints, they ignore economic imperatives, they fail to make the connection between commitment and the quality of the work experience. These shortcomings can be the result of inexperienced trainers or insufficiently committed managers and union officials.

The first redesign task force will be followed by others. With subsequent task forces, beware of shortcuts, especially those based on the assumption that it has been done once and the organization therefore knows how to do it. The reality of individual paradigm change intrudes here. Many wheels, though not every one, must be reinvented by a new set of participants. Local union officials have fine-tuned sensitivity in this area and their opinions are worth heeding.

MULTIPLE ACTIVITY TRACKS:
ACTION ON MANY FRONTS

The success of the first redesign task force and the beachhead that follows—the centerpiece of the change process—is tied to the timely accomplishment of multiple, codependent activities. As in the new plant, the amount of activity to look after can seem over-whelming. A helpful method for effectively managing the many activities is the creation of multiple, simultaneous activity tracks that pace the change and identify who does what. The use of this method can go far to ensure that needed things and conditions are in place when the task force comes forth with its proposal, thus avoiding the high probability of fade-out that is associated with a serial approach.

Some activity tracks are "union only," some "management only"; others are managed jointly. Some are for the steering com-mittee, if such a unit has been formed. Others may be managed by existing or newly created groups. The term or life span of these activity tracks vary, some having a predictably limited life span. Some are "temporary" with an unpredictable life span. Others are "ongoing" and will continue far into the future.

Individual Paradigm Change Track. The speed at which one can move in the plant as a whole is a function of success in initiating individual paradigm change. In this track one endeavors to see that opportunities for familiarization and discovery are afforded people in the various segments of the plant, that is, senior man-agers, middle managers, staff and support groups, first-level su-pervisors, senior union officials, and shop floor committeemen/ stewards. A plan to encourage and monitor these individual para-digm changes is then formulated. Too often, managers will forget their own change, the time it took, and the circumstances. Forget-ting this they expect others to undergo the same change in much less time and with fewer resources. It is an ongoing activity track.

Enabling Functional Area Preparation Track. This activity is very similar to "getting it right at the center" presented in Chapters 5 and 6. One must be resigned to having one foot in the old paradigm and one in the new for a good long spell.

Personnel from some of these in-plant functions will take part in redesign task forces. Others will be involved in analyzing and rewriting new roles. All should be involved in awareness sessions, training in what new-paradigm organizations are all about, elements of structure required if self-regulation is to function well, and how to design a system. Some stimulus to begin redesign of the functions prematurely will arise. This must be managed carefully in the context of the strategy to create the first beachheads in the core processes.

Sustaining Functional Area Preparation Track. Also similar to Chapters 5 and 6, sustaining functional areas are those that may not change their way of doing business until the task force recommendations are implemented. The preparation step, study of changes in functional philosophy, processes, and procedures required to accommodate the redesigned areas, begins at once. Because they will be giving up certain tasks and responsibilities to operating teams, a timetable for the transfer should be established. Sustaining functional areas will, for some time, have two kinds of relationships to the operational areas they service, the unchanged parts of the plant and the altered beachhead and subsequent breakout areas.

Boundary Management Track: Management. The plant is undertaking intensive change with a center-out model but at the division and corporate levels it is periphery-in. Without appreciation, some, if not most, division and corporate executives will not understand how they and their units or functions should relate to intensive change on the periphery. In this, the plant manager can apply the technique described in the last paragraph of the main text in Chapter 7. Boundary management is an ongoing track managed mostly by the senior managers in the plant.

Boundary Management Track: Local Union Officers. Intensive change may be new to key officials in the international union, although not so much now as formerly. For certain it is new to local membership. The political risks were discussed earlier in this chapter. This ongoing track belongs to the union.

Role Redefinition Track. As intensive change is brought about through the redesign process, roles must change. Role redefining should begin early, at first-level supervision in the core processes, and then extend upward and outward, so that it is complete and understood once the task force recommendation is made and implementation begins. The activity here is in many ways similar to the sustaining functional area track. Study and anticipation is required. Once the new team leader role is implemented, change in the role of the bosses should not be far behind.

Internal Resources Track. This is a temporary track. Training needs for a manufacturing plant in transition can scarcely be overestimated. This book devotes an entire chapter (see Chapter 13) to the subject. At this point in the paradigm shift, training resources are in short supply. The experience gap is prevalent in the training community where unlearning is as painful as anywhere. An estimate of training needs should be drawn up. The pace of change is limited by the availability of trainers. Potential trainers exist in all ranks, including the union, but participating in a redesign task force does not itself a trainer make.

New Technology Introduction Track. New technology applications won't wait. In this track comes formulation of a design philosophy and a participative process for incorporating new technology in a manner that gets the most out of the capital dollars spent and does not do violence to the new philosophy and goals. When engineers continue to design in the same old way, credibility of those espousing the new way of operating is seriously eroded. Furthermore, opportunities to design good work through joint optimization are lost.

Strategy Reviews Track. In this track management and the union engage in joint reviews of progress, failures, and dilemmas in order to make mid-course corrections. Similar to a self-regulating team, they learn from error correction.

STARTING THE FIRST BEACHHEAD

Once the redesign task force recommendation is submitted the decision rests with the management and the union. Implementation should be a joint effort although in the nature of things a line manager takes the lead. Chapters 8 and 9 on new plant start-ups have useful recommendations, especially for training the operating team members.

In a large measure, prospects for early success reflect the care, effort, intelligence, and dedication that has been put into bringing matters to this point. If things have gone well the quality of team design is high, the change is intensive, and team members may cross a threshold from psychologically impoverishing work experiences to a work life that is potentially better, albeit at this point in time, unproven. With a changed work experience, commitment should be forthcoming.

The enabling and sustaining functions in the plant are ready to make adjustments and task transfers, and have been trained in the art of interacting with new units with new values.

The foreman, with recast role and new title, has had exposure and considerable training in the anatomy of self-regulation, how to intervene, how teams develop, and his or her role and responsibilities in that process. The team leader's boss (if that position still exists) knows the role modifications called for.

The union officials are committed and involved. Workers in the first operating team have no more than modest doubts about union sanction.

Unlike a new plant start-up, the technical system is a functioning unit and the skills to make it so are present, even if multiple skill proficiency is lacking.

A rigorous and thorough technical analysis has produced new information about the old technology and an elegant operator decision support system is in place.

In spite of these considerable accomplishments, there is work to be done. Only a few team members have had involvement and discovery opportunities, understand the principles, and are enthusiastically disposed to make the new way succeed. Predominant in number are team members with little exposure and no discovery. Attitudes in this group will range from wanting to disprove to some willingness to give it a try. For a time some team members will interpret everything they see and feel to justify their belief that "this can't happen here."

Team members face the terror of having to decide. The challenge for this disparate group and their team leader is to create the discovery laboratory as they make the discovery. Considerable quantities of experienced support are advisable.

If the anatomy of self-regulation has been made right the team will soon pull together. It is a thrill to be directly involved and to see people and teams develop and performance improve. Soon one begins to hear that they never want to go back to the old way. QWL then has its greatest meaning.

In start-up and for some time after, the paradoxical complications described in Chapter 2 are to be expected. Some we/they feelings and behavior are inevitable. Conflict with suppliers and users will develop and must be managed. It pays to become well schooled in the enduring phenomena associated with the creation of something radically different, substantially better.

A more commonly occurring condition is the one in which an ill-conceived change strategy and shortcomings in the preparatory steps have given rise to beachheads that require alterations. All teams are not created equal. Usually, more than one thing needs redoing.

Team design is the most frequently encountered particular needing corrective measures, and—because bad design has many derivatives—the most serious. Far too often, managers expend time and energy on the derivative problems instead of attending to the root problem—the design itself. For example, faulty team design can lead to an hourly paid worker evolving into a de facto foreman. Intensive training for one forced into such a role is of little avail.

Team leader shortcomings have serious consequences, especially in the early life of the beachheads. Shortcomings can often be traced to insufficient up-front training (before beachhead start-up), wrongful training based on faulty theories and models, especially on how teams develop, and ineffective or absent mentoring.

A failure to make timely alterations in stated middle-and-up management roles complicates matters. Even with alterations, deeply ingrained manager habits will resurface, usually unbeknownst to the sincere manager striving to meet the new role requirements. Questions that managers ask, orally and in writing, and the forms the team and team leader are required to fill out, enable the workers to decode what management is really thinking. In some cases the clues are found in the many "boundary conditions" attached to delegation that leave so little room for creativity on the part of self-regulating work groups. The answer the manager wants is clear and subordinates can see that only the wanted answer is acceptable. These actions indicate that "good soldier" behavior on the part of subordinates is valued.

Not all managers exhibiting these behaviors are casualties but one must be expected now and then. The tendency in the early stages of the change process to bypass managers who appear to be potential casualties has serious consequences in the critical stage of beachhead start-up. While it is not easy to know when someone should be declared a casualty and drastic action taken, the responsible manager must legally and fairly face up to this problem that won't go away.

Frequent evaluation of the beachhead is important. This does not mean written questionnaires passed out to the new team! It does mean hands-on assistance from resources experienced in the process of self-regulating team development.

BREAKING OUT
OF THE FIRST BEACHHEAD

The cardinal rules-of-when for the second beachhead are "Leave the anomaly hanging out on a limb no longer than necessary!" and "Don't await manifest success in the first beachhead before chartering the second redesign task force." The urgency of much discovery by many, and scarce training resources initially limit the number of redesign task forces that can operate simultaneously. As a foundation of experience is gained, the process of redesign can accelerate.

The first rule favors locating the second beachhead in an immediate upstream unit that supplies materials to the first, creating a cluster of experience. Those who began upstream in the core production process should give first consideration for the second beachhead to the immediate users of the beachhead's outputs. If for some reason neither is feasible, try a service and support area that is interconnected with the beachhead.

MANAGING IN THE TRANSITION

Managers of established plants in transition alter the way they deal with the outside world—the company and the wider environment. Theirs is far more complex than acting at the point of discontinuity between the old way and the new way as do senior managers in a new plant. Without the luxury of a plantwide-at-once move to the new paradigm, senior managers in the plant-in-transition must contend with two competing paradigms within the plant.

Under the best circumstances, the beachheads must be nurtured, developed, and the shrinking unredesigned parts adjusted, all at a carefully monitored pace.

Uncontrollable events will intrude. A union election can drastically change the character of the union-management relationship and the union's participation in the redesign efforts. Key and middle managers may leave, a situation compounded when unprepared senior management sends ill-suited replacements, challenging even the best plant-level new-manager assimilation process.

Crowd-out remains a potential when things have not been made right at the corporate center. Seasoned innovators with well-established innovations still struggle with counterproductive actions by misunderstanding or conformity seeking senior managers.

Intensive change requires lots of continuing training and evaluation. The next two chapters in this book are devoted to these important facets of remaking an organization.

PART V

Training and Evaluation

THIRTEEN

New-Paradigm Training in a Paradigm Shift

GENERAL

Training, the deliberate and systematic use of theory-based concepts and methods, is an important complementary component to the extended array of activities necessary to effect and sustain an organizational paradigm shift. Training is the primary vehicle by which organization members are enabled successfully to bring about intensive organization changes. Training must carry the burden of helping people learn to work and manage in the new way. Union officials must be enabled to find a role in the organization change effort and in the subsequent ongoing setting.

A broad spectrum of training needs exists in every category, a daunting prospect in a context where there are as yet few mentors. The training investment—person-time and the cost of trainers and facilities—will be high for some time to come.

Much training was covered in earlier chapters of this book, especially Chapter 5, "The Work of the Second Echelon," and the chapters on new (Chapters 7, 8, and 9) and old (Chapters 10, 11, and 12) plants. This chapter is, so to speak, a supplement on this very important subject.

The new training is a transformation, far more than cognitive acquisition. Beginning with individuals as they are, training considers the new demands and expectations of the organization members and endeavors to alter what they can do and what they are motivated to do. The new way is founded on responsible autonomy exercised by people throughout the organization, not just by the key managers. Responsible autonomy carries with it the need for analytical thinking, broad and deep awareness of reality, and the presence and continuing development of judgment. When perceptions of reality are blurred, distorted, or incomplete, a person's resulting acts are faulty and most likely not in the best interest of the individual or the organization.

The transformation is designed and attempted in a context that includes what it is like in the workplace back home and what is going on immediately outside this workplace. The context bears heavily on the transformation attainable.

Learning from experience being central to life in the new organization, systematic training is the off-the-job complement of on-the-job experiential learning. The two together constitute the necessary and sufficient conditions. The effectiveness of the latter is limited without the former, but the former by itself does not lead to the requisite complete understanding and buy-in to the new paradigm by individuals and groups.

Close linkage between the training and the workplace is essential. Some examples of mismatch include training a team leader in intervention skills when the anatomy of self-regulation back home is critically deficient; training the team leader in interpersonal competency appropriate for the power relationships of old-paradigm settings when self-regulating teams exist back home; training supervisors to conduct team meetings when there are no teams back home and no prospects for teams for some time.

In the way that a redesign task force serves as a laboratory for discovery, training experiences can bring about some discovery. Axioms must be examined. Models must be illuminated, challenged, and supplemented. Other opportunities for personal paradigm change arise spontaneously and the effective trainer will make the most of them rather than mechanically sticking to a text.

There is no clear distinction between the new complementary and connected training and other activities. To regard things done away from the usual work setting as training and that done in the usual work setting as work is a false dichotomy. Management—plant, division, or corporate—away from the usual site engaging in the act of appreciation is "work" of the most basic sort. Yet they must learn—be trained in—this art. Cognitive notions of organizational paradigm, paradigm shift, and individual paradigm change must be acquired. This is done while assisting them in real-life managing activity. In the act of appreciating they learn how to do it better, as well as more about themselves and their environment, present, past, and future. Their knowledge of personal paradigm change is enriched as they experience it.

At the shop floor time spent in making widgets is usually regarded as "productive" time. Time away from the shop floor for training is "nonproductive" time. But facilitating the functioning of the work group in its weekly team meeting is training of a sort. The pause for reflection and learning is a keystone feature, scarcely nonproductive. The manager who understands the new way will view the weekly team meeting as a built-in training feature, part of the essential anatomy of self-regulation and vital to productivity and rapid response to new conditions.

The new training requires reliance on the use of concepts and models and rejection of a cookbook approach to training. People need explicit models—a framework—a way of thinking. The essential theory is not all that complex and obscure. One has a base of experiences in life against which to match the concepts. It is unlike math or chemistry in this respect.

The cookbook approach to training makes the assumption that the participant cannot learn concepts. Procedures and rote are prescribed. A cookbook tells you how to mix ingredients and bake a cake. A cookbook doesn't tell you how to look at a faulty cake (cake with variances), determine what is wrong, where it went wrong and how to use the bad experience for learning. A cookbook always assumes certain unvarying conditions. They never are. Variability of individual human beings is almost infinite. Variability of groups of human beings is of an even greater magnitude.

In a cookbook it is also assumed that conditions are controllable. They are not. Thus a cookbook would have to be a very thick, many paged book even to begin to cover all the situations that arise.

Cookbooks are expected. Those seeking and expecting cookbooks are frustrated and angry when the cookbook is not forthcoming and the trainer endeavors to persuade them that learning concepts is more suitable. Most managers have deeply entrenched aversion to theory. Theory, rather than being an explanation for what is seen and felt, is seen as impractical and unpragmatic. One manager possessing a PhD confessed that he was turned off every time the trainer used the word *concept*. Common is the reaction, "I don't like to use new words." Another would say, "You have to make it simple for me." One exasperated workshop participant on the final day of a three-day workshop repeatedly pleaded "Tell me what I must do differently when I return to the plant on Monday!" Trainers new in the field should not be surprised at the strong resistance to the idea of concepts instead of cookbooks.

Off-site formal training is advantageous. One plant-level redesign task force conducted all of its business at rooms in a nearby university. Providing the participants an opportunity to step out of their usual environment and routine gives them a distant viewing perspective that lends a dispassionate air to deliberations about this usual environment. An away-from-the-site training location is also symbolic that they are there to learn, not to work. It will be a different activity.

Off site, the usual distinctions of rank and privilege tend to blur as coat-and-tie supervisors and blue-uniformed hourly paid workers all come clad in sport shirts. Male executives also come in sport shirts, leaving at home their white shirts, conservative ties, pinstripes, and gray flannel suits. It is the same with the female gender.

Of great value is the getting away from the distractions of the work place—telephone calls and messages.

The remote classroom carries a symbolism of sanctuary. There is less risk in exposing one's ignorance and incompetence, especially when those senior are present. The remote classroom is also a symbol that providers of the training are taking seriously the training and the trainee. Away from the site it is feasible to give adequate time for rumination without the trainees being seen by others in the plant as loafing, on the gravy train. Rigid schedules for lunch hour and breaks can be safely ignored, giving way to trainee autonomy (discovery).

New way trainers must accept a wide spectrum of participants and back home conditions. Those to be trained—workers, senior executives, middle managers, specialists, and union officials—are products of an old-paradigm culture. Abundant trainee skepticism, founded on the trainees' plentiful past experience with programs-of-the-year and old operational paradigm values is initially evident. The contradiction between one's past experience and the values expressed by the new training material and methods spawns disbelief. "They really don't believe this up there" is the dominant feeling and provides an eminently logical reason for the trainee to dismiss the training as impractical, unrelated, theoretical, and the like. Much time is spent as the trainees test the limits in an attempt to justify their skepticism.

Sometimes trainee skepticism is based on the fact that they have never before had any training experiences.

A source of cynicism stems from past experience with old training methods based not on unique needs of people at a particular time and place, but on a curricular philosophy under which corporate training centers become the purveyors of canned programs thought to be good for everyone, aimed at enabling the trainee to function better in the old-paradigm organization.

Trainee distraction is common. It is easy to imagine that a crisis of some nature will erupt in their absence, be it a spill, emission, product failure, personal injury. They know they will be held responsible even though their absence has been sanctioned.

The nature of management in the old paradigm with its strong focus on short-term activity and the need for managers to be the glue that holds disparate parts together is also a distracting factor. Middle-level managers will complain about the length of the lunch and break periods, saying that too little time is allowed to enable them to keep in touch with the plant. Trainers must work hard to get sessions restarted after a short break or lunch period. First- and second-line supervisors seem to be the least dispensable back home.

Early in the change process a need for the trainee to save face will arise. For many, the training will be their first exposure to the concepts. Soon they realize that the ideas have been around a long while and embarrassment can set in.

Some will be slow to make the personal paradigm change. Later, as the buy-in progresses, they will blame the trainer for the delay, testing the trainer's helping skills.

Some will not make a paradigm change. In one plant years into the change process, a reluctant manager pretending to buy in, was fond of recalling that "Mr. X" (referring to the long since departed initiating manager) "made it awfully hard to buy in." Subsequent events over a considerable period of time made it clear that buy-in was never seriously considered.

Training extends over a period of time and changing conditions are inevitable.

An ever-changing cast of characters is the rule. The "trained" will depart and the trainer must begin anew with the replacements. The failure to maintain training in face of turnover (especially of managers) and other factors has been quite disastrous in several major projects in the early days such as the regression in the Shell project in the United Kingdom after four years and in the new refinery particularly. This threat is no less potent today. Short tenure is more common in the ranks of management than in the union. However, union officials are not always reelected.

In one plant making the move to the new paradigm, the future went from rosy to uncertainty to the certainty of inevitable downsizing. A shrinking market for their products led to a circumstance in which there were too many workers and too many supervisors. The workers had the protection of seniority, which in this case simply determined who would be terminated first. The supervisors, having no such protection, were told that the last to go would be the most competent. Rationally, they might be expected to work very diligently to unlearn the old and learn the new so that they could survive in this smaller new-paradigm plant. When anxiety takes over, however, rationality disappears; learning is severely handicapped. Motivated learners then become otherwise.

Training conditions are much more favorable when the out-moded periphery-in strategy has been abandoned and replaced by the center-out strategy with its proviso to get-it-right-at-the-center first.

An especially unfavorable condition at the plant level is the lack of shared values, beliefs, axioms, theories, and models among the key managers of the plant, the plant manager, and his direct reports.

As a plant in one company diligently pursued socio-technically based change, corporate management promulgated Deming's 14 points. Shortly thereafter they modified Deming's list into their own. In each case, the points were imposed. The key managers in the aforementioned plant held three views. One view had it that Deming's 14 points, the corporate 14 points, and socio-technical systems were but three different ways to say the same thing. A second view deemed that socio-technical systems is a "complete" approach to analysis, planning, and managing. Specific tools such as statistical process control are helpful and can be applied when appropriate. A third opinion had it that the Deming and corporate 14 points are a complete approach and "we will do socio-technical things when it is convenient." The simultaneous existence of these dissimilar beliefs created great confusion in the ranks and had other bad effects on the change effort.

Trainers must invent the transformation process. The art of using the right concept with the right people at the right time is prized. Training sessions should contain a balance of the abstract and the concrete. Trainees must be stretched but not overwhelmed and an optimum quantity of new material covered to ensure that they do not get so much that it is not remembered.

Trainers should revisit the concepts from time to time and be prepared to hear, "Why didn't you tell us that at first?"

Training sessions must allow enough time for the experiential.

The initial conditions, the content, and the transformation sought together dictate group size and make up. Bosses and subordinates are often better trained together rather than separately but having too many levels present can discourage participation.

There is a need for private exposure to the concepts and issues. The trainer should endeavor to mix the group training with one-on-one discussions.

Trainers must cope with responsible managers who fail to recognize truths about unhappy learning. Speaking of this problem in the training of first-level supervisors, one plant-level training manager sadly noted, "You send 'em off for a day and they come back feeling good, saying 'The greatest training I ever had.' The plant manager, seeing that they feel good, says to send more. But a day or two after they return it is as though they had never gone. It has no practical application and all is forgotten."

Serious trainers with an advocacy orientation, believing in the need for individual paradigm change and understanding that individual paradigm change unavoidably involves unhappy learning, may come into conflict with peer trainers believing their role is to assist the client do whatever he or she desires. The latter sometimes provide an easy alternative to managers facing unpleasant introspection. Reluctant managers are thus provided a convenient path of retreat from confrontation of their personal paradigm.

Before deciding on the transformation process the trainer, acting in a consulting relationship with the manager involved, should participate in the diagnosis of the problem and situation. The interested manager's diagnosis is often invalid.

Trainers must ever be learners. Those with a relatively narrow experience base should resist the temptation to apply a learned bag of tricks whether appropriate or not. It is equally bad for the trainer to uncover many problems but work only on those that fit the familiar bag of tricks.

METHODS

In earlier chapters of this book a wide array of training methods was depicted. They include the best job/worst job—best boss/worst boss exercise, a job content interview in which explaining the questions and terms has proven to be a potent form of concept training while clearly communicating the values of the new paradigm, appreciation at the corporate level and the established plant, mapping new plant design activities, the technical analysis, the Traditional Model exercise as an appreciating tool, and the learning cycle for supervisor development.

Matrix of Experience for Initial Group Formation. Training for the purpose of organization change is vastly different from mere impartation of knowledge—facts, information, skills—from experts to learners. If Ohm's law is being taught, some get it and some don't. The trainer goes on to the next group. One expects and tolerates uneven returns.

In a participatory change process, multidisciplinary groups engage in many activities including validation, analysis, recommending, and deciding. These activities extend over a considerable period of time. At its beginning, a group is in an undeveloped state with the many deficiencies peculiar to that condition. If the change process is not to founder, go down blind alleys, and fade out, the multidisciplinary groups must be quickly developed into units that can effectively perform the requisite tasks. Recommendations and decisions are faulty if made on incomplete analysis or incorrect interpretation and weighting of the facts, hallmarks of underdeveloped groups. The trainer must keep uppermost the need for the group to be developed early.

Underdevelopment in a newly formed group is rooted in its innate heterogeneity including factors such as age, gender, formal education, training experiences, assertiveness, appetite for the conceptual, length of service, position in the organization, career aspirations, and the like. There is richness in diversity, yet therein lie the seeds of potential impediments to mission accomplishment be it knowledge acquisition, discovery, or analysis. Every opinion, perspective, fragment of information unique to a particular individual in the group is needed. Typically in newly formed groups one who has had some exclusive training will use words that the others do not understand and may feel a sense of superiority, forgetting that a little knowledge can be dangerous. Of greater consequence, those without previous exposure are apt to be shy, unsure, awed, or daunted, and thus will deskill themselves, that is to say, hold back and permit the presumed "expert" to make the comments, decide what is right, wrong, good, bad, and how it really is. The deskilled ones will learn less than they could.

Common in new groups is a so-called natural leader who dominates. Inexperienced trainers or those trained in an old-paradigm orientation will mistake such a person as a positive force who keeps the group moving on whatever task is immediately before them, forgetting that the foremost objective is to develop the group into one that uses all of its resources. In truth the dominating natural leader, the trainer, and the other group members are unconsciously colluding in this activity. Two undesirable results ensue. The first, relatively minor, is that the immediate proceedings are deprived of the other members' contributions. The second, far more serious, is the deprivation sure to occur in the future. Vital group development is delayed or shut off. A good trainer accepts the responsibility for group development, for ensuring that a group gains access to all of the available pertinent facts, that vital information is not withheld through shyness or other causes. There is never just one thing being accomplished. The trainer has multiple objectives.

These conditions gave rise to the Matrix of Experience method. It fits into a general framework of a larger method of subdividing each of a series of training transformations into a preparation phase, the transformation itself, and a post phase of preparing the participants to reenter the workplace from whence they came.

The preparation phase for the first in a series of training endeavors includes "who are we?" "why are we here?" "what are we here to do?" and "how shall we go about it?"

Before the training session the trainer works with a knowledgeable inside person to find out what training and other relevant experiences the trainees have had. Some have served on redesign and other task forces. Some have been to various outside conferences and training sessions such as NTL, the Ecology of Work Life Conference, the George Meany Center, and so forth. It is common today to find members with past training as quality circle coordinators where the theory and goals are old-paradigm-based. Difficult unlearning is ahead.

Other items such as gender, union membership, management experience, union officer, departments in which one has worked are included along with items such as "possessing common sense" and "being a mature adult," "being one who cares what happens in this plant."

A matrix is prepared. The training, experiences, and characteristics are placed in a column on the left. Blank spaces are available so participants can add their situation if it is not covered. Participant names head up the vertical columns (see Figure 13.1).

Separately, each participant fills in the column reserved for him or her. The information is then shared by each individual, every participant filling the columns in his or her matrix.

Those who have had a training experience not shared by others are asked to describe briefly the experience and relate a bit of their feelings regarding the exclusive experience. In so doing the strangeness is dispelled and the unknown is demystified. Deskilling and potential arrogance are minimized. Group development— the molding of a collection of people into a group capable of performing real work—is initiated. In this up-front development the meek discover their worth and the dominant discover the worth of the others.

EXPERIENCE/TRAITS	NAME									
Adult										
Intelligent										
Common sense										
Care about this plant										
Stakeholder										
Union member										
Former union member										
Union official										
Management										
Work in area target area										
Maintenance										
Engineering										
Personnel										
Dept.										
Dept.										
Other										
Other										
Other										
Other										
Other										
RELATED TRAINING/ CONFERENCES/PARTICIPATION										
Foreman role task force										
Redesign task force										
Train the trainers										
Plant visit										
Ecology of work										
Statistical process control										
Team leader network										
Other										
Other										
Other										
Other										
Other										

Figure 13.1 Sample Matrix

The Triad Learning Process. The combination of deskilling and unfamiliarity with the conceptual is not immediately solved. A proven on-going supplementary method for coping with deskilling and unfamiliarity with the conceptual, begins with subdividing the participants into groups of three. One person in each triad is designated as "explainer." The other two are designated as "helpers." It is explained that these are temporary roles. The trainer gives a "lecturette," presenting a limited point or concept to the entire group. Within each triad the explainer then recaps for the helpers the first point. Paraphrasing is encouraged. So is relating the concept to some personal life experience. The helpers then critique the explainer's recap, clarifying, noting omissions, differences, and agreements. The triad attempts to reach a "consensus of meaning."

The explainer in each triad in turn reports its consensus of meaning to the large group. A large group consensus of meaning is sought. One cycle is complete.

For the next cycle, roles in the triad change; one of the helpers assumes the role of explainer. A lecturette on the next point or concept follows and the triads endeavor to reach a consensus of meaning on the second point or concept. Public sharing follows and a third cycle begins.

Trainers must draw on all of their helping skills. Participants must be corrected in public without feeling demeaned. Generally the triad is greatly appreciated by the participants, easing their fears and helping them gain knowledge, expressions that are heard in public and made privately to the trainer.

For the more sophisticated, a third role is introduced. An explainer explains to a helper while the third member assumes the role of a consultant for the purpose of observing the pair's respective telling and listening skills. The scope of learning is thus multiplied.

Worker Attributes and Worker Performance. This exercise helps trainees of many categories clarify their thoughts and develop their theory of motivation at the micro level. It is suitable for plant-manager level and more senior levels of management.

Table 13.1

Compliant	Intractable
Deferential	Irreverent
Teachable	Uncurious
Malleable	Rigid
Unsocial	Gregarious
Collaborative	Competitive
Mature	Developing
Assertive	Taciturn
Independent	Conforming
Anxious	Assured
Prideful	Humble
Limited Potential	Unknown Potential
Dutiful	Apathetic
Hopeful	Despairing

Participants are instructed to reflect on their experience and identify three good and three poor performers they have known. The names are not disclosed. The trainer then presents a list of word pairings, not necessarily antonyms. See Table 13.1 for examples.

Next, the participants are asked to select privately from each pair the term that best describes the good performers he or she has in mind, a forced choice. Participants then do the same with their lists of poor performers.

Each participant in turn reveals the choice from the first pair. As this is done many past personal experiences are shared, secondarily affording some team building. Stereotypical thinking is exposed. The participants are continually forced to compare their experience with people in an old-paradigm setting with conjecture about people and their behavior in a new-paradigm setting. A discussion of the choices follows and for each pair some implications for the new or redesigned organization are teased out. A form

might include, "What does this have to do with making the processing equipment in our plant run reliably? producing more in-
specification product per shift? hiring specifications, practices and
processes? supervisor selection criteria and process? pay distribution practices? individual worker performance appraisal?"

Once the conclusions from the first pair have been drawn, they
proceed to the second, doing each pair in turn. By the time the
entire list has been processed the participants have engaged in
fruitful identification and discussions of key issues. Typically the
discussions include what people are and are not, adaptive behavior, how people are molded by the organization, that one can forget
the need to learn, plateaus, atrophy and recovery versus being de-
stroyed and gone forever, is there such a thing as an unteachable,
and how life experience in a traditional context has molded our
ideas regarding what people are like. Some unpredictable probes
occur such as the low credibility of information issued by management in the old way and how different it can be in the new, the
extensive and dramatic changes that occur when the job-and-per-
son building block is replaced by the team with a common purpose.

You Must Build a New Plant. This method is useful in circumstances
such as familiarizing the local union officials with the quality of
working life field or assisting a new plant design team to articulate
their paradigm of choice.

The participants are asked to assume the roles of busy corporate
vice presidents who must get a new plant in a remote location built
and brought on stream. The instructions outline the background
and specify the task:

> You will build a new plant to make an established product X
> on a site in a hard to get to location more than 3,000 miles from
> the corporate office. You have hired from the outside a plant
> manger, personnel manager, industrial engineer, and produc-
> tion manager. The time is short and being new with the com-
> pany, the new hires know little about corporate policies in the
> area of organization design.

You have decided to proceed by presenting them with your philosophy of job design and some criteria (general specifications) that the jobs in the new plant must meet. In this way you can delegate to them the design and feel that it will be done with satisfactory results, in accord with your wishes.

Prepare in writing a statement of your philosophy of job design and criteria for jobs in the new plant.

This method is best used after at least a day of introductions to the subject of innovation. Care must be taken because the assignment has the potential to overwhelm those not accustomed to reducing their thoughts to writing.

PUBLIC EVENTS

Public seminars, workshops, and conferences help to meet the multitude of training requirements occasioned by the paradigm shift. There are several types.

One type is the one-shot seminars one to three days in length given repeatedly in regional locations on various single subjects. Another type is to be found in universities offering a menu of workshops with various subject matter and objectives. One can partake of one or many but it is not a progression, one leading to the next. They tend to be suited best for those just getting started in the field of innovation.

An example of a third type is the ongoing series, The Ecology of Work, that began in 1979 with more than 100 participants. In the intervening years, more than 7,500 have attended Ecology of Work conferences in the United States and Canada. Besides the awareness raising accomplished in these conferences, they afford presenting opportunities for people from many innovating organizations.

Another form of public training is the major conferences. In 1973 the International Conference on the Quality of Working Life was held. Almost a decade later came Quality of Working Life and the

'80s. They tend to mark major phase change in the field. The participant gains a sense of being part of an international movement; meets an extraordinary variety of people, ideas, and procedures and hears some of the leading figures.

A rarer, more comprehensive form of public workshop has high connectivity to the goings-on in an organization. It requires five sessions spaced at four-week intervals, with each session leading to the next in a cumulative fashion.

Networks are a unique form of public training.

The potential benefits of public training are several. Training expertise and experience not available in-house can be found and utilized. Many companies without internal training staffs regularly and effectively make the most of the public training opportunities.

Those with internal staffs are not always in an enviable position. Typically, in-house staffs are old-paradigm-oriented and are neither inclined nor equipped to serve the new training needs that vary in major ways from old-paradigm-based impartation of knowledge from experts to passive receptors. It takes a long time to retrain an old-paradigm training organization to operate in the new way and to do so can mean excessive delay in the change process; delay has its risks and its costs. Turf battles are typical. And you can't hire experienced new-way trainers at this time because they are in such scarce supply.

Public training affords a superior milieu in which to learn the general principles and distinguish the general from the unique. The trainee associates counterparts who operate in other technologies, in a variety of social settings that includes unions, no unions, large unit, small unit, and variations in corporate and plant change strategies.

Bringing together people from a variety of situations often serves to break down or soften the line, "You must understand, ours (mine) is different. Even though this works elsewhere it won't work at our place." More difficult to break down is the hard-core resister who adopts a waiting posture, waits to be shown a successful innovation in a plant of like size, technology, type of product, union, industry, regulatory agency requirements, and so forth. Demonstrations are rare and seldom can all of the requirements be met. Clever resisters have elastic specifications.

One advantage of public training arises in the trainee's opportunity to save face, thus getting buy-in that did not occur at home. If the person didn't get it all the first time at home, it is more natural to think and to say, "I'm against this" than "It went over my head." One can blame the back home trainer: "What I am hearing at this workshop today is different from what they were saying back home."

In public sessions the trainer must help some trainees cope with deflation. At an end of the first-day hospitality session of a public training event one trainee expostulated, "This morning I put my chest out and now, after what I experienced today, I realize that we aren't doing (expletive) back home!" Fortunate is the trainer whose trainee can own up to such feelings.

Managers should not attempt to train their way to organization change. A manager at one company sent large numbers of people from one large plant to several Ecology of Work conferences when little or nothing had been done to prepare the way for change in the plant and with the union. The attendees were energized but returned home to a situation where there was no constructive outlet for this energy. It was described as an attempted revolution. Nothing positive came of it.

COMPLEMENTARY TRAINING
FOR TEAM LEADERS

When public training makes the proper linkage between the classroom and the back-home situation a powerful result ensues. An example of fully complementary training is found in that designed and conducted by Alan Ketchum for those who connect the self-regulating team on the shop floor to management. The decision to create this training arose from a recurring theme among plant managers, "We just don't do right by our team leaders," an expression of somewhat uncertain regret regarding an insufficient quantity of training effort versus the appropriateness of the training itself. These same managers equated the cost of underdeveloped team leaders to the savings from the innovation, an expression revealing the extreme importance of the team leader.

Ketchum was of the opinion that an insufficiency of training quantity was universal and was compounded by off-target training goals and content. He conceived a way of looking at the team leader role by stating it in goal terms. In general terms the goal of the team leader is a team that continually increases its capability to self-regulate. After confirming the role-as-goal statement with plant managers on the leading edge of workplace innovation he factored in his belief that the anatomy of self-regulation must be complete and correctly arranged if the primary goal is to be achieved. The team leader therefore must become the custodian of team design, at least until the experience gap back home is narrowed. In this regard the limitations of the team leader's power to make structural change must be taken into account.

Ketchum further detailed the team leader's role as one of knowing what causes behavior, correctly discerning "good" behavior from "bad" behavior, pinning down the root causes of dysfunctional behavior, and taking action, action being to foster (change) conditions that diminish the bad behavior without undue reliance on rules, rewards, and punishments and the use of authority power, and without weakening the team's ability to function.

The goal for team leader training became the enabling of team leaders to learn from experience. The training employs concept presentations, some practice in their use, and teaching and structuring (and encouraging) how to learn from experience. A copious supply of carefully prepared handouts—notebooks, charts, models, diagrams and matrices—are furnished to help them remember and apply when they get back home.

The quantity of training to offer was a trade-off between the needs—a major sized experience gap to be overcome—and affordability. Managers may confess in the abstract that the cost of underdeveloped team leaders is high but shrink from making the requisite investment. Time away from the shop is a second dimension of affordability.

In the context of so much for the trainee to learn and experience, Ketchum was guided by the principle: "Only so much can be learned in the classroom at one time." Five three-and-one-half-day modules spaced at five-week intervals comprise the training.

Another guiding principle had to do with the psychological dynamics of personal paradigm change. Some unhappy learning is inevitable, so teach about it while it is being experienced. Knowledge of the dynamics of personal paradigm change is crucial to understanding the behavior of self and others in a paradigm shift, crucial to knowing how to achieve the team leader's primary goal.

Participants are solicited from sites with work teams in place or soon to be, justifying the claim, "This training is not for everyone!" Persuasion that the new-paradigm way is the right way is not the primary intent of these sessions; yet extraordinary changes in attitudes and postures occur.

A five person per site minimum is imposed and it is suggested that the effectiveness of the training is enhanced if participants occupy a cluster of roles on the back-home site. Enrollment of the team leaders' boss is mandatory.

Team members, union stewards, and officers are optional but welcomed. Their inclusion has served to enrich the training.

Connectivity is achieved by appropriate design features coupled with the cooperation of sponsoring plant managers. Prior to the first session the plant manger assembles the trainees, the managers to whom they report, and other key stakeholders in the plant. They review Ketchum's statement of objectives for the training, the plant manager's reason for sponsoring a group from that plant, and the key objectives for the in-plant self-regulating teams and team leaders for the next 12 months.

Those designated as trainees receive from Ketchum a pre-meeting assignment that leads to reports by company groups at the opening of the first session at midafternoon on Monday.

Each session concludes with company teams accepting an assignment to generate separately a plan for back home actions to be taken between sessions. Recommendations to the plant manager for both the short- and long-term are included.

Upon the trainees' return home the plant manager reassembles the same group to hear a summary of what the participants learned, to receive the recommendations, and to initiate planning for implementation of these recommendations. Objectives for the trainees to accomplish at the next session are collectively formulated.

At the opening of the subsequent session each company group reports what they set out to do and how it all came out.

Session one concentrates on job and team design—parts of the anatomy of self-regulation. The end-of-session assignment is to examine the design in their area back home and critique it against their newly acquired knowledge. Invariably the participants find the back home anatomy for self-regulation wanting.

The subject matter is not as sharply drawn as session titles indicate and throughout the series the concepts of the first and succeeding sessions are expanded and developed.

Session two introduces the role of one who connects the shop floor self-regulating team to management. The concept of team processes is central to this session.

Until midway through session two the participants have existed in two configurations, their company group and the total body of participants. A third configuration is introduced; learning teams comprised of strangers from several sites are formed. Having learned about the anatomy of self-regulation, they put the necessary anatomy in place for themselves and get a taste of the frustrations and joys known only to those who have been members of a newly formed and undeveloped self-regulating team. Each team writes its permanent (for the workshop's duration) mission, develops its measures of performance, and spells out its processes. Their mission is real, not a simulation, and has parallels with self-regulating teams back home. They are asked to regard the lecturette and work assignments as an equivalency of the self-regulating team on the shop floor doing its "business" during the week. When a segment of concepts is completed the team has a meeting, a pause for learning-how-to-do-their-(here and now)-job better, a parallel to a shop floor team meeting.

Team development comes sometimes quickly and sometimes slowly. Participants begin to understand team life as a people-transforming process. Empathy with team members back home is enabled. The experience gap narrows.

Session three covers team meetings, their purpose, structure, and format. Additional features of the anatomy of self-regulation and the team leader's role are introduced.

Session four addresses team boundary management and across-boundary relationships. With the former the trainees are asked to replace the notion rooted in manager timidity of boundary-as-limit, with attainment of a balance between much desired team cohesion and not so desirable exclusivity. Team cohesion is shown to be a function of the congruence of natural division points in the technology and team groupings determined by administrative relationships. Theory and practice in maintaining suitable across-boundary relationships are pursued.

The final session—*Behavior analysis and intervention planning when things go wrong*—brings still more refinement and expansion of the team leader role and serves to integrate the contents of the previous four sessions. Session five entails some necessary psychological concepts not yet encountered in the workshop.

In various configurations the participants have been getting two components of experience, one feeling, one seeing. There has been a rich diversity of behaviors to observe. They have experienced the formation of a new community with a common purpose, made up of individuals with a range of reasons for being present. Some came to learn and some came with another agenda. In this respect the workshop is not unlike an in-plant redesign task force where conflicts and issues in the plant carry over into the task force. They experienced this community as it formed and developed into what it has become.

Besides the community, each has had experience in a company group that began embryo-like. They experienced and contributed to (or perhaps hindered!) its development.

Each participant has been in a position to observe other company groups as they began undeveloped and grew into more developed states. At the start they were not all alike. Nor have they developed in the same way nor to the same degree. One company group began in a typical way with a "natural" leader present. He was their thought leader and more articulate than the others. Although the norm for company group reporting was to consider the reporting out as part of the learning, thus rotating the reporting role, this company group's reports were always made by the same person. The quality of the report was high but the development opportunity for the others was cut off. Observers began to wonder if the opinions presented were considered opinions of the group and if the others could report. A medical problem intervened and kept the "leader" away from the fourth session, whereupon the others began to report and two of them seized upon the development opportunity, showing themselves that they, too, could make good reports.

Participants have experienced and observed company groups cope with absenteeism, dropouts, and changing makeup.

Each has had dual opportunities in yet another group, the learning team, experiencing its formation and development as it coped with absenteeism, loss of members, and staff arranged changes in its makeup forced by people external to the group, people with the power of authority.

At the same time they have had opportunities to observe other newly formed groups cope with formation, development, absenteeism, dropouts, and forced changes in membership, the unique ways the learning teams reacted to authority. They have an appreciation for "the terror of having to decide."

They have experienced and observed between-session and after-hours goings-on.

As individuals they have made varying degrees of change in the way they view the world about them. This was not always without some pain—the pain of unhappy learning. Most of them now know how unhappy learning feels.

Each has had the opportunity to observe others make similar changes and experience pain.

Along with having observed how individuals and groups have dealt with authority under these circumstances, they have watched the authority figures attempt to model the team leader role, in this case operating with the purpose of getting the greatest learning opportunities for the greatest number, with due regard for the rights of all.

Every person has contributed to the amassing of this experience and it would be difficult to name the most valuable player; the most valuable players might be those who exhibited extremes in behavior.

A behavior model—things that, taken together, strongly influence behavior—is presented. The model puts the work experience into a broader context and provides insights into group behavioral norms, showing the basis for the group norms to be group values (Katz & Kahn, 1966). Team leaders and others learn that group values can be changed and that they can be strengthened, and how to do it in a state-of-the-art organizational context.

With the behavior model as a base, they are provided, as a practical analytical tool, a step-by-step model for behavior analysis and the planning and tracking of interventions. Explanations are followed by company teams applying the newly acquired concepts on a case of real behavior from their plant.

The final planning at the close of session five begins with individuals being asked to contemplate what they will do when they return to their jobs back home. Three questions are given:

"What will I do to make my 'experience of work' better?"

"What will I do for/with/to my team so that it becomes more effective at accomplishing its mission and ensures a better experience of work for all team members?"

"What will I recommend to the key managers at my plant?"

TRAINING WITH NETWORKS

A unique complementary form of public training that has proved its value is networking in a permanent organization for managers who share a common interest and involvement in workplace innovation.

At the most basic level the justification for networks is to be found in the paradigm shift and the many faceted accompanying phenomena. At a second level one can point to the periphery-in change model. These have already been treated at some length in this book.

Under these conditions, a plant manager bent on finding a better way is lonely, and needs continually to get his bearings confirmed, to dispel doubts, to be told that something being contemplated has worked elsewhere or is being tried elsewhere. The first organization to meet these needs, the Plant Managers' Network,™ convened in 1976 and since has met for two-and-one-half days, twice each year.

The network's origin is traceable to the first author's experience in General Foods in the early seventies. After initiating and overseeing the creation of the Gaines pet food plant in Topeka, it was apparent that it was both a business and a people success. It was an activity in which he took great satisfaction. Accordingly, he proposed a new position that would endeavor to secure for all of General Foods the immense latent potential thought to be available through widespread applications of the new principles that were working so well in the Gaines plant. He became its first incumbent.

Soon thereafter, working intensively with two or three plant managers, he noticed a marked similarity between their current feelings and those he had experienced in the mid to late sixties as he pursued change from his old-paradigm thinking and acting. He began a practice of frequently, about every three months, bringing these lonely managers together in a low structure atmosphere wherein all could discuss the successes and travails of the change process in the large, old-paradigm system. Membership in this network was informally gained by invitation, a practice intended to ensure that the focus remained on finding a better way, not to argue the merits of the search.

In the eyes of its members the newly created forum was eminently successful. With the assistance of the second author, within three years the group size grew to almost a score. Unexpectedly, the phenomenon associated with a paradigm shift then intruded; the ugly face of politics appeared. Some of the division operations executives who, as a group, earlier declined a request that they act as a steering committee for the change effort, began in a most accomplished Machiavellian style to make it risky for the plant managers to attend the network meetings. Shortly thereafter the first author left the company to start a general consulting practice and never again did the plant managers' network meet as such.

Now on his own, the first author believed that there was a need for a similar network in the larger universe. Confirmation came with a few phone calls to innovative plant managers he knew personally. An invitation letter followed, noting that:

> In today's fast changing world of work, innovation is vital to organizational health and individual career survival. The work force is changing at a rate that promises to increase rather than subside. Managers successfully coping with these changes find themselves breaking new frontiers, gaining new insights, encountering unfamiliar problems, and often lonely. Resources are not abundant.

The network was announced as a new resource, and a low-risk place in which participants could discuss their successes, failures, doubts, dilemmas. Mutual supportiveness was a major objective.

The practitioners were considered the experts. Intuitively, a limit of 20 members was fixed.

The original membership was comprised of managers of most of the prime innovations in existence at the time. Participants at the first meeting included two of the designers and original managers of General Foods's Gaines plant, Edward Dulworth and Robert Mech. Also included were plant managers from two Jamestown, NY, plants. Comic relief was provided by a manager from a large automotive plant in the midwest as he described his plant, the union, and 17,000 pending grievances.

Enthusiasm was high and the meeting was a success. One manager of a greenfield automotive parts plant about to start up was later to tell of an impressive quantity of money he saved for his company by gaining reinforcement for some ideas he was otherwise too timid to try.

News of the network spread by word of mouth. Screening was limited to a verbal assurance that the prospective member was serious about innovation. A waiting list grew and a second network was formed. Subsequently it was found that the 20-member limit was invalid and the networks were combined.

A strong fraternal bond developed. The reception at the first evening took on the aura of a happy reunion of very good friends. One member likened it to a reunion with his college fraternity brothers.

As time passed, new members came and were inspired. One manager in the early planning stages of a new plant start-up was urged by a consultant in his company to join the network. He did so and his first meeting was a revelation. He returned home, scrapped all of his previous plans, and began anew to strive for a state-of-the-art plant.

They came and were deflated. At the first evening social get-together and in his introduction, one member boasted of his innovation. By the end of the second day he sheepishly confessed how far behind his plant was. One second-generation manager of a greenfield plant in start-up remarked after his first meeting, "There is a lot more to this that I ever realized."

Meetings were not without confrontations. A second generation manager of a very successful greenfield plant proudly presented his plan for gain sharing and was dismayed by the strong, relentless criticism his presentation evoked.

One plant manager related to his discussion group that some of his staff did not share his beliefs regarding the high and unused potential of workers, whereupon advice—"you must get your staff with you"—was heaped upon him. Shortly thereafter, as the same discussion group explored "How much [responsibility] can/should we put into teams?" he was compelled to remark, "You guys sound just like my staff."

Often a member plant hosts the meeting. An impressive assortment of technologies has been visited including circuit boards, packaging materials, petrochemicals and other chemicals, engines, frozen foods, furniture, dog food, synthetic fibers, CRTs, surgical instruments, gauzes, corn products, antibiotics. One can scarcely tell who benefits the most, visitors or host. Presentations, touring of the plant, and team meeting observance greatly benefit the visitors; yet these same activities serve to develop those in the host plant. In a similar symbiotic way, hosts and visitors benefit when host plant hourly paid workers, union officials, and managers attend the network sessions and the accompanying social events.

One host, a notably successful innovative plant and performance leader in its industry, saw in the network meeting hosting a marketing opportunity. They developed a similar format of presentation and display for senior executives of their valued customers. Significant sales volume increases resulted.

Making a network fulfill its training role in a paradigm shift requires more than rap sessions. Merely finding out what is happening elsewhere is insufficient.

Turnover of network members makes role fulfillment a major challenge. Turnover gives the network some characteristics of a one-room school. There is continual exiting and a continual influx of new members. There the analogy ends. All new entrants are not neophytes, all who exit are not graduates, nor by any means are long-term members those who have failed the course and must be held back.

Turnover is occasioned by retirement, promotion, termination, reassignment to staff position, the company falling on hard times, and slashed travel budgets. At times past it has seemed that possibly the innovators were retiring faster than new ones were emerging. The last founding manager to retire, Mr. Richard Pruett, did so after more than a decade in the network.

Other reasons given for resignations have been heavy demands for the plant manager's time and energy occasioned by the EPA and other environmental concerns, upper level management support for what they were doing was not forthcoming, "I was giving more than I was getting."

Some exit after learning that the intensiveness of the change represented in the network is well beyond what the member had in mind for his plant.

Hiatuses have been common. Budget crunches have turned out to be temporary. One hiatus arose with the assignment of a member to a staff position. After completing the developmental assignment he was reassigned to a more senior line position and returned to the network. A change in senior management caused one member to announce that dropping out was part of his need to go underground with his innovation. Sometime later another change in senior management occurred and he returned to the network.

Network membership reflects the state of affairs in the present phase of the paradigm shift. Of late they are mostly male, and vary in age, time in present position, and career prospects. They manage units ranging in size from large to small, in many technologies. Theirs are greenfields, nonunion redesigns, and unionized plant redesigns. New entrants (into innovation) coexist with a small handful of plant managers who have been at it for more than a decade.

Their efforts to find a better way stem from varied motivations. A minority have distant planning horizons, have correctly assessed the state of affairs, past, present, and future, internal and external, and have come to believe that dramatic changes in the way things are done are in order. Commensurately, they are the most committed. Others have tired of modest change such as quality circles and employee involvement and have come to realize that change of a more substantial quality is required. A typical progression: short interval scheduling, incentive pay, quality circles, just-in-time, and then socio-technical systems.

With new entrants the better mouse trap theory is widespread and tends to persist.

Members differ in their knowledge of essential concepts; how to change an organization, how to design a good one, what a good one looks like, how to manage a good one. Overall, they lack sufficient knowledge of socio-technical concepts and how they are applied. They find it difficult to acknowledge the existence of an experience gap and accept its implications.

What I Would Tell the Plant Manager About Job Design, Team Design and Team Functioning If I Had the Chance to Tell Just One Thing (Statements made by trainees in the Team Leader Network Training™)

"To try to tell the plant manager one thing about all of this would just confuse him/her. He/she needs to know something about it in order for me to talk to him/her."

"We need more than the support of the plant manager. We need him/her to understand the concepts around self-regulating teams. One of the reasons he/she needs this understanding is so he/she can influence the corporate management to get their support for what we are trying to do."

"Expecting the first-line supervisor to start teams all by him/herself is unfair."

"We need to raise awareness about how long this will take."

"You must go through the whole design process completely, with no shortcuts. If you can't buy this, don't do it."

"We need more support and commitment through the plant staff."

The most fundamental difference of belief among those who seek a better way has to do with the question: Is there such a thing as an organizational paradigm shift and are we attempting to bring one about in our organizations? Those who say yes to the two part question have difficulty communicating with those who answer no—and vice versa—but they continue to share experiences and debate the question, the need, utility, and attainability of intensive change. Some arguing for modest change can be seen inching their way toward believing that dramatic change is needed.

Within the group seeking intensive change is a conflict of ideas regarding, "Can intensive change be attained without microlevel discontinuity?" Common to all in this group is the buy-in problem—getting others in the plant back home and in the corporate office to agree that change is needed, what this change is, and how to go about it. None have succeeded in getting all of their direct reports committed to their goals and knowledgeable enough to do a fair share of the effort required to make the paradigm shift. Common to all is their lack of sufficiently knowledgeable internal resources.

Variety in network meetings, makeup, and content is the key to successfully coping with the conditions of the one-room school. Meetings must range from being heavy on sharing, to a mix of sharing with teaching, to full teaching workshops. Still more variety is gained by incorporating case study presentations by members.

Whatever the current meeting design, the network sponsor must stay mindful that network must remain a safe place to learn. Meeting structure that stimulates critical examination of personal beliefs and what is being done back home is appreciated by some, resented by others.

Efficient interchange of data is important. Discussions can be kept efficient and fruitful by the collection, maintenance, and distribution of key background data on the members' plants. A complementary activity in this regard is a member-by-member review at the meeting opening of the most significant happenings in the past six months and the outlook for the next six months. These and other structural features equip the members to contact each other by letter, phone, and visits between meetings.

The value of networks as a training and transforming forum will remain high for some time to come.

The next chapter takes up another form of transformation, evaluation for learning.

FOURTEEN

Evaluation as Learning

The earlier chapters in this book covered a center-out process for remaking the company to strengthen the likelihood of continuing successful existence in that future environment. Mainly, however, they told of how to start the passage from the old paradigm to the new. Life goes on after getting started.

Little is known about changing large-scale organizations in the magnitude of a paradigm shift. It hasn't been done yet, so it is new territory for which there are no maps. The ignorance is compounded by the increasing rapidity of environmental and technological change. With so little to go on, special effort must be exerted to create this critically important requisite knowledge; and evaluation as learning is a means to do so.

Bold steps are required. Evaluation in center-out will be according to new values, new views of reality. They include changing the underlying philosophy of evaluation from the judgment of many by a few, to the enablement of vitally needed learning for all.

In the new evaluation one makes a basic affirmation that one has to be continuously critical of what one is doing. It increases openness and the exploration of the new—is experimental, looking for confirmation or for disconfirmatory evidence. It is bad for sacred cows.

Evaluation, being cross level, will have important consequences for organizational democracy. There is no class of "the always right" and one does not have to lose very much face in admitting that one is wrong. Evaluation alters the shame threshold in the organizational culture. It maintains humility and prevents megalomania. It is the best guarantee we have not only of honesty but of keeping in touch with reality. The genuine acceptance of a basic evaluation posture will profoundly affect (for the better) the politics of the organization.

Evaluation will not go smoothly at first. It won't begin with a spirit of learning. The spirit will develop. The great residue of experience with evaluation in the old paradigm must first be overcome.

Old-paradigm evaluation is founded on the belief that outside audits that exert the greatest coercive force are a sure road to excellence. The "outsider" is frequently a staff unit auditing on behalf of management senior to those being audited, auditing something against a known standard or quantity.

It may be a comparison. General Foods in the mid seventies once conducted an evaluation of two plants in a single division to prove to the skeptics in GF's senior management that the innovation that had emerged on the periphery of the organization, the Gaines pet food plant in Topeka, was making an above normal contribution to the bottom line. Prove this, the reasoning went, and these skeptical managers would embrace the underlying ideas. The evaluators chosen were the corporate controller and industrial engineering departments, people who were considered "neutral." The evaluators were to, "Determine the differences in manufacturing costs of products common to two plants producing the same products and the reasons for those differences." Two categories of costs were specified: (1) Those that clearly were not attributable to the different organizational concepts in use at the two plants, and (2) those that "may to some degree be attributable to the differences in organizational concepts."

Despite its large-scale (4 to 9) disadvantage, the smaller, new-paradigm plant came out slightly better on variable costs per unit.

Fixed costs per unit in the smaller plant were substantially lower. After adjusting for the scale difference (from 4 to 9, to 8 to 9), the bottom-line product cost difference favoring the Topeka plant became quite substantial.[1]

The evaluators dealt neither with the separate cost categories nor the "reasons for those differences." Nowhere in the report was commitment mentioned. Instead, despite their knowledge that the old-way plant had large maintenance and quality control departments and the new-way plant had neither, they made note of cost reduction opportunities in quality control and maintenance departments in the old-way plant. If only these departments could be made more efficient, the report seemed to say.

All told, the study consumed significant management resources and by far produced more negatives than positives. At corporate and division headquarters the report was greeted with massive inattention. They simply went on believing what they had believed before. One division operations vice president, some time after the completion of the study, remarked, "I don't really know that the Topeka plant is any better." Another, some years later, astonished one of the Topeka plant designers by asking, "As you look back, do you really believe that the Topeka plant was a good business proposition?"

It exacerbated the already existing schism that had developed between people in the new and old plants. As in most organizations, the managers of the old-paradigm organization were proud and, by old-paradigm plant performance standards, had cause to be. They did not relish being held up to a close scrutiny, being compared to a rate buster. And there had already been comparisons aplenty in the media, always holding the old plant up as the epitome of all that was bad, a Phoenix from whose ashes the new utopian Topeka system had arisen.

People in the Topeka plant found the study disconcerting, and reinforcing of their already present doubts about division and corporate executive attitudes toward their innovation. They knew the limits of numbers in a plant comparison. They knew that old-paradigm cost accounting principles and procedures, good enough for comparing two or more old-paradigm units, are not suitable for comparing an old- with a new-paradigm unit. They knew that only hard, quantifiable data would be used, and any difference between the two organizations that could not be quantified would be ignored. They knew that neither plant was an undisturbed model. The study is replete with "adjustments" for equipment changes, running of tests for the marketing department, shutdowns, and so forth. Throughout the study these adjustments were the source of endless arguments between personnel of the two plants.[2]

The new evaluation is multidimensional, affects all levels, and has to be repeated. As a learning process it is not just for the organization's center nor just for a manufacturing plant.

At each concentric ring outward from the center the time frame and scope of inquiry tend to be different but the motive—organizational learning, performance improvement, and faster change— is the same throughout. Evaluation will be done more frequently at the periphery.

Many things are evaluated. A list of "whats" includes performance, the conjectured environment, the fit of the goal paradigm with the latest conjectured environment, theories and models in use, structure, processes, behavior, the many aspects of decision making, consistency and absence of crowd-out, and the gap between the operational paradigm and the goal paradigm.

Evaluation examines the critically important rate-of-change accomplishment. Not good enough is a photo flash picture giving, as it were, an absolute value of achievement to that moment. Past achievement plus the current rate of change of each "what" are used to judge movement.

The process of the critique has to be shared, not that this means everyone has to be public about everything all the time, but appropriate limits have to be set and reset.

Organizational learning is one goal; but action must result. The action component is not to be underemphasized. From time to time, the "action" may be necessarily harsh to those obstructing the re-making of the organization.

Action requires that meetings produce written, specific plans, delineating who does what by when, or else the pressures of the day-to-day problems will crowd out the action requirements that emerge in the evaluation activity. Written statements of what was learned are also necessary. Senior managers can profit by studying the shop floor teams where team processes are given appropriate cycle times and learnings are recorded.

EVALUATION AT THE CORPORATE CENTER

Are things sufficiently "right" at the corporate center? This general question will have several subparts. Does the goal paradigm exist? What of its adequacy and appropriateness? Is it business related? Is the goal paradigm clear to organization members—the difficulty of making it so should not be underestimated. Does the goal paradigm ignore any relevant claimants—customers, shareholders, employees, suppliers, community, governments? Is the operational paradigm acknowledged? What about the gap between the operational paradigm and the goal paradigm? How do corporate officer perceptions of this gap compare with those in the field units?

The rightness-at-the-center questions should include: Is the strategy of intensive change and discontinuity, with beachhead laboratories for discovery, understood and adopted? Are the enabling functions moving fast enough? Are all functions adjusting nicely to accommodate intensive change? Are these functions now anticipating changing work in their areas from "bad" to "good?" Is the crowd-out in evidence? Is QWL for everyone? What are the entitlements? And what are the obligations? Many more questions will become evident from a review of Chapter 4 on getting-it-right-at-the-center.

The *decision audit,* a periodic review of already made key decisions, is a tool created for the early stages of center-out, a time when powerful executives, operating on a meager experience base in unfamiliar territory, unknowingly tend to make inconsistent decisions that deter innovation and cause fade-out. The difficulties of individual paradigm change will be evident and it takes some time for it all to sink in.

It is necessary to take measures that ensure that this audit activity is a learning-from-experience process and not one of finding the guilty and meting out appropriate punishment. Accordingly, the audit's dual purposes, to enable senior executives and others to learn more about the intricacies of changing their organization, and to regulate the remaking of the company, are made known. Categories of key decisions are identified and might include executive appointments, plant closings, labor relations strategies, negotiating plans, new plant plans, and programs requiring major expenditure of time and money such as just-in-time, education for quality, and computer integrated manufacturing.

For each decision it is necessary to determine who should be involved in the audit—who were the decision makers and who can supply the information needed in the audit?

The audit reviews the original rationale by which a key decision was made. Did the thinking process consider the long-term goals of the organization? Auditors then seek to ascertain if this decision did or has the potential to accelerate or slow movement toward the corporate goal of a remade company. Whatever the conclusion, a why-is-this-so analysis is made and is followed by two final steps:

From our experience with this decision we have learned: (list)
Having learned these things, we should: (list)

Another method for overcoming inconsistency is the *corporate future impact statement,* requiring those who develop proposals that need high-level approval to prepare a statement of the effect the proposal's acceptance (or rejection) will have on movement of the corporation toward its chosen goal. Will it aid and abet or will it deter?

Of itself the requirement is a powerful statement of corporate intentions, more powerful than a philosophy statement. Besides communicating intent, the corporate future impact statement puts the burden to investigate what is happening in the change process upon those who otherwise might not be curious enough to ask.

The impact statement encourages proposers and deciders to expand the criteria as they dialogue about the merits of a proposal. It has utility in the preparation of annual capital spending plans. Normally the organization will bring up far more items on which money can be spent than there is money. The new impact statement can be an additional criterion for choosing among otherwise equally important projects.

Requiring the corporate future impact statement to accompany appointment recommendations is a potentially fruitful application of this novel technique. In every organization there is extensive "appointment watching" and the messages received from watching appointments are the strongest possible, outweighing almost any profession of policy. Part of appointment watching is observing what appointing executives charge the named one to do. It is one thing to name a manager to head up an innovative unit and charge him or her to learn from the experience as well as see to its sustenance and development. It is quite another to charge him or her with making the innovative unit come into harmony with the old unchanged parts.

At the end of Chapter 6 on old plant redesign was an example: a promising joint labor-management project's quick demise was due to a thoughtless process for naming a replacement for a promoted plant manager. Had the responsible executives prepared a corporate future impact statement with the appointment recommendation they would have confronted the issue, "What future state is this division striving to achieve?" Logic would dictate their investigating the strategy of this plant and the progress it had made so far toward the future state. Had they done so they would have included these facts in discussions among themselves and candidates vying for the job. Upon arrival at the new station the successful candidate would have sought the facts surrounding the embryonic intensive change activity. But things in division management had not been made right. He received no mandate to pursue the socio-technical strategy for survival. The message to managers, workers, and union officials in the plant was that it is okay to run first this way and then that and this too shall pass.

Safeguards must be devised to ensure that the new requirement is kept in perspective and doesn't result in approval delays. It is easy to imagine that some executives might engage in a going-by-the-book action.

Some criteria against which to judge the impact statement might include accuracy—direction—magnitude—cause and effect logic—the message that the organization will receive if the recommendation is approved (or not approved).

Some thought must be given to what is to be done when proposers submit a substandard statement, how to evaluate the procedure's effectiveness, and for how long the new procedure will be required.

EVALUATION FOR LEARNING IN THE PLANT

This chapter on evaluation has so far been directed to the practice of center-out. Because periphery-in prevails in contemporary corporate America, the plant section of evaluation for learning is directed to plant managers who have achieved some intensive change in parts of the core manufacturing process. With the state of affairs disturbed, it is now necessary to make some sense of the boiling cauldron. Immediate challenges include preserving and developing the good teams, fixing the poor ones, creating new good teams at a faster rate, getting on with the adjustments we have described in Chapter 6, and seeing to basic paradigmatic change at the plant center. This, too, is new territory and evaluation for learning will serve plant management well.

Our chosen sequence of presentation begins at the plant periphery and moves toward the plant center.

The work team at the shop floor is an object of evaluation for learning at the basic subsystem level, the atom of the molecule constituting the larger organization. In a well-designed system a healthy anatomy of self-regulation exists. In its hour-to-hour, day-to-day functioning, the team focuses on its given mission, measures of performance, and processes. Weekly, however, the team pauses for an evaluation-for-learning session. The stated purpose of the meeting is to "integrate scattered, incomplete information into a cohesive, meaningful whole." All then learn from the shared information and this is truly "system" learning.

An occasional evaluation checks out things like the appropriateness of work team technical boundaries. Is the concept of team processes well understood? Is each assignment on the team "good" (not psychologically impoverishing) work? Are the team needs for information adequately met? Is there a team generated code of behavior and is it being constructively used? Are team meetings effective? Do the team structure, processes, and behavior accommodate individual team member differences?

A probe of team processes is essential. What of the appropriateness of team processes? Does the number of processes reflect adequate scope? After scope comes efficacy. Is the team adequately regulating each of its processes? Then comes the calculus: A work team is a learning system; as its capabilities increase, its activity scope, especially that of decision making, should be expanded. Operating units tend to absorb certain maintenance and control functions. They become capable of setting their own machines. The problem-solving capability on day-to-day issues increases. They negotiate for their special needs with their supply and user departments. As time goes on, more of the members acquire more of the relevant skills. Increase in scope means modification in other parts of the organization. The team leader role, for example, must stay consistent with the scope of team activities.

Is the team getting control of variances? A self-regulating team should continue to improve with experience. This is the essence of learning. Therefore the unit should be evaluated against itself.

Is the team staying in tune with its environment? Team goals, like products and technology, can become obsolete. A well-designed team has evaluation structured into its functioning. It has built in mechanisms and expectations that the team will stay in tune with its environment and will adjust its mission and other aspects of its structure as indicated. In addressing the staying in tune with the environment question, one asks, "What in the team's environment has changed?" and the important related questions, "Has the team sensed the changes? If so, have they commensurately altered their mission, measures of performance, structure, processes, and behavior?"

What is the level of team member commitment? Are they supportive of others in and outside the team? What about initiatives? In what area ? Do they act as if the plant is theirs? A memorable part of NBC's "First Tuesday" showed a team member in the Gaines Topeka plant saying, "We know what needs to be done and we know how to do it, and we do it! That is why I say it is our plant."

What is the quality and quantity of team members' skills? And how many does each have? Are members acquiring the difficult skills as well as the easy ones? While the system should accommodate the lack of desire of some to gain a broader scope of skills, the lack of breadth is a symptom of learning disincentives. With insufficient skill breadth, high performance is impossible.

Does the team successfully maintain good across-boundary relationships?

Does the team function well under conditions of variability and uncertainty? Designing a unit that can perform well in stable conditions is easy. In the new paradigm a successful team is one that gets the job done in varying and uncertain conditions.

Every shop floor team must be connected with management. Generally the connector is a former foreman, now called a team leader, acting in a new way in a changed milieu. In a large measure the connection is evaluated in terms of the conditions one finds in the operating team. The primary function of the team leader is to see to it that his or her team(s) develop ever greater capacity for self-regulation. Conditions necessary for self-regulation are a requisite.

The time the team has been in existence is a factor shaping the probes. Evaluators should ask about team meeting frequency and duration; what is the team meeting like? Does the team leader understand and make the most of the concept of team processes? What are the critical team needs at this point and what are the team leader's plans for filling these needs? Does an explicit and apt role statement for the team leader exist?

The team leader's understanding of the technology is probed along with his or her understanding of available resources and how to use them.

The evaluation progresses into management. Many of the evaluation questions asked at the team and team leader levels should be asked in some form at the department and plant level. Much of the time a "wrong" answer to a question at the shop floor leads directly to middle and upper plant management. Once beyond the basic socio-technical unit, one should begin to find managers engaged in three sets of activities: doing, auditing what others do, and regulating their own processes. Doing includes being engaged to one extent or another in design, redesign, development, training or teaching. Is the managers' knowledge of new-paradigm organizational principles and theories adequate for the task?

Doing includes intervening. Do they retrospectively test their interventions? Do they and subordinates and/or teams learn in this endeavor?

Managers should be found in logical groupings and one should detect a difference in what each level of managers does. A level should not be doing the same things as the level above or below it. When found, this condition indicates that there are too many levels.

Do manager groups waste many hours of precious meeting time by confusing what they are to do as individuals with what they are to do as a team?

The assimilation of new members is an important process throughout the plant. Are new people made into functioning members? And are the values and beliefs in the paradigm preserved? Does the organization adjust to take advantage of some special skill or experience brought by the new person?

Are the sustaining functions fully ready, are they giving support to the beachheads, and are they adjusting?

The technical knowledge of the plant management group is to be challenged. After doing a thorough and rigorous technical analysis it is not unusual to find managers conceding an insufficient knowledge of the technology.

Are the meetings of the managers effective? Do they use their own meetings as opportunities to learn about group dynamics from the here-and-now experience of the group? Have they established the anatomy of self-regulation for themselves?

Does the behavioral evidence indicate a genuine striving for movement toward the goal state of affairs or is it just another case of professing while ignoring? To be sure, middle managers, supervisors, workers, and union officials are continually making this evaluation.

Is there within the plant managing group an excessive divergence of views regarding beliefs, values, assumptions, theory, and models? Too much divergence has unfortunate consequences. Leaders should lead and the organization members below the level of the plant manager should be spared unnecessary confusion.

Does senior plant management spend too much time and energy on an internal focus as compared to the external? One looks for a heavy focus on the environment wherein managers seek to establish smooth, harmonious, and effective boundary crossings. In the old paradigm, fire-fighting managers seldom find the time to discharge their external responsibilities. In the new, excessive time and effort on the internal is a signal that self-regulation is faulty. One who made it to the new paradigm said, "Before it was mostly crisis intervention, long hours and highly stressful. Now it is much less toward the internal and that only to facilitate process development and maintenance. I now have time to be involved in bound-ary management."

Does the time spent on the external produce the wanted results? Is senior plant management effectively managing its relationships with important entities in its environment?

Being mindful of the enduring phenomena associated with the paradigm shift, senior management of a plant in transition must reach out to "significant others" in its environment in and out of the company. The essence of managing the relationship of the plant to other entities lies in gauging the disparateness between one's image of self and the image a significant other has of the plant. One also investigates both sides' perceptions of the relationship be-tween them. A disparity of images and perceptions indicates that all may not be well. Being innocent can contribute to destructive across-boundary relationships.

The image of self involves many unit performance factors, busi-ness and social, quantifiable and not quantifiable. Relevant catego-ries for a plant would include responsiveness to business needs, product quality, assurance of product quality, scheduling relia-bility, productivity and productivity improvement, good manu-facturing practices, information made available on cost and other matters, handling of new products, handling of new technology, efforts in cost reduction, capital planning and budgeting, goal set-ting, manager development, profit plan budgeting, return on funds employed, efforts and achievement in equal employment activity, and record and efforts in safety. This list is not exhaustive. What is important in one business is not in another so the list should be tailored.

After developing "How do we perceive our unit's performance and the quality of the relationship with them?" plant management ascertains, even if only by conjecture, "How do people in these external entities view our unit's performance and the quality of the relationship with us?" Action steps become evident.

Because there is a politics of leading and a politics of lagging, it is important for plant management to examine how the plant organizational paradigm compares with that in various parts of the larger organization. Typically, innovating plant managers tend to think that they are the only ones in the corporation trying for this new paradigm. In the past that has been generally true.

The plant manager and staff must confront the data developed in the evaluation. This can be an unsettling business. One plant manager took his staff off site to pause and ask the hard questions: Where are we now? Where do we wish to be? Do we have clear, appropriate goals and is the feeling about these goals shared among us? Are we making acceptable progress toward these goals? Such was not the case. It was left to the consultant present to advance a hypothesis: (1) The serious business condition, the union, and the consultant are the major forces propelling and sustaining change in the plant. Withdraw these and the plant will quickly revert to an earlier undesirable managing mode, attitudes, and level of performance. (2) There is no organizational paradigm at the top. (An organizational paradigm, it was pointed out, is a shared set of values, beliefs, axioms, theories, and models.) (3) There is polarization in the senior managing group regarding an appropriate paradigm. Meanwhile, a new paradigm is being established at the bottom of the organization. Now your middle managers are confused. This condition is unstable. You are training them in one set of theories, structure, models, behavior. These have become beliefs for the bottom. At the top you are struggling and are perceived by others in the organization as not practicing these same ideas. You are not effectively resolving this unstable condition. There is trouble ahead; performance deterioration will set in.

The lively discussion that followed, demonstrated the validity of the hypothesis. Considerable "working through" was accomplished. Candor rose. Importantly, out of this meeting came learning. The manager had been operating in the belief that goals were clear, that the group had settled these issues long ago. The working through process made his wants clearer. Socio-technical concepts cleared up for some. Also, each participant saw himself as others saw him in ways he had not realized before. This was not pain free. Importantly, through newly acquired ability to confront some realities, they wound up with a clarified goal and greatly increased commitment to this goal. Some concrete action plans were agreed to and subsequently carried out.

INITIATING EVALUATION
FOR LEARNING IN PERIPHERY-IN

In the nature of things at the present stage of the paradigm shift, a knowledgeable and committed plant manager is the one most likely to initiate evaluation for learning. Given the limits of power inherent in the position it is unlikely that one has enough influence to initiate evaluation for learning by the corporate level. The results of one plant manager's efforts were mixed. His was a five-year-old greenfield plant existing in a strategic business unit alongside an old-paradigm plant at a distant location. Sensing danger when the plant manager of the other plant was made SBU manufacturing manager, he proposed an evaluation with a fourfold purpose: (1) Gain an improved conceptual and operational understanding of the innovative plant by members of the unit and those closely related to the unit. (2) Reclarify and unite goals relating to organizational innovation in the corporation, SBU, and plant. (3) Identify and verify economic and other contributions this plant has made and is making to the business unit and the corporation. (4) Assess the yet undeveloped potential of this plant while identifying structure, processes, and behavior, both internal and external, that stand in the way of achieving this potential.

The plant manager pointed out some strategic issues:

Is this plant to be compared with one or more other operating units? Is there an undisturbed model available for such a comparison? What are the pitfalls of the comparative approach to evaluation?

What is the involvement of company employees in the evaluation, particularly in the design, data collection, data analysis, and conclusions?

What is the role of the consultants in the process? Are they to be "doers" or are they to be collaborators, teachers, model suppliers, and learners?

A comparison was not wanted. Noting the plant's participative nature, the president said that the employees would participate in the evaluation. The role of the consultants as collaborators, teachers, and model suppliers was easily settled.

With regard to purpose, the president accepted item (1), ignored item (2), considered unnecessary item (3) because he was "already aware of these contributions through the business data I regularly receive." He especially liked item (4), "Assess the yet undeveloped potential of the plant; identify structure, processes, and behavior, both internal and external, that stand in the way of this achievement."

Despite his rejection of the proposal to clarify corporate goals as they related to innovation, the plant manager and his consultant were elated. But it was not to last. It turned out that the entire evaluation was internal to the plant. Lost were SBU sponsored learning for those "closely related to the plant," and consideration of beyond the plant boundary "things that stand in the way of achieving the plant's potential."

Initiatives must be taken by key corporate officials if company wide evaluation is to happen at all. The preferred initiator is the CEO but this is not to say that other officers should not make the attempt. The many difficulties having to do with giving up the old values of evaluation for the realization that capacity to go on learning in a rapidly changing environment is primary both for the individual and the organization mean postponement of evaluation that is an extension of training in the new way.

We are destined to remain for some time in new territory with uninvented wheels.

NOTES

1. The cost differential continued to grow for a decade.
2. The General Foods evaluation experience does not in itself prove that objective comparisons can't be made. They were as long ago as the original Tavistock studies, but those in power chose to put other factors before cost. This is not so easy to do now.

PART VI

Conclusion

FIFTEEN

A Look at the Future

This book has described a three-faceted problem of monumental seriousness. The first-order problem of organization performance arises in a second-order problem that in turn has its roots at yet a deeper level, the mismatch between people in industrialized societies and the firms and institutions that employ them. There is something wrong with work. It is hard to imagine, much less estimate, the loss of effectiveness in U.S. manufacturing stemming from uncommitted workers and managers in old-paradigm organizations.

The predicament of the mismatch and its consequences is not static. A nonlinear interplay of multiple factors continues to enlarge the mismatch, making the consequences more grave.

One factor contributing to the widening of the mismatch has been people's continuing retreat from docility and belief that work, no matter the form or condition, is good for a person. A second contributor has been the rapid increase of mechanization and automation of ever greater sophistication. The latter, accomplished while the philosophy of scientific management remained dominant, further reduced opportunities for people to develop and contribute their skills. By and large, the nature of most work has psychologically worsened just as people need, more than ever, work that is to be found in "learning organizations," work that allows them to develop and contribute their skills.

The consequences of the mismatch are several, and the stakes have been raised. Substances not known as hazardous have became known as hazardous, and have proliferated. As emissions have become more harmful, the consequences of error have grown more grave, even as advances in technology with its irreversible thrust toward greater complexity continue and bring new imperatives that workers be knowledgeable, committed, informed, awake, and alert.

Business firms are expected to do ever more and do it better. On the one hand the requirements of certain regulatory agencies have broadened and become more stringent, bringing unprecedented claims on corporate resources from environmental protection acts at local, state, and national levels. On the other hand there has been deregulation of entire industries in that individual firms had been protected from competition, both foreign and domestic. Competition on quality, price, and variety intensifies. In every way, what was good enough in the past, even the recent past, has become insufficient.

As noted at the close of Chapter 3, if one chooses to fix the beginning of the current organizational paradigm shift as the early 1950s, we have already traversed about 40 years. To be realistic, we must expect a good many years to elapse before the shift is complete.

Taking into account the distance we have traveled, are we in a race against time, an apocalyptic view, or is the situation more benign? Given time, will the problem go away, be solved by unemployment, or by some new breakthrough in technology?

Our disposition to take a long-term view together with our belief in the validity of the third-order diagnosis with intensive change as the remedy, see that there is good news and there is bad news.

In the conspicuously large rise in activity level we see some good news. By activity we mean the entire gamut of effort that in some way raises the level of employee involvement, be it one or a combination of employee involvement, quality circles, application of statistical process control, total quality management, gain sharing, teamwork, self-managing teams, empowerment, or socio-technical systems. If this rise in activity manifests a broader recognition of a problem, then it is good news.

The bad news is that the rise in activity may be confirming evidence that the problem has become more serious, and gives no assurance that we are gaining.

In the quality of the heightened activity there is bad news. The nature of most of the heightened activity does not reflect managements' acceptance of the third-order diagnosis, the need for commitment and the principle that commitment is conditional on the work experience. Where socio-technical system principles and theories are not crowded out, periphery-in and microlevel gradualism are dominant. Only parts of organizations are being made over and where this is occurring the pace is exceedingly slow.

Yet there is good news. The activity itself may be leading to consideration of a paradigm change and move us further along in the paradigm shift. Corporate America is now expending considerable sums of money and energy to make modest change. A rechanneling of these resources into intensive change with the center-out model could result in more speedily transforming entire organizations.

Two scenarios can be imagined.

> Modest change gives way to intensive change, applied with gradualism and periphery-in. Slowly, only parts of organizations are changed and fade-outs persist.
>
> Modest change gives way to intensive change, applied with the center-out model. Whole organizations are remade and the pace quickens.

Periphery-in has brought us to the beginning of the transition that we are in now. Center-out must now begin to take over. This will not be smooth as it will create other problems we can't foresee.

In 50 years someone may look back and see the period 1950-1995 as a time of transition during which there was some movement from the old paradigm with a periphery-in change model. The period 1995-2010 might be seen as a time when the periphery-in model was replaced by a center-out change model. Companies began making intense and sustained change efforts throughout the company instead of only in parts. The paradigm shift moved beyond the flat part of the exponential curve.

Retrospectively, one then may see when the paradigm shift got underway in lawmaking bodies, regulatory agencies, educational institutions and the like.

With much more confidence we say that preserving the status quo will not give survival in the new century; bold steps in the new paradigm may.

References

Ackoff, R. (1974). *Redesigning the future: A systems approach to societal problems.* New York: John Wiley.

Argyris, C., & Schon, D. (1974). *Theory in practice: Increasing potential effectiveness.* San Francisco: Jossey-Bass.

Bierce, A. (1911). *The devil's dictionary.* New York: Thomas Y. Crowell.

Blue collar blues. (1971, May 17). *Newsweek,* pp. 80-86.

Bower, J. (1970). *The amoral organization: An inquiry into the social and political consequences of efficiency.* Unpublished manuscript.

Byrne, J., & Jackson, S. (1986, January 20). Business fads: What's in—and out: Executives latch on to any management idea that looks like a quick fix. *Business Week,* pp. 52-56.

Davis, L. (1971). The coming crisis for production management: Technology and organization. *International Journal of Production Research, 9*(1).

Davis, L., & Cherns, A. (Eds.). (1975). *The quality of working life.* New York: Free Press.

Donahue, T. (1989, March). [Remarks presented to the City Club Forum, City Club of Cleveland, OH, 26501 Emery Industrial Parkway, Cleveland, OH.]

Driggers, P. F. (1967). *The open systems model of organizations.* Assen, the Netherlands: Koninklijke Van Gorcum.

Emery, F. (1964). *Report on the Hunsfoss Project.* Tavistock Documents Series. London: Tavistock.

Emery, F. (1976). *Futures we are in.* Leiden, the Netherlands: Martinus Nijhoff.

Emery, F., & Davis, L. (1983). Learning from the design of new organizations. In H. F. Kolodny & H. Van Beinum (Eds.), *The quality of working life in the nineteen eighties.* New York: Praeger.

Emery, F., & Emery, M. (1976). Searching: For new directions, new ways . . . for new times. In J. Sutherland (Ed.), *Management handbook for public administrators.* New York and London: Van Nostrand Reinhold.

Gooding, J. (1970, July). It pays to wake up the blue-collar worker. *Fortune,* pp. 68-71.

Gooding, J. (1972). *The job revolution.* New York: Walker.

Guest, R. (1979). QWL learning at Tarrytown. *Harvard Business Review, 57*(4), 76-97.

Herbst, P. (1974). The product of work is people. *Socio-Technical Design.* London: Tavistock.

Hoerr, J., Pollock, M., & Whiteside, D. (1986, September). Management discovers the human side of automation. *Business Week,* pp. 70-76.

Jaques, E. (1956). *Measurement of responsibility: A study of work, payment, and individual capacity.* New York: Dryden.

Katz, D., & Kahn, R. (1966). *The social psychology of organizations.* New York: John Wiley.

Ketchum, A. (1971). [Data from job content interviews]. Unpublished data.

Ketchum, A. (1987). *Design engineer in the '90s; Lone Ranger or joint optimizer?* Paper presented at the 13th annual Advanced Control Conference sponsored by Purdue Laboratory for Applied Industrial Control and *Control Engineering Magazine.*

Kiefhaber, M., & Cochren, S. (1990, June). Remarks made in discussion following presentation of their paper, *The impact of membership in a high-performing work system on personal life, family life, and the community,* at the Ecology of Work Conference, Louisville, KY.

Kuhn, T. (1962). *The structure of scientific revolutions.* Chicago: University of Chicago Press.

Latest moves to fight boredom on the job. (1972, December). *U.S. News and World Report,* pp. 52-54.

Lopez, J. (1990, October 5). When "big brother" watches, workers face health risks. *Wall Street Journal,* p. B1.

Luther, D. (1991, January). *Continuous quality improvement: The ever-widening network.* Paper presented at Conference Board Conference on Total Quality Management, New York.

Maccoby, M. (1976). *The gamesman.* New York: Simon & Schuster.

National Institute for Occupational Safety and Health. (1987). *Stress management in work settings.* Washington, DC: Government Printing Office.

Nixon, R. M. (1971). Labor Day address. *Public papers of the presidents of the United States, 1971,* pp. 934-937.

Price, C. (1972, March). *New directions in the world of work: A conference report.* Kalamazoo, MI: W. E. Upjohn Institute for Employment Research.

Senate Committee on Labor and Public Relations. (1972). *Worker alienation.* (Hearings before the Subcommittee on Employment, Manpower, and Poverty of the Committee on Labor and Public Welfare.) Washington, DC: Government Printing Office.

Shepard, N., & Herrick, N. (1972). *Where have all the robots gone?* New York: Free Press.

Smith, M., Sainfort, P., Rogers, K., & LeGrande, D. (1990, May). *Electronic performance monitoring and job stress in telecommunications jobs.* Madison: University of Wisconsin, Department of Industrial Engineering, and Washington, DC: Communications Workers of America.

Stern, G. (1991, June 18). As the going gets tougher, more bosses are getting tough with their workers. *Wall Street Journal,* pp. B1, B3.

Trist, E. (1978, January). Adapting to a changing world. *Labour Gazette, 78,* pp. 14-20.

U.S. Department of Health, Education, and Welfare. (1973). *Work in America: Report of a special task force to the Secretary of Health, Education, and Welfare.* Cambridge: MIT Press.

Vickers, G. (1965). *The art of judgement.* New York: Basic Books.

Vonnegut, K. (1952). *Player piano.* New York: Dell.

Work in America. (1971, October). [Special Section.] *Atlantic,* pp. 60-105.

Zaleznik, A. (1970). Power and politics in organizational life. *Harvard Business Review, 40*(3), 47-60.

Index

About the Authors

Lyman D. Ketchum received a BS degree from Kansas State University. For the past 15 years he has been a consultant to America's leading companies. His 30-year business career included a rich variety of managerial assignments for both large and small companies. He became involved in the socio-technical field during his years with General Foods when he began to question the viability of an organization set up along traditional lines. These doubts coincided with training at the National Training Laboratories, the Menninger Foundation, and a consulting relationship with Dr. Richard Walton. As an operations manager for General Foods, Ketchum created a new Gaines pet food plant in Topeka that received worldwide attention. Its success and the complications that followed led to a highly valued association with Eric Trist with whom he has worked for the past 20 years. He is an associate member of the Columbia University Seminar on Organization and Management, a member of the International Federation of Automatic Control, and was theme chairman for Work Redesign-North America at the International Conference, Quality of Working Life and the 80s. He currently resides in Leawood, KS.

Eric Trist was born in England and educated at Cambridge University. He was a founding member and later chairman of the Tavistock Institute, where he took part in many action-research projects. He and Ken Bamforth, one of his students, introduced the concept of socio-technical systems in 1951. He joined the faculty of the School of Management at UCLA in 1966 and the Wharton School of the University of Pennsylvania in 1969. He is a Fellow of the International Academy of Management and the Academy of Management. He is currently retired, and is editing a three-volume work, *The Social Engagement of Social Science,* which presents innovations emanating from the Tavistock Institute in three perspectives: socio-psychological, socio-technical, and socio-ecological.